Inclusion in the American Military

Inclusion in the American Military

A Force for Diversity

Edited by
David E. Rohall, Ph.D.,
Morten G. Ender, Ph.D. and
Michael D. Matthews, Ph.D.

LEXINGTON BOOKS
Lanham • Boulder • New York • London

Published by Lexington Books
An imprint of The Rowman & Littlefield Publishing Group, Inc.
4501 Forbes Boulevard, Suite 200, Lanham, Maryland 20706
www.rowman.com

Unit A, Whitacre Mews, 26-34 Stannary Street, London SE11 4AB

British Library Cataloguing in Publication Information Available

Library of Congress Cataloging-in-Publication Data Available

Names: Rohall, David E., editor of compilation. | Ender, Morten G., 1960- editor of
    compilation. | Matthews, Michael D., editor of compilation.
Title: Inclusion in the American military : a force for diversity / edited by David Rohall,
    Morten G. Ender, and Michael D. Matthews.
Description: Lanham, MD : Lexington Books, [2017] | Includes bibliographical
    references and index.
Identifiers: LCCN 2017023773 (print) | LCCN 2017014182 (ebook) | ISBN
    9781498560849 (Electronic) | ISBN 9781498528603 (cloth : alk. paper)
Subjects: LCSH: United States--Armed Forces--Minorities. | United States--Armed
    Forces--Women. | Gay military personnel--United States. | Sociology, Military--
    United States.
Classification: LCC UB417 (print) | LCC UB417 .I54 2017 (ebook) | DDC
    355.3/3080973--dc23
LC record available at https://lccn.loc.gov/2017023773

Printed in the United States of America

Dedicated to Mady Wechsler Segal and David R. Segal
Scholars, Teachers, Mentors

Contents

Acknowledgments

Morten G. Ender and Mike Matthews would like to acknowledge a number of colleagues, friends, and family who contributed in vital ways either pragmatically or inspirationally to buttress the research, writing, and editing and made this volume possible. Their commitments to diversity, inclusion, and social justice are worthy of recognition. The folks include in no particular order Remi Hajjar, Diane Ryan, Everett Spain, Aaron Belkin, Lissa Young, Samantha Ross, Todd Woodruff, Laura Weimar, Anita Howington, Tony Espinal, Juliza Ramirez, Tony McGowan, Brian Reed, Michael Barlow, Janelle Bass, Bob Tully, David Frey, Allyson Robinson, Sue Fulton, Robert Goldstein, Sue Fulton, Rick Black, Elizabeth Velilla, Jess Dawson, Mary Tobin, David White, Robert Caslen, Dan White, Irv Smith, Jozlyn McCaw, Sharon Edens, Ericka Rovira, Ty Seidule, Karlos Febus-Traphagen, Mady Segal, Judy Rosenstein, Tom Kolditz, Bernie and Candace Banks, Jacob Absalon, Brian Reed, David Segal, and Ryan Kelty. Morten gives all thanks and praises to his family including Corina, Ilka, Ingrid, Brittany, Tee, CJ, and Axel for their support. He is far less complete without them in his life. David gives a special thanks to Lisa Kreis for her work on this project and the support of his wife, Molly.

We extend our gratitude to the authors of each chapter. Your passion and expertise about diversity and inclusion in the military are evident in each of your contributions. Thank you for helping us create this timely and important contribution to the discussion of diversity in the military.

All this being said, the views of Michael D. Matthews and Morten G. Ender are their own and do not purport to reflect the position of the United States Military Academy, the Department of the Army, the Department of Defense, or the United States Government.

Morten G. Ender
Michael D. Matthews
David E. Rohall

Chapter 1

Diversity in the Military

David E. Rohall, Morten G. Ender and Michael D. Matthews

In a strict sense, diversity is simply about variety. There are many types of diversity; one can own an ice cream stand with a variety of flavors or a lumberyard with a variety of different types of wood. The goodness or badness of diversity in these cases is that diversity gives customers more options and the business owner who can maintain a larger, more diverse stock of items may be able to make more money by providing more choices for consumers.

Social diversity refers to variations in social statuses in society. In this case, it is not a consumer model; there is no supply and demand for different types of people unless you are in something like the film industry where you need to fulfill a variety of roles. Social diversity can have a moral dimension unlike the diversity found in other areas of life. No one has a moral concern if the local market has an appropriate representation of candy bars in the aisles but many people are concerned that there is equal access to societal resources, such as jobs, based on sex (being male or female) or race. America is one of the most diverse countries in the Western world and Americans believe that people from different backgrounds should have equal chance at obtaining their goals in life (Williams, 1970; Wolf, 1998).

Americans also dislike racism and bigotry. Polls regularly show that people believe racism and sexism are wrong. For instance, while there is still some debate about the morality of same-sex attraction, it is also clear that Americans do not support any kind of bias against gay and lesbian people in the job market (Gallup, 2016). It is also clear that there are people who resist diversity, and there is a concept called institutional bias in which organizations can manifest bias without necessarily espousing it. Organizations may even develop policies forbidding any kind of bias but people can still feel the impacts of bias in their everyday interactions within the workplace. Universities, for instance, are among the most politically liberal institutions in the world yet many of them in the last several years have seen riots and demonstrations against the organization and its members based on race or sex and identity politics.

The military is an interesting place to study diversity because it has a long history of diversity and it is a great place to test our ability to be fair to people from different backgrounds. Military leaders have more control over the personnel compared to their peers in private businesses and other government agencies. The military organization is not a democracy and military leaders have more latitude to order people to do any number of things compared to other organizations in society. If diversity initiatives cannot be successful in the military, it will be difficult to develop and implement them in any other organization.

THE VALUE OF DIVERSITY FOR ORGANIZATIONS

Besides the moral imperative of social diversity in the military, there may be a value to diversity for organizational effectiveness. Research shows that having people with diverse backgrounds may provide solutions to problems that would otherwise be limited by demography. Diversity is an antidote to the common problem of groupthink in organizations, the tendency to put limits on decision-making processes, to think "outside of the box" and apply novel approaches to existing problems (see Janis, 1971). Social diversity often reflects cultural diversity; African-Americans, for instance, bring a subculture with them to a job and so do women and Hispanic-Americans. Subcultures are cultures that exist within a larger culture. As a result, people from these subcultures may have a unique way to see and address problems that occur in organizations that provide any number of solutions to those problems. In the case of the military, diversity can provide a commander more options from which to make decisions. This is especially important in making decisions that may lead to mass casualties or the allocation of large sums of money and resources. Irving Janis, for instance, applied the concept of groupthink to explain the errors surrounding the decision to invade Cuba in 1961, otherwise known as the Bay of Pigs invasion (Janis, 1972). This event led President Kennedy to change the way he made important decisions to include people with different perspectives as a way to limit monolithic thinking processes.

Types of Diversity

When it comes to human diversity, there are almost no limits. We can discuss social statuses such as a race and gender but also sexuality. Consider the wide range of racial diversity. In the United States, the distribution of races is clear:

African-Americans, Caucasians, Asian-Americans, and Native Americans to name just a few. However, things become more complex when you bring in the concept of ethnicity. Though Hispanic-Americans currently outnumber African-Americans, being Hispanic refers to an ethnic, not a racial, identity. To add to this confusion, Asian-Americans can come from any number of countries that can represent racial and ethnic groups including China, Japan, and Korea.

Diversity also relates to gender and sexuality. Sex refers to the biological differences between men and women, while gender refers to the attributes and mannerisms we generally associate with being a man or woman in society. Women in the western world are more likely to wear dresses than men are for instance. We also expect women to act differently than men and most people are heterosexual, thus attracted to each other. However, unlike racial minorities, women are considered a minority status not because of their numerical position in society but because of their historically diminished social status. Women make 79 cents for every dollar that a man makes (American Association of University Women, 2016) and they are less likely to be in high-level leadership positions. According to Forbes business magazine, less than 20 percent of corporate officers (e.g., Chief Financial Officer) in the 500 largest US corporations are women (MacDonald & Schoenberger, 2007). As of 2015, only 19 percent of the 535 members of the US Congress are female and 20 percent of the Senate. Less than 10 percent of chief executive officers are female (Center for American Women

Table 1.1   Age, Sex and Racial Distribution of the US

Total population	314,107,084	100%
Gender		
Male	154,515,159	49.2%
Female	159,591,925	50.8%
Age		
Median age (years)	37.4	(X)
18 years and over	240,329,426	76.5%
Race and ethnicity*		
White	231,849,713	73.8%
Hispanic or Latino (of any race)	53,070,096	16.9%
Black or African-American	39,564,785	12.6%
Asian	15,710,659	5.0%
American Indian, Alaska Native, Pacific Islander	2,565,520	1.0%

*Percent does not add to 100% because Hispanic/Latino designation overlaps with racial categories.
Adapted from the 2014 American Community Survey retrieved from: https://www.census.gov/programs-surveys/acs/.

in Politics [CAWP], 2016). Similar distributions exists in the military where women represent less than 10 percent of general grade officers from any of the services (Sagalyn, 2011).

Sexual minorities may include any number of diverse groups. In terms of numbers, less than 5 percent of men and women would identify themselves as gay or lesbian (Bradbury & Karney, 2014; Michael, Gagnon, Laumann, & Kolata, 1995). It becomes more complicated when we consider the fact that some men identify as women and vice versa, reflecting the idea of transgender. Finally, there is the idea of intersex, men and women born with unclear sex characteristics such as being born with no genitalia or both forms of genitalia. These variations in sex and sexuality can lead to discrimination in organizations and society.

Diversity can take on so many different forms that it is difficult to include all of the types of social diversity that exist. Diversity can come in the form of religion, disability and even veteran status is a form of diversity. Hence, diversity may be a matter of relative proportion in a group or society or it may be about relative status or power (Blaine, 2013). The important thing about diversity is that it can provide both positive and negative outcomes in an organization. We have already reviewed some of the positive things about diversity; let us examine the negative side of diversity.

The Downside of Diversity

There are two ways to approach the role of diversity in organizations. Current thinking is that diversity is good for organizations because it protects us against the effects of things like groupthink and provides new ideas from which to make decisions. However, diversity is also a managerial challenge because organizational decisions affect people from different cultures in different ways. Consider the 2010 French law outlawing the use of burqas or head coverings by Muslim women. While this is a long-standing tradition among some Muslim cultures, the French government decided that the practice prevents clear identification of persons that may pose a security risk for law enforcement personnel. While it is clear that the law puts limits on diversity in French society, it was supported by the European Court of Human Rights (Willsher, 2014). Europeans espouse all sorts of diversity in lifestyle but their leaders decided to put limits on religious freedom because, they argued, it is for the good of the community.

The same logic is applicable to developing policies in any organization including the military. Consider the challenges of wearing a gas mask while maintaining a beard. Beards are generally not acceptable in the US Armed Forces, in part, because they restrict soldiers' ability to seal their gas masks. Soldiers have less than a minute or two to take out their masks and seal them during a chemical attack. Having a beard makes this process very difficult, if not impossible. However, some religions forbid or put limits on men from shaving and even the US Supreme Court has ruled that Muslim prisoners may grow a beard even though the practice goes against regulations (Totenberg, 2015). So how can a military commander allow for diversity while maintaining the efficiency and the lives of his or her soldiers? Unfortunately, there are no easy answers coming out of today's culture, a culture where people embrace diversity but also want organizational efficiency.

It is also important to note that diversity is one of the largest predictors of conflict (Hewitt, Wilkenfeld, & Gurr, 2012). Diversity is not just about individual freedom of expression but larger affiliations and perspectives that may conflict with other views of the world. Allowing diversity to flourish in society is one thing but managing all varieties of diversity in the workplace can be a challenge as differences lead to conflict about any number of things. Symbolic representations of these differences like clothing and hairstyle represent ideological differences. These differences not only cause anxiety for members as they navigate different value systems but can also produce differing opinions about how to deal with a particular issue or problem. The military organization is one of the most challenging places to understand diversity because leaders make life and death decisions every day. While leaders have the right to make decisions without much input from the people they lead, most of them are aware of the impacts of their decisions. Consider the concerns among Hispanic soldiers—many of whom are first generation Americans—as you engage in hostile action in Latin America or Muslim soldiers participating in operations in Iraq and Afghanistan. Having access to people who have knowledge of these places can be very useful to a commander but it also produces some anxiety among those troops. American military leaders need to have this kind of knowledge to optimize their decision-making processes.

The diversity of the human condition can be viewed as a problem for managers who simply want to manage an organization, to achieve its goals without much reference or caring for the types of people who work under them. We argue that leaders cannot afford to ignore social diversity if they are going to be successful in today's military. There has always been personality diversity but modern organizations also have social diversity. They must know how to make decisions with more information, information from these multiple perspectives, and they must resolve issues that arise from these differences. Consider managing people from the Northeastern United States as well as the Deep South, atheists and Satanists, gay people, Asian-Americans, and other groups, each with their own subcultures with different ways to manage life in the military. These differences can make it difficult to manage and achieve goals because leaders must consider these multiple perspectives before making important decisions. It is a lot of work! All managers of organizations have had to deal with some level of diversity but managers of the US workforce—and the military forces—have a greater number of perspectives to manage and more groups are seeking inclusion among minorities.

Social diversity can become a goal itself, adding to an already long list of things that a commander must consider in his or her day-to-day activities. It is important to note that not everyone accepts every type of diversity. Perhaps you have no animosity toward Muslims but you believe in banning the wearing of burqas. Muslims may have issues with their Jewish counterparts and vice versa. You may support affirmative action but do not agree with the homosexual lifestyle. If you are military leader, you still have to manage a diverse force and learn ways to deal with types of diversity even if it makes you feel uncomfortable. The goal of this book is not to convince you that you should embrace every form of diversity but we hope that it gives you the information you need to manage a diverse force. If you are not a military leader, this information is essential if you want to understand the diverse nature of military culture today and ways to deal with diversity in society. If the military organization cannot positively manage diversity with a focused policy run by leaders who follow those policies, it is going to be almost impossible to do it in a democracy in which multiple views collide with no clear guidelines.

THE MILITARY CONTEXT OF DIVERSITY

Armed forces in the United States and many western nations represent a democratic anomaly: They defend democracy yet maintain the least democratic organizational structure in existence. In the United States, there are four branches under the Department of Defense including the Army, Navy, and Air Force. The Marines, technically, serve under the Secretary of the Navy. Although under civilian oversite, service leaders make policies on almost every area of military life. In some cases, these policies are made with little civilian intervention while in other cases, the civilian government dictates policies in the military. For instance, Army Regulation 600–20 4–14b prohibits any social relationship that would undermine the authority of the chain of command. While it has been updated over the years, this situation almost always precludes senior ranking people from having sexual relationships with junior soldiers (e.g., Non-Commissioned Officers (NCOs) and junior enlisted troops or officers and enlisted personnel) (Schlosser, 2014). This regulation clearly is out of line with American culture that emphasizes individuality and freedom but one can argue that this and other rules exist for the maintenance of discipline and order. The important thing to consider is that the military both reflects American society among its members and its organizational structure operates outside of the democratic norms that exist in the larger society.

These dynamics are essential to understanding diversity in the military because policies related to diversity can come from within the organization or they can come from congressional or presidential orders. All branches of the armed services had policies banning homosexual relationships for much of the twentieth century; however, the well-known Don't Ask, Don't Tell Policy, which started in 1993, officially ended when President Barak Obama signed a new law allowing gays and lesbians to openly serve in the military in 2010 (Jelinek, 2010). Whether service men and women wanted to allow gays and lesbians to serve openly had little bearing on the decision to diversify the armed services in this way. Now, the military organization is more diverse with regard to homosexual relationships relative to many US states!

One could argue that the single most important event in the organizational history of the armed services in the United States is the end of the conscription or "the draft" in 1973. President Richard Nixon had campaigned in the 1960s to end the draft or conscription, which coincided with the end of the war in Vietnam. Huge changes needed to occur within the military organization in order to field an all-volunteer military. Military pay rates increased to entice more young people to join the services but many jobs in the military require extensive training so new soldiers would be required to sign a contract in order to offset the costs associated with training. Under this plan, the military gets some form of commitment while individuals have the freedom to join and, eventually, leave the military.

Unfortunately, for diversity, the all-volunteer force (AVF) creates no mechanism by which to control the diversity of its forces. Theoretically, a good draft should produce a random selection of rich and poor, men and women, black and white people, among other groups. The draft was not always this fair but, in principle, it is possible to do so utilizing this method. The AVF offers no such hope as it can only attract people who are predisposed to join the military or have some need to do so, such as financial issues or a court order. At any rate, a stereotype of the military as predominately working-class, white male from the Southeastern United States is accurate today through the AVF (Joyner, 2014).

The AVF has produced some anomalies; African-Americans, both males and females, have historically been overrepresented in the enlisted forces but underrepresented among officers. It is important to note that most officers have a college degree and African-Americans are less likely to graduate from college than whites and Asians. However, Asians are underrepresented in both the officer and enlisted forces in every branch of service even though they have higher education levels. In this case, social class is part of the story but so is race and ethnicity. That is, enlisted forces typically do not have a college degree and they come from the working class compared to the officer corps that is largely college-educated, middle- and upper middle-class men and women. Since 82 percent of the armed forces are enlisted ranks, it has a disproportionately higher number of working-class people relative to the general population. According to the National Center for Educational Statistics, 35 percent of Americans between the ages of 25 and 29 had a college degree or higher in 2015, a basic requirement to be a member of the officer corps. Hence, a disproportionately smaller number of people with a college degree are in the armed forces. Finally, women continue to represent less than 20 percent of the forces even though almost every position has been opened to them. Statistically, the military represents a male, working-class organization primarily white and African-American by race.

CURRENT STRUCTURE OF THE ARMED FORCES

There are currently 1,326,273 service men and women in the US military. There are also over one million reserve service members and almost 900,000 civilian Department of Defense employees (Military One Source, 2014). These figures represent the largest single employer in the United States and one of the largest militaries in the world, second only to China with India close behind. This size is important because India and China have two to three times the population of the United States.

Much like the US population, the military is primarily white (68.9 percent) but unlike the larger population, it is more male (85 percent) and less likely to have a college degree, as represented by the small number of the officer corps (18 percent) (Table 1.2). Also like the US population, most service members report being only one race (97 percent) but Asian-Americans are slightly underrepresented in the military compared to the general population while Native Americans (including Alaska natives and pacific islanders) are over-represented at 3 percent compared to about 1 percent of the general public.

Status comparisons are very important in the study of diversity in society. Do minority people have access to the same status as their majority counterparts? Utilizing officer and enlisted ranks as measures of relative status in the military, it is clear that being a minority varies with relative status in the military. That is, about 27 percent of officers in the Army are of a minority background compared to only 21 percent of the officers in the Navy and 19 percent in the Marines and Air Force. It is important to remember that being an officer typically requires a college degree but only 19 percent of African-Americans, for instance, currently have a college degree (*Journal of Blacks in Higher Education, 2016*).

Table 1.2 **Branch, Rank, Sex and Racial Distribution of the US Military**

Total active-duty population	1,326,273	100.0%
Branch		
Army	504,330	38.0%
Navy	321,599	24.2%
Marine Corps	187,891	14.2%
Air Force	312,453	23.6%
Rank		
Enlisted	1,090,939	82.3%
Officer	235,334	17.7%
Gender		
Male	1,125,581	84.9%
Female	200,692	15.1%
Race and ethnicity*		
White	914,203	68.9%
Black or African-American	228,148	17.2%
Hispanic or Latino	158,000	12.0%
Asian	52,891	4.0%
American Indian, Alaska Native, Pacific Islander	32,161	2.5%
Other/unknown	56,602	4.3%

*Percent does not add to 100% because Hispanic/Latino designation overlaps with racial categories.
Adapted from 2014 Demographics: Profile of the Military Community. Military One *Source*. Retrieved from: http://download.militaryonesource.mil/12038/MOS/Reports/2014-Demographics-Report.pdf.

THEORETICAL CONSIDERATIONS

There are at least two approaches to the study of diversity in the military. From a functional perspective, one can view the ways that diversity helps or hinders the military organization. Under this framework, diversity is like an independent variable and military efficiency is the outcome. The current thinking on this matter is that diversity allows organizations to prosper by providing alternative ways to resolving issues that come along and help us avoid things like groupthink (Janis, 1971). This framework focuses on the utilitarian value of diversity in organizations. Utilizing this perspective, the challenge for military leaders is to figure out how to manage and best harness the energy of a diverse workforce.

Another prospective in the social sciences approaches diversity from a moral dimension. The conflict perspective views diversity in the form of antagonism. Different groups in the military—and every other organization—compete for status and resources. This framework is useful for understanding why minority groups are upset when their group is underrepresented in higher ranks or perceive unfair treatment. For example, though American troops were desegregated in 1948 with President Truman's Executive Order 9981, scholars have argued that African-Americans were overrepresented in combat relative to white people in the Vietnam War (Butler, 1999). From this perspective, military leaders need to cope with different groups who view their service utilizing different frameworks from which to judge their leadership.

We want to emphasize a third perspective on the role of diversity in the military, one that emphasizes microlevel, every day interactions among people and the role of diversity in those interactions. First, identity theory focuses on the impacts of social statuses in our day-to-day lives, the ways in which the norms associated with different roles and statuses in society influences our values and beliefs—and our behaviors (Rohall, Milkie, & Lucas, 2015). Women experience the world differently than men and African-Americans carry a unique history from other racial and ethnic minorities. Understanding the people's backgrounds helps us in understanding their thought processes in everyday life. Men, for instance, are typically more conservative in their political values than women are; African-Americans are much more likely to vote with the Democratic Party than whites although they hold more conservative views on some issues and report higher levels of religiosity than whites (Newport, 2015). Imagine the challenges of working with and managing people every day with very different statuses. Each decision affects people in these groups differently and managers must take those differences into account when they make decisions that may produce some pushback.

Military affiliation is another form of social status. Rhetoric around the military mindset associated with aggression and war abound. Consider the popular movie *Dr. Strangelove* in which one of the main characters is General "Buck" Turgidson who loses his sense of reality and initiates a nuclear war. He is portrayed as both aggressive and insane. It does not take long to find similar portrayals such as another more recent popular film *Avatar* in which the character Colonel Miles Quaritch is also portrayed as aggressive and psychotic. Even the main character, Jake Sully, is an aggressive Marine who has a revelation that his perspective on life is wrong and fights against his former commander to save the indigenous people on another planet.

In one sense, these stereotypes are true: service men tend to be more hawkish then their civilian counterparts (Rohall & Ender, 2007). However, these differences are explainable with other social characteristics, especially gender. Women in the military are more hawkish relative to civilian women but less so than their male counterparts. These findings are important only because they provide a more complete understanding of diversity within the military and it gives us a sense of how service men and women differ from civilians.

It has also been argued that the military is more than just a job. The well-studied "Institutional-Occupational" model portrays the military as both a job and an institution (Moskos, 1977). As an institution, the military serves to protect society. Soldiers have rights to do things that other members of society are not, including the taking of lives if necessary. They wear special clothing that make them distinct from the rest of society and they have a sub-culture with unique norms and standards. From this perspective, the military organization gives its members a new framework from which to view the world, in addition to their other statuses.

The theory of intersectionality goes a step further than identity theory by incorporating the idea that people are more complicated than any one social status, that we develop our identity based on multiple, overlapping statuses and roles in society. This theory emphasizes the unique ways that individuals bring diversity from society and into organizations like the military. Utiliz-ing this framework, we cannot simply look at a particular race or gender—or military status; rather, we must see people as a culmination of many differ-ent cultures and backgrounds. African-American women, for instance bring a different set of characteristics into the military compared to white men, African-American men, or Hispanic women. It is more than just gender or race. It is not enough to understand the perspective of someone's gender or race or sexuality but the culmination of these things.

Military identity is only one of many statuses that service men and women hold and they are not defined by this single status. Consider the fact that Afri-can-Americans associated with the military were significantly less supportive of the wars in Afghanistan and Iraq than their white counterparts, controlling for a number of other background characteristics, but more supportive than their civilian counterparts (Ender, Rohall, & Matthews, 2015). If you want to understand individuals' attitudes toward war, it is not enough to know some-one's military status or their race but both. The theory of intersectionality provides the perspective by which to put these statuses together to understand people's perspectives on life.

The military organization provides a new status to men and women who join the services but they bring their own set of characteristics to the military. It is important to understand the military status as well as other major char-acteristics in society. In this book, we try to provide a framework for under-standing two sets of characteristics in each chapter because each one will include military status in addition to other social characteristics. Gay service members have unique lifestyles and perspectives relative to their counterparts in the civilian world and heterosexual military women have similar and dif-ferent experiences in the workforce compared to civilian women.

We believe that this volume is an important starting point for understand-ing the intersection of military status and other important characteristics. We believe that knowing how service members from each unique area of American life will give you insights into the talents that each group brings to the services. In addition, we want to show the unique challenges they face as they enter the services.

STRUCTURE OF THE BOOK

This edited work is the most comprehensive and up-to-date book to provide an overview of many forms of diversity in the US military including, race, class, gender, and sexuality with a short historical background of each group, an assessment of their current state of integration in the services, and predictions about the future of diversity in the services. We document the range of diversity that currently exists in the US military services by examining the history of inclusion and exclusion of each group and we provide a portrait of diversity in the military as it stands today. Each subject matter expert brings an extensive knowledge of each minority group and utilizes their specialized knowledge to help military leaders, service members, and students of the military better understand the unique and shared features that each group brings to the military organization. Ultimately, the goal of this book is to provide insights that will make the armed services capitalize on diversity and inclusion to create a more cohesive, professional military.

The second chapter, *African-Americans in the US Military*, JooHee Han emphasizes the important history of African-Americans' service in the military. In many ways, the African-American legacy is a model for understanding diversity in the military representing both the challenges and successes of diversifying the services. The goal of this chapter is to provide a heuristic device for understanding the inclusion of other minority groups, their triumphs and challenges.

In chapter 3, Dr. Karin De Angelis examines the increasing role of Hispanics in service today. She examines the changes in representation of Hispanics in service and their disproportionate representation in the Marine Corps. She argues that the presence and history of Hispanic soldiers are less studied than other minority groups but they represent the demographic future of the United States and the military since the military relies on the general public to supply its workforce.

In chapter 4, *Fighting to Belong: Asian-American Military Service and American Citizenship*, Dr. Deenesh Sohoni examines the roles of Asian-Americans in the services. Here, Dr. Sohoni tries to unpack the role of the military in immigration and naturalization processes more broadly and with Asian-Americans more specifically.

Dr. William Meadows gives us a view of another important ethnic minority group in the military, Native Americans, in chapter 5. Less is known about this small group in society (less than 1 percent of Americans are native) but they have a long history in the services. Indians participated in the Scouting Program in early American history and served in the Spanish American War, World War I and most other wars. They have a unique history during World War II as "code talkers," which is also reviewed in this chapter.

The second section of the book examines the role of sex, sexuality, and religion in the military today. The first chapter in this section is by Dr. Janice Laurence. She examines the rich history of women officially and unofficially serving the military as "camp followers" during the Revolutionary War in which they supported the troops by doing laundry and cooking for the troops. This chapter follows the long history of women in service while examining the current findings related to increasing opportunities for women to serve in combat.

Chapter 7, *Lesbian and Gay Service Members and Their Families*, addresses the newest minority groups formally recognized by the military: gay, lesbian and bi soldiers. Dr. David Smith and Dr. Karin De Angelis review the legal history leading up to the formal inclusion of these groups and then addresses the relative size of this group and the issues they face in today's military, including acceptance both at the unit and organization levels.

Chapter 8, *The Integration of Trans People into the Military*, is by Dr. Judith Rosenstein. Dr. Rosenstein focuses on a very specific group in the military: transgendered personnel. She examines what it means to be transgender in the first place before examining current policies with this population in service. As of this writing, the US military has repealed the ban on transgender service members and the author discusses changes and accommodation that will be necessary for full inclusion.

Dr. Michelle Sandhoff reviews the role of *Religious Diversity in the US Armed Forces* in Chapter 9. First, she provides an overview of the history and role of religion in the US military such as the function of the military chaplaincy as well as religiosity in the services (e.g., Stouffer and colleagues research on prayer during World War II). Finally, she examines current issues in addressing religious diversity in the services and policies that address those issues.

The last section of this book employs the social psychology of identity and the theory of intersectionality to the military by adding military status as a distinct one amidst race, ethnicity, gender, sexuality, and religion. How do the authors integrate military and minority statuses in each chapter? How does this knowledge help us better understand these intersecting identities? Our goal is also to assess how multiple statuses may combine in ways not specifically addressed in each chapter. How are lesbian, African-American women different from their heterosexual, white or black counterparts? We take some time to explore such intersections in a way that helps us understand the unique impacts of military identity on the lives of its diverse membership.

This time period is exciting for people who study the military and diversity more broadly. Society is changing with regard to inclusion of people from different backgrounds. The military organization will continue with its mission of defending the nation. The question is how the military will manage this diversity in the process of defending the nation. There are no easy answers to this question but we hope that this book will provide some insights into the matter and readers will learn something about the unique subcultures that people bring with them into the services and perhaps consider how the military subculture intersects with the other ones.

REFERENCES

American Association of University Women. (2016). *The simple truth about the gender pay gap*. Retrieved from http://www.aauw.org/research/ the-simple-truth-about-the-gender-pay-gap/

Butler, J. S. (1999). African Americans in the Vietnam War. In J. W. Chambers (Ed.), *The Oxford companion to American military history*. Oxford and other locations: Oxford University Press.

Center for American Women in Politics. (2016). *Women of U.S. Congress 2015*. New Brunswick, NJ. Retrieved from: http://www.cawp.rutgers.edu/ women-us-congress-2015.

Ender, M. G., Rohall, D. E., & Matthews, M. D. (2015). Intersecting identities: Race, military affiliation, and youth attitudes toward war. *War & Society*, 34(3). Retrieved from http://www.tandfonline.com/doi/full/10.1179/0729247315Z.00000000056

Gallup. (2016). *Gay and lesbian rights*. Washington D.C.: Gallup. Retrieved from http://www.gallup.com/poll/1651/gay-lesbian-rights.aspx

Hewitt, J. J., Wilkenfeld, J., Gurr, T. R., & Heldt, B. (2012). *Peace and conflict 2012*. College Park, MD: Center for International Development and Conflict Management, University of Maryland.

Janis, I. L. (1972). *Victims of groupthink: A psychological study of foreign policy decisions and fiascoes*. Pp. iii, 276. Boston, Mass.: Houghton Mifflin

Janis, I. L. (1971). "Groupthink." *Psychology Today* 5(6): 43–46, 74–76.

Journal of Blacks in Higher Education. (2016). More than 4.5 million African Americans now hold a four-year college degree. *The Journal of Blacks in Higher Education*. Retrieved from http://www.jbhe.com/news_views/64_degrees.html

Jelinek, P. (2010). DADT Repeal: Obama signing 'Don't Ask, Don't Tell' repeal bill into law. *Huffpost Politics*. Retrieved from: http://www.huffingtonpost. com/2010/12/22/dadt-repeal-obama-signing_n_800126.html

Michael, R.T., Gagnon, J. H., Laumann, E. O., & Kolata, G. (1994). *Sex in America*. New York: Little, Brown.

Military One Source. (2014). Retrieved from http://www.militaryonesource.mil/

MacDonald, E., & Schoenberger, C. R. (2007). "The world's most powerful women." *Forbes*. Retrieved from: http://www.forbes.com/2007/08/30/power- women-merkel-biz-07women-cz_em_cs_0830powerintro.html

Moskos, C, Jr. (1977). "From institution to occupation: Trends in military organization." *Armed Forces & Society*, 4: 41–50.

Newport, F. (2015). "Religion, race and same-sex marriage." *Gallup Report. The Gallup Organization*. Retrieved from: http://www.gallup.com/opinion/polling- matters/182978/religion-race-sex-marriage.aspx

Rohall, D. E., and Morten G. Ender. 2007. "Race, gender, and class: Attitudes toward the war in Iraq and President Bush among military personnel." *Race, Gender, & Class, 14*(3–4): 99–116.

Rohall, D. E., M. Milkie., & J. Lucas. (2015). *Social psychology: Sociological perspectives,* 3rd Edition. Boston & other locations: Pearson.

Sagalyn, D. (2011). "Report: U.S. Military Leadership Lacks Diversity at Top." *PBS Newshour.* Retrieved from: http://www.pbs.org/newshour/rundown/military-report/

Schlosser, T. (2014). *Army updates reg defining inappropriate relationships.* Retrieved from http://www.army.mil/article/138222/Army_updates_reg_defining_inappropriate_relationships/

Totenberg, N. (2015). *Supreme Court rules for Muslim inmate in prison beard case.* Retrieved from: http://www.npr.org/sections/thetwo-way/2015/01/20/378639564/supreme-court-rules-for-muslim-inmate-in-prison-beard-case

Willsher, K. (2014). France's burqa ban upheld by Human Rights Court. *The Guardian.* 1 July 2014. Retrieved from https://www.theguardian.com/world/2014/jul/01/france-burqa-ban-upheld-human-rights-court

Williams, R., Jr. (1970). *American society: A sociological interpretation,* 3rd Ed. New York: Knopf.

Wolf, A. (1998). *One nation, after all: What middle-class Americans really think about God, country, family, racism, welfare, immigration, homosexuality, work, the Right, the Left, and each other.* New York: Penguin.

Part I

RACE AND ETHNIC DIVERSITY
IN THE MILITARY

Chapter 2

African-Americans in the US Military

JooHee Han

Racial diversity in the US military is not limited just to the racial composition of the armed forces relative to their peers in the civilian population. Even if the racial composition in the US military is comparable to that of civilian population, there may also be uneven distributions in power and authority within the military. For example, there may be a smaller proportion of racial minorities in officer ranks who have relatively higher status in the services compared to the enlisted ranks. There are also issues of race relations within the military. For instance, there were periods when African-American soldiers were segregated from other races in the military and assigned to lower-status occupations or overrepresented in combat positions. This segregation extended beyond military bases as many minorities were unwelcome in off-base facilities such as barbershops, bars, and theaters; many faced hostility from civilians in communities surrounding military bases. Many incidents of racial conflict occurred after the death of Martin Luther King in 1968, for example, when white servicemen set fire to crosses and hung confederate flags as a sign of deep-rooted racism against African-Americans even among "brothers in arms" (Höhn & Klimke, 2010; Terry, 1971).

A formal ban on discrimination against racial minorities began in 1948 but some diversity issues remain unresolved and new ones have emerged following the all-volunteer force (AVF) in 1973. There are still concerns that African-Americans have lower rates of promotion than whites and concerns over their disproportionate exposure to combat continue to plague the discussion of race relations within the services.

In this chapter, I briefly introduce and discuss some of those diversity issues as they pertain to African-Americans. African-American service men and women have a history that goes back as far as the military services themselves. I focus on the major periods of American conflict to show the

19

changing relationship between African-Americans and the military both reflecting changes in American society as well as times and ways that the military has been more progressive than many civilian institutions. A special emphasis will be placed on the Army because that is where African-American participation has been largest, especially for males in the active duty component of enlisted ranks.

THE RIGHT TO FIGHT

African-Americans have fought for the United States throughout its history going back to the Colonial era. While officially excluded from joining militias going into the 19th century, over 3,000 African-Americans fought in The War of 1812; 180,000 and 29,000 African-Americans served in the Union Army and in Navy (respectively) during the Civil War (Lutz, 2008). Whenever there was a "manpower" shortage, blacks were allowed to serve. This dynamic (manpower shortages leading to more inclusion) would continue throughout American military history. In the colonial wars, the Revolutionary War, and the Civil War, the main reasons for prohibiting black participations was to keep the racial order of white supremacy and the fear of blacks' retaliation with arms as well as concerns over the loss of the labor in the civilian market. Discriminatory provisions were passed very early on in colonial history; in 1639, for instance, Virginia mandated all Virginians to arm, except for blacks. Similar provisions were passed in Massachusetts in 1656 and in Connecticut in 1661. However, these provisions were rescinded when there were not enough whites to fight against Native Indians and French (Foner, 1974). During the Revolutionary War, blacks were initially barred from joining the military but later this prohibition was lifted as the British military started to recruit black slaves in exchange for freedom (Lutz, 2008). During the American Civil War, President Lincoln called for volunteers, including free blacks, but they were often turned away at the recruiting centers. However, with the shortage of volunteer manpower Lincoln signed the Conscription Act in 1863, which included blacks (Foner, 1974). In a similar situation, in 1862, the Confederate army officially allowed free blacks to serve. In the meantime, black slaves were mobilized in menial labor such as construction and growing crops for the Confederate army and their income was paid to the slave owners (Young, 1982). In the early years of World War I, black volunteer enlistments were allowed only to fill the vacancies in all-black regiments, which resulted in enlistments of only 4,000. In comparison, 650,000 white volunteers, for which there was not such restriction, were accepted into the ranks (Foner, 1974).

Going into the 20th century, the US Congress passed the Selective Service Act of 1917, by which all able-bodied American male citizens aged twenty-one to thirty-one should be registered at local draft boards. It expanded African-American participation in the US Armed Forces. By the end of the war, about 2,291,000 African-Americans registered for draft constituting 9 percent of all registered men; 367,710 black men were inducted into the armed forces constituting 13 percent of all men drafted for service (Foner, 1974). Larger number of blacks served during World War II; over 900,000 in the Army (about 9 percent of the Army), 167,000 in the Navy (about 4 percent of the Navy), 17,000 in the Marine Corps (about 2 percent of the Marine Corps) (Lutz, 2008). Right after World War II, although many young men were drafted yet more African-Americans voluntarily enlisted in the Army, with 17 percent of enlisted men being black while the proportion of African-Americans in the US male population was 11 percent, aged 18–37 years (Young, 1982).

Continued support for integration appeared in laws passed during the World War II era. On September 16, 1940, for instance, an anti-discriminatory provision was produced: Section 4(a) of the Selective Service and Training Act stated, "there shall be no discrimination against any person on account of race or color" in selection and training of inducted men. This act, however, did not mention anything about segregation. As of 1939, blacks could serve in a small number of segregated units including 24th and 25th Infantry Regiments and 9th and 10th Cavalry Regiments. These units, Mershon and Schlossman (1998) argue, were legacies of the Reconstruction Era when the public began supporting blacks' civil rights for their contributions toward the victory of the Union Army. With such social support, these segregated units became institutionalized by Reconstruction laws that began to give blacks access to many public institutions, including the Army but in a segregated way, justifying the doctrine of "separate but equal."

In a move to end the institution of military racial segregation, President Harry S. Truman issued Executive Order 9981 in 1948, which states, "segregation as a form of racial discrimination" is outlawed in the military (Lutz, 2008, p.172). This initiative is particularly important because it happened before the US Supreme Court officially ended school segregation in 1954. However, segregation effectively continued in the military into the Korean War, and military leadership was resistant to ending segregation, especially in the Army where most of blacks served. For example, in the testimony to the Fahy Committee, Secretary of the Army Kenneth C. Royall insisted that segregation with assigning blacks only to their qualified tasks is a rational division of labor, implying the inferiority of black servicemen in learning complex tasks. Despite these concerns, manpower shortages during the Korean War moved ahead the cause of equality in the forces. Army officers started to implement desegregation measures, with the support of the Truman's Executive Order at this time, which were later expanded to units in the United States and around the world (Mershon & Schlossman, 1998). By the end of the Korean War, the US Army became integrated, at least formally, with only about 10,000 of a total of 250,000 African-Americans serving in segregated units as of January, 1954 (Young, 1982).

Even before the services were formally desegregated, scholars began to question whether there was an unequal burden of military service for African-Americans. On October 9, 1940, the White House released a statement regarding the Army's enlistment policy, which specified that "the number of Blacks in the army should correspond to the proportion of Blacks in the total population" (Foner, 1974, p.138). This policy helped to make the representation of the blacks in the total armed forces, as well as in the Army, proportionate with the civilian population as it increased from 7.3 percent in 1955 to 11.1 percent in 1972 (Moskos, 1973). However, during the Vietnam War, specifically between 1961 and 1966, blacks were found to be more likely to be drafted than whites with blacks constituting 14.8 percent of total draftees while constituting about 11–12 percent of the eligible age group (Moskos, 1971). This overrepresentation of black draftees likely resulted from the fact that a larger proportion of blacks were disqualified for the draft based on their lower mental ability scores and poor health conditions, which left smaller proportions of them eligible for draft. However, when taking the disqualified blacks into account, Fligstein (1980) notes, African-Americans had been underrepresented in the military during the World War II period, the Korean War period, and in the Vietnam Era controlling for demographic attributes such as socioeconomic status, education level, and age.

Although blacks had been disqualified at higher rates than whites, they had also been less likely to obtain occupational or student deferments, which were granted more to whites than blacks (Moskos, 1971; 1973). During World War II, deferments were granted to those who worked in occupations essential to national interests such as health and safety, agricultural workers, clergymen and divinity students, and public officials. By 1945, only 4.4 percent of these deferments were given to blacks, with an exception of agricultural deferments (Murray, 1971). Selective deferments expanded to college students, fathers, and married men for limited periods during the Korean War. This expansion, however, had a negative impact on African-Americans since few blacks attended college and many of them did not have occupations which qualified for deferment except for agricultural jobs (Murray, 1971). Thus, this process favored white students and professionals from the middle classes at the expense of lower socioeconomic groups, including blacks (Laurence, 2004). While some people wanted an end to deferments as a way to increase military manpower, military officials responded by loosening enlistment qualification standards leading to an even higher proportion of African-Americans being drafted into service (Murray, 1971).

A well-known recruiting program, which led to higher rates of enlistment among African-Americans, was called, "Project 100,000." Introduced in

1966 as a part of President Lyndon Johnsons' War on Poverty, this program drew on blacks and youths without high school diplomas, accepting more people with lower aptitudes and physical health problems than in previous times—people who would have otherwise been deemed ineligible. Many of them served as infantrymen in the Vietnam War (Laurence, 2004). It is clear that the primary motive of the program was to help staff the armed forces in Vietnam but it had little benefit to the poor and otherwise unqualified servicemen who joined the military as a result of the program (Murray, 1971). These processes clearly create a dynamic, which both helps provide equality in the forces by bringing people from more diverse walks of life but later created unfairness as those same people are differentially exposed to harm and lack access to higher statuses and pay within the services via promotion.

African-Americans in the Early AVF Era

The US military lost some of its ability to control racial composition of the forces by transitioning to the AVF system, which relies completely on volunteers. Critics believed that the AVF would likely recruit from socially disadvantaged groups including racial minorities and people with less education. This system, they believed, may lead to a disproportionate number of them being put into combat. As anticipated, the proportion of African-Americans in the US military increased when the AVF was implemented when the proportion went from 9.7 percent in 1964, a year before the Vietnam War, to 15.7 percent in 1974, a year after the transition to AVF, and further to 18.4 percent as of March, 1978 (Janowitz & Moskos, 1979). Black overrepresentation continued to increase to 22 percent in the total US Armed Forces and 33 percent in the Army in 1980 (Armor & Gilroy, 2010) including many black women.

Black overrepresentation in the military is closely associated with qualification standards for nonprior service-enlisted accessions. The military, intentionally and unintentionally, accepted many people from among the lower end of the aptitude scale in the early AVF era after the Vietnam War ended because many American youths lost interest in military service. Thus, the military had the challenge to staff the services without having an adequate pool of recruits. By lowering standards, the military could access a larger potential pool of recruits. The Army initially planned to set a goal of a ratio of high school graduates to dropouts at 70:30. Later, however, it settled on a ratio of 50:50 (Bailey, 2009).

Between 1976 and 1980, the proportion of blacks in the nonprior service accessions dramatically surged again, from 18 percent in 1975 to 26 percent in 1979 (Armor & Gilroy, 2010) and to 37 percent in the Army in 1980 while their percentage of civilian youth population was 13 percent (Armor, 1996). In this period, with Armed Forces Qualification Test (AFQT) scoring error, known as the "mis-norming error," the military unintentionally allowed a large number of less qualified applicants who would not otherwise be eligible to enlist. Many recruits whose scores ranged between 10th and 30th percentile (AFQT Category IV or "Cat IV") were accepted with this error and they comprised about half of the total nonprior service-enlisted accessions in the Army and a third in the total armed forces during this period (Armor & Gilroy, 2010).

The mis-norming error invoked concerns over the quality of the military manpower. The error was corrected in 1980 and Congress made efforts to ameliorate quality concerns by investing more resources into personnel such as increased pay, benefits, and financial support for college education as a way of attracting better qualified youths (Armor, 1996). The military successfully raised enlistment standards in the 1980s. As a consequence, the quality of recruits improved considerably but many less qualified applicants, mostly blacks, were cast off from the military service opportunities. The proportion of recruits with AFQT Cat IV decreased to about 5 percent in this period and has remained below it since 1990 (Armor & Gilroy, 2010). In addition, the proportion of accessions without a high school diploma in the total armed forces decreased from less than 70 percent in 1980 (55 percent in the Army) to 6 percent (9 percent in the Army) in 1987 (US Congressional Budget Office, 1989). Fixing the AFQT mis-norming error likely impacted blacks more severely since they were disproportionately distributed in the lower quartile of the AFQT scores at the time (Angrist, 1998; Laurence & Ramsberger, 1991).

The size and quality of the armed forces increased during the 1980s. In 1991, when the first Gulf War occurred, the military experienced a sharp drop in black representation in enlisted accessions by five-percentage points (Armor & Gilroy, 2010). The military experienced another sharp drop of five-percentage points in 2002, a year after the 9/11 terrorists attacks on the World Trade Center (Armor & Gilroy, 2010). Scholars attributed the decrease in the black representation in the enlisted accessions in this period to a change in the supply side, that is, a drop in the level of willingness among young African-Americans to join the military (Segal, Bachman, Freedman-Doan, & O'Malley, 1999). Propensity for military service is measured by proportion of respondents who indicate that they will be either "definitely" or "probably" serving in the military in the next few years on survey questionnaires. The most well-known study of this topic comes from the "Monitoring the Future" longitudinal survey of American youths. Research using these and other data sources show that African-Americans' propensity to serve persisted at higher than 30 percent until 1989 and then it dropped to about 16 percent in 1992. Whites' propensity to serve remained relatively stable during this time period at about 10 percent (Armor & Gilroy, 2010).

Black representation in enlisted accessions bounced back after a sharp decline. The proportion of blacks (including Hispanic blacks)[1] increased from

11.8 percent in 2003 to 19.3 percent in 2014 (Office of the Under Secretary of Defense, Personnel and Readiness, 2015). This increase was found in all branches except for the Navy, where black representation declined in this period.

Equality within the Military

Having an adequate ratio of races within the military does not necessarily mean that forces are equitable. Moskos (1973) raised concerns over the racial inequality in terms of representation in different ranks and grades that determine power, authority, prestige, and compensation. He pointed out that black representation was highly concentrated in the enlisted ranks (E1–E4) and the low noncommissioned officer ranks, constituting 23.9 percent of E6 (staff sergeant) and 19.6 percent of E7 (sergeant 1st class) in the Army in 1972. On the other hand, only 3.9 percent of the officer corps in the Army was black, 1.7 percent in the Air Force, 1.5 percent in the Marine Corps, and only 0.9 percent in the Navy.

As the military transitioned to the AVF system, however, the power differential through the distribution of blacks in different ranks or grades have improved in many ways. For example, African-Americans' access to the office corps expanded to as much as 4 percent of the total officer corps in 1987 and 6.4 percent in the Army (Jankowitz & Moskos, 1979), far greater than in the pre-AVF era. According to the Office of the Under Secretary of Defense (2015), both black representation in the officer corps and gains in the office corps continued to expand throughout this time period. The proportion of non-Hispanic they in the total Department of Defense officer corps increased to 9.6 percent in 2001 and 13.5 percent in the Army while they constituted only 8.2 percent of the comparable civilian population (twenty-one- to thirty-five-year-old population in the noninstitutionalized civilian population). This led to increasing representation of African-Americans among the total officer corps from 3.4 percent in 1976 to 8.5 percent in 2002 (5.3 percent and 12.1 percent, respectively, in the Army). Since then, however, the proportion of blacks (including Hispanic) among the officer corps decreased from 8.8 percent in 2003 to 6.9 percent in 2014 (12.5–8.4 percent in the Army). Despite the decrease in black gains in this period, the proportion of blacks in the total officer corps stayed stable around at 8.5 percent between 2004 and 2014 and around 12.5 percent in the Army.

Another way to assess racial and other forms of inequality in the military is the rate of promotion people experience within their respective groups. In this case, do African-Americans get promoted at the same rate as other racial and ethnic groups? Once again, rank is associated with both pay and relative status in the services. The Congressional Black Caucus raised the issue of institutional racism against blacks on active duty based on testimony that it was more difficult for blacks to get promoted than whites (Butler, 1976). Institutional racism includes the ways in which organizations maintain inequality through their rules and regulations. Examples in the civilian world include problems finding loans and obtaining adequate housing among minority populations (Phillips, 2011).

One could justify racial differences in promotion rates by attributing them to their lower levels of education, AFQT scores, and occupation. (Note that people in different Military Occupational Specialties [MOSs] get promoted at different rates.) However, after analyzing the administrative data from the Enlisted Master Tape Record (EMTR), which contains information on all service members, Butler (1976) concluded that the mean time to be promoted to rank for African-Americans was longer than whites even after controlling for education levels, AFQT scores, and MOS. Hauser (1978), however, refuted the validity of this conclusion arguing that the analysis did not take into account those people who were promoted to upper ranks more quickly but then left the military, which can create upward bias of the time to promotion.

Later, Daula, Smith, and Nord (1990) reexamined this question by adjusting censoring of those who left the military and thus were not reflected in the previous analysis. Analyzing the Enlisted Panel Research Database, which contained promotion histories of a 25 percent sample of all Army enlistees who joined between 1974 and 1987, they found that there was a variation in promotion time depending on military occupations, with minorities promoted faster than whites by 3–4 percent in mechanics and administration but slower by 3.5 percent in infantry among some enlisted personnel (E4–E5). They insisted that the seemingly slower promotion of blacks was because blacks were more likely to stay longer than whites when faced with slow promotion whereas whites were more likely to leave. However, they also warn that these results do not mean that there is no institutional discrimination against African-American soldiers in the Army. Among officers, Baldwin (1997) found that promotion rates of African-Americans exceeded that of whites to the rank of captain (O6) in the Navy. This variation shows the complexities of organizational life in the military and the challenges of monitoring fairness with regard to rank and status as it pertains to diversity in the military.

The military is one of the few institutions who have authority to put Americans in harm's way. As a result, another way that discrimination may manifest itself in the military has to do with exposure to danger, which may yield one of the worst forms of discrimination, death, and injury. While African-Americans experienced organizational discrimination in the form of racial segregation, as discussed above, they were also assigned to lower-status support occupations and their right to fight in combat units was often denied until World War II. Controversies over segregation reversed and critics became concerned as to whether African-Americans were put at a greater risk of death. For example, African-American leaders criticized US defense policies arguing that disproportionate numbers of blacks were sent to the Gulf War as a "cannon fodder" (Armor, 1996). However, systemic analyses of casualties by race have been relatively scarce with a few exceptions.

In the Vietnam Era, Moskos (1973) pointed out that an increasing proportion of blacks were being assigned to combat arms including infantry, armor, and artillery whereas decreasing proportion of whites were assigned to them. In 1945, 1962, and 1970, respectively, the percentage of total black personnel in combat arms increased from 12.1 percent, 33.4 percent, and 26.0 percent whereas it decreased from 48.2 percent, 24.9 percent, and 23.4 percent for whites. Moskos continued to argue that a disproportionate number of black casualties in the Vietnam War might be caused by their concentration in combat arms. Black proportion of the killed-in-action was as high as 20 percent in the army and 16 percent in the total armed forces between 1961 and 1966 but decreased to 9.1 percent in the Army and 8.8 percent in the total armed forces in 1970. The black proportion of the cumulative total casualties in 1961–1970 was 12.5 percent in the total armed forces and 13.3 percent in the Army, marginally different from that in the civilian population.

Utilizing Cook County (Chicago) area casualty data, which contained all Army personnel killed in action between 1964 and mid-1968 and all branch personnel killed in action between mid-1968 and 1972, Badillo and Curry (1976) tested whether blacks actually had higher risk of casualty in the Vietnam War. They found that low socioeconomic status rather than race increased the risk of death.

In the more recent Iraq War, two studies found that African-Americans were less likely to die in combat. Gifford (2005) documents that blacks comprised 14.0 percent of total casualties (643), between 2003 and 2004, similar to the US population of eighteen to thirty-four-year-olds (13.4 percent), but considerably lower than the proportion in all active duty military (20.3 percent).[2] Ender (2009) finds similar lower proportions for African-Americans among all 3,807 American fatalities in Iraq from March 2003 through the so-called surge in Iraq in 2007.

IMPACTS OF MILITARY SERVICE

Perceptions of Military Service

Most of the analysis in this chapter has emphasized statistical comparisons of placement within the military structure and other barriers to full racial integration of the services. The question remains as to how African-American service men and women experience military life. Research suggests that many of them perceive military service positively. For example, African-Americans have higher reenlistment rates than whites (MLDC, 2010). In another study utilizing data from the Pentagon's 1999 Survey of Active Duty Personnel, Lundquist (2008) finds that African-Americans and Hispanic military personnel report higher levels of perceived benefits, job satisfaction, and quality of life compared to white males.

Impacts of Military Life on Families

Military scholars continue to monitor the impacts of military life on families. The military is often called a "greedy institution" because it requires an exorbitant amount of time and energy from the people working for it (Segal, 1986). Concurrently, the military also provides benefits to people from all walks of life; it can serve as a "leveler" of sorts for people coming from disadvantaged backgrounds. A number of studies show that military service does have a positive impact on families, especially among otherwise disadvantaged groups. For example, marriage rates of African-American active duty personnel are found to be similar to that of whites while there is a significant difference between black-white marriage patterns among civilians with blacks being far less likely to marry than whites (Lundquist, 2004). Furthermore, it is found that infant mortality and preterm birth of black women in the military are considerably lower than civilian black women although the black-white differences remain even in the military setting suggesting that white women benefit even more from the military health care system (Lundquist, Elo, Barfield, & Xu, 2014).

AFRICAN-AMERICAN VETERANS

With relatively high levels of pay and benefits, the military has always been an alternative to civilian careers for many Americans but especially for African-Americans and other disenfranchised groups in the civilian world. Given the standards by which the military selects potential recruits, one could argue that blacks are positively selected into military service. Mare and Winship (1984) argue that as better educated and more competitive black youths either join the military or go to college, it results in sustaining an unemployment gap between black and white civilians, despite blacks' increasing educational attainment in general. The positive selection of black youth into the military leads to a long-standing important diversity issue for the relationship between the armed forces and society because it contributes to the bifurcation of the African-American labor market.

A regular debate among military scholars is whether the services give working-class veterans an advantage in the civilian labor market because military service provides real job experience to people who would otherwise have little or no consistent professional work experience (Kleykamp, 2007). Browning, Lopreato, and Poston (1973) argued that the military provided World War II and Korean War minority veterans with a "bridging career." They found African and Mexican-American veterans had higher average incomes compared to nonveterans while white veterans had an income penalty relative to their civilian counterparts. However, Cutright (1974) refuted the "bridging career" argument after analyzing earnings of Korean War veterans in 1964. He found that accounting for time-lost in the civilian labor market during the service produced negative effects for white veterans and a negligible earnings premium for African-Americans, which even yielded negative results when education levels were controlled for. Nevertheless, in a more recent study, Teachman and Tedrow (2004) found that African-American veterans from World War II had a relatively high veterans' premium in earnings. They explained that this premium resulted from occupational training while in the military and more investment in vocational training and college education after the World War II compared to nonveterans. African-American veterans' earnings were higher than nonveterans controlling for education, family background, and other factors.

For the AVF-era veterans, the positive effects of military service among blacks are found to have continued although the effects and their duration vary depending on education level. Teachman and Tedrow (2007) examined the income trajectories of veterans who served during the early years of AVF era and found that African-American veterans without high a school diploma had a long-term income premium but the income premium for those with a high school degree persisted only for a short period. Similarly, Angrist (1998) found that military service yielded a long-term increase in the civilian earnings as well as higher employment rates of nonwhites veterans. Meanwhile, military service had a negative impact on white veterans' civilian earnings.

Scholars have also examined the possible impacts of military service on the life course. Life course sociology examines the ways that life events create different trajectories for people over time (Elder, 1994). Given that most veterans come from lower middle- and working-class backgrounds, military service can give these people an opportunity to break out of bad relationships and lifestyles that would otherwise have negative consequences for them later in life. Utilizing data from a famous study by Eleanor and Sheldon Glueck at Harvard University conducted after World War II, Sampson and Laub (1996) analyzed data of 1,000 underprivileged men raised in the Boston area to examine the effect of military service over their life course. They found that overseas service reduced the number of arrests and dishonorable discharges significantly for those who had delinquent pasts. Thus, military service seems to have mitigated the negative life histories of these men. Most of the impacts of military service on the life course come from improving job prospects and increasing marriage rates. The military provided these men a stable source of income and benefits that they would not have had otherwise; having a stable job and family is negatively related to criminal behaviors.

More recent research has shown similar impacts of military service on the life course but findings vary by race and ethnicity. Bouffard (2005), for instance, tested veterans from the early years of the AVF era and found that the deterrence effect of military service on violent offenses is limited only to African-Americans. Similarly, Craig and Connel (2015) found that military service in the early AVF era increased desistence of criminal behaviors for nonwhite veterans only. As a consequence, black veterans from the Vietnam War and from the early AVF era were found to have lower risk of incarceration relative to age-matched nonveterans (Greenberg, Rosenheck, & Desai, 2007).

THE FUTURE OF AFRICAN-AMERICANS IN THE MILITARY

African-Americans have played a part in American military history going back to the country's origins. Unlike most other minority groups who came to the military through immigration, African-Americans began fighting discrimination in the form of slavery. There were free blacks and slaves who served the military in different capacities but it creates a nonlinear narrative in which African-Americans had to fight for formal recognition both in the services and in the civilian world, even though they have been involved in the military from its inception. This struggle paid off in many respects as African-Americans have come to be a major part of the military, especially in the Army, at every rank. But it is also clear that the struggle is not over because there is a pattern of discrimination that must continually be monitored given the ways that promotions and exposure to harm has varied over the years. That is, it appears that African-Americans have experienced more exposure to harm at some periods of time compared to other times and access to high-status positions has also varied over time, even though it has been consistently better over the last decade.

It is also important to monitor recruitment levels of African-Americans over time. Levels have varied dramatically over the last half century but their representation has declined relative to the early years of AVF era. As decreasing number of African-Americans join the military, Segal and Segal (2005) warn that this may result in failing to maintain necessary manpower in the Army, which depends largely on blacks in meeting recruiting and reenlistment goals. This may necessitate a change in recruiting strategy, pay, and benefits. A decline in enlistment is a loss to both the military and the

African-American community. About 8–9 percent of black men aged sixteen to thirty-five were estimated to serve in the military during the late 1970s and early 1980s (Kleykamp, 2007). However, in the first half of the 1990s, military drawdown eliminated about 500,000 jobs. This decline in the military personnel size affected blacks stronger than whites since blacks disproportionately comprised the armed forces. However, Kleykamp (2010) finds that many of these African-Americans who would otherwise have joined the military went to college rather than seeking employment in the civilian labor market; she estimates that military downsizing accounts for about a 10 percent increase in blacks' college enrollment rates.

Other scholars have argued that the military still serves as a major source of employment among the African-American population who face poor economic and social conditions in the social world. The incarceration rate among African-American men has skyrocketed since the early 1980s. The cumulative risk of prison incarceration at the ages of thirty to thirty-four for birth cohorts between 1965 and 1969 is 20.5 percent, twice that of the older birth cohorts between 1945 and 1949. As black men increasingly experience imprisonment at a higher rate than military service or earning a bachelor's degree, Pettit and Western (2004) point out that the prison emerged as a "major institutional competitor to the military and the educational system, at least for young Black men with little schooling" (p. 156).

The data in Figure 2.1 presents the estimated percentages of black and white men in the military (dots) and prison/jail (solid lines) out of the total male population of each race age sixteen and above in 1980–2010. The simultaneous increase in incarceration and decrease in military service since 1980 has resulted in a crossover of the two populations of affiliated black men in the early 1990s (Gupta & Lundquist, 2013; Han, 2016). By comparing the two cohorts of National Longitudinal Survey of Youth 1979 and 1997, Han (2016) finds that military downsizing and the change in qualification standards since 1980 cast off many low-skilled African-Americans from military service opportunities and that many of these newly unqualified were channeled into the penal system as a consequence.

Considering that a large number of black youths are at risk of imprisonment instead of having opportunities to serve in the military for the country, it will be necessary to expand ways to give disadvantaged minority youths an alternative or a second chance to be a good citizen of the American society. One way would be expanding the current criminal history or "moral" waiver program, which grants applicants who faced criminal charges before joining the military eligibility. Although most of these men were charged with misdemeanors, some were charged with felonies. About 20 percent of the total enlisted accessions in 2006 were moral waivers and the proportion of moral waivers was 54.3 percent of the Marine Corps accessions (Boucai, 2007). In

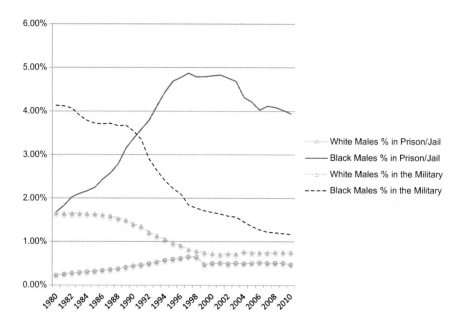

Figure 2.1   Proportion of the Military Population and Incarcerated Population by Race among Men Age 16 and Above (1980-2010). Author's calculation based on Census, Bureau of Justice Statistics, and Department of Defense data.

a recent study, Lundquist, Pager, and Strader (2016) find that moral waivers perform as good as or sometimes outperform regular recruits. However, due to lack of applicant pool data, they could not assess whether a moral waiver is given to black and whites at the same rates.

There are several critical topics that need further discussion but were not included in this chapter. Here, I briefly address two of them. First, it is necessary to note that African-American women representation in the military has been increasing. Moore (1991) documents that African-American women increasingly comprise a larger proportion of military personnel; black women constituted only 0.56 percent of total active duty armed forces in 1974 but 3.7 percent in 1989. Among female active-duty personnel, enlisted black women increased from 14.4 percent in 1971 to 33.7 percent in 1989. This overrepresentation of blacks among female military personnel persists today. In 2010, about 31 percent of female military personnel were black (Patten & Parker, 2011). Like many black men, black women pursue military careers as a better alternative to civilian labor market (Melin, 2016). Thus, the over-representation of African-American women in the military is expected to continue unless the prospect of the civilian labor market for them improves substantially.

Another important topic that was not sufficiently addressed in this chapter relates to racial tensions between black and white military personnel that have not been fully resolved. After series of race-related incidents that occurred at the end of the Vietnam War, the Department of Defense established the Defense Race Relations Institute (DRRI) in 1971, which was later renamed as Defense Equal Opportunity Management Institute (DEOMI) in 1979. This organization is charged with helping to resolve racial tensions and to shape the military as a more racially integrated institution (Dansby, Stewart, & Webb, 2001).

Research on race relations in the military suggests that the military services have a lot of work to do. Nteta and Tarsi (2015), for example, show that white veterans in the AVF era expressed more racial resentment toward African-Americans than civilian whites and pre-AVF era veterans. Further efforts will be needed to identify what generates such negative views against racial minorities among the white military personnel and how to improve race relations more broadly. The authors suggest that one explanation is self-selection into the different MOSs causing less formal and informal interaction among blacks and whites than in the past.

Like American society, the US military must manage a highly diverse group of people. African-Americans represent some of the worst and best experiences of minorities in military service and they have had a relationship with the American military from its earliest days. Findings from this chapter can show how the military can be a great resource for people from otherwise disenfranchised backgrounds but also a source of frustration and discrimination. By monitoring the well-being of troops—especially given the rocky history of African-Americans in service—the military can be a model of managing diversity for the rest of American society. And, the lessons learned from the long history of African-Americans' service may aid the military as it continues to further integrate women, gays, lesbians, bisexuals, transgender, and other historically discriminated people into its ranks.

NOTES

1. There was a change in the way DoD reported race/ethnicity data in 2003, collecting race data separately from Hispanic ethnicity.

2. For the detail number of American casualties in major wars, see Congressional Research Service (2015). "American War and Military Operations Casualties: Lists and Statistics." Available online at: https://fas.org/sgp/crs/natsec/RL32492.pdf.

REFERENCES

Angrist, J. (1998). Estimating the labor market impact of voluntary military service using social security data on military applicants. *Econometrica, 66*(2), 249–88.

Armor, D. (1996). Race and gender in the U.S. military. *Armed Forces and Society, 23*(1), 7–27.

Armor, D. & Gilroy, C. (2010). Changing minority representation in the U.S. military. *Armed Forces & Society, 36*(2), 223–249.

Badillo, G. & Curry, D. (1976). The social incidence of Vietnam casualties. *Armed Forces & Society, 2,* 397–406.

Bailey, B. (2009). *America's Army: Making the All-Volunteer Force.* Cambridge, MA: The Belknap Press of Harvard University Press.

Baldwin, N.J. (1997). Equal promotion opportunity in the United States Navy. *Journal of Political and Military Sociology, 25*(2), 187–209.

Boucai, M. (2007). Balancing your strengths against your felonies: Considerations for military recruitment of ex-offenders. *University of Miami Law Review, 61*(4), 997–1032.

Bouffard, L. (2005). The military as a bridging environment in criminal careers: Differential outcomes of the military experience. *Armed Forces & Society, 31*(2), 273–295.

Browning, H. Lopreato, S., & Poston, D., Jr. (1973). Income and veteran status: Variations among Mexican Americans, blacks and anglos. *American Sociological Review, 38,* 74–85.

Butler, J. (1976). Inequality in the military: An examination of promotion time for black and white enlisted men. *American Sociological Review, 41*(5), 807–818.

Craig, J.M. & Connell, N.M. (2015). The All-Volunteer Force and crime: The effects of military participation on offending behavior. *Armed Forces & Society, 41*(2), 329–351.

Cutright, P. (1974). The civilian earnings of white and black draftees and nonveterans. *American Sociological Review, 39*(3), 317–327.

Dansby, M., Stewart, J., & Webb, S. (2001). *Managing Diversity in the Military.* New Brunswick, NJ: Transaction Publishers.

Daula, T., Smith, A., & Nord, R. (1990). Inequality in the military: Fact or fiction? *American Sociological Review, 55*(5), 714–18.

Elder, G.H. (1994). Time, human agency, and social Change: Perspectives on the life course. *Social Psychology Quarterly, 57*(1), 4–15.

Ender, Morten G. (2009). *American Soldiers in Iraq: McSoldiers or Innovative Professionals?* NY and London: Routledge.

Fligstein, N.D. (1980). Who served in the military, 1940–1973? *Armed Forces & Society, 6*(2), 297–312.

Foner, J.D. (1974). *Blacks and the Military in American History.* New York: Praeger.

Gifford, B. (2005). Combat casualties and race: What can we learn from the 2003–2004 Iraq conflict? *Armed Forces & Society, 31*(2), 201–225.

Greenberg, G.A., Rosenheck, R.A., & Desai, R.A. (2007). Risk of incarceration among male veterans and nonveterans: Are veterans of the All-Volunteer Force at greater risk? *Armed Forces & Society, 33*(3), 337–350.

Gupta, S. & Lundquist, J.H. (2013). The converging proportions of the U.S. adult population in the military and in prison, 1960 to 2010. Paper presented at the annual meeting of the Population Association of America, New Orleans.

Han, J. (2016). *Where did prisoners come from: Military to prison channeling of male youths 1980–2010*. Working paper.

Hauser, R. (1978). On inequality in the military. *American Sociological Review, 43*(1), 115–118.

Höhn , M. & Klimke, Martin. (2010). *A Breadth of Freedom: The Civil Rights Struggle, African American GIs, and Germany*. NewYork, NY: Palgrave Macmillan

Janowitz, M. & Moskos, C. (1979). Five years of the All-Volunteer Forces: 1973–1978. *Armed Forces & Society, 5*(2), 171–218.

Kleykamp, M. (2007). Military service as a labor market outcome. *Race, Gender & Class*, 14, 65–76.

Kleykamp, M. (2010). Where did the soldiers go? The effects of military downsizing on college enrollment and employment. *Social Science Research, 39*, 477–90.

Laurence, J. & Ramsberger, P. (1991). *Low-aptitude men in the military: Who profits, who pays?* New York: Praeger.

Laurence, J.H. (2004). *The All-Volunteer Force: A historical perspective.* Office of Under Secretary of Defense, Washington DC: RAND.

Lundquist, J.H. (2008). Ethnic and gender satisfaction in the military: The effect of a meritocratic institution. *American Sociological Review, 73*(3), 477–496.

Lundquist, J., Pager, D., & Strader, E. (2016). *Does a criminal past predict worker performance?: Evidence from America's largest employer.* Working paper.

Lundquist, J., Elo, I., Barfield, W., & Xu, Z. (2014). Racial disparities in US infant birth outcomes: A protective effect of military affiliation? *Race and Social Problems, 6*(2), 161–180.

Lutz, A. (2008). Who joins the military?: A look at race, class, and immigration status. *Journal of Political and Military Sociology, 36*(2), 167–188.

Mare, R. & Winship, C. (1984). The paradox of lessening racial inequality and joblessness among black youth: Enrollment, enlistment, and employment, 1964–1981. *American Sociological Review*, 49, 39–55.

Melin, J. (2016). Desperate choices: Why black women join the U.S. military at higher rates than men and all other racial and ethnic groups. *New England Journal of Public Policy, 28*(2) (Article 8), Available at: http://scholarworks.umb.edu/nejpp/vol28/iss2/8

Mershon, S. & Schlossman, S. (1998). *Foxholes and Color Lines*. Baltimore, MD: Johns Hopkins Press.

MLDC. (2010). Reenlistment rates across the services by gender and race/ethnicity. Issue Paper #31 downloaded on December 21, 2016 from: https://www.hsdl.org/?view&did=716162.

Moore, B. (1991). African-American women in the U.S. military. *Armed Forces & Society, 17*(3), 363–384.

Moskos, C. (1971). Minority groups in military organization. Pp. 271–289 in *Handbook of Military Institutions*, edited by Roger Little. Beverly Hills, CA: Sage Publications.

————. (1973). The American Dilemma in Uniform: Race in the Armed Forces. *The Annals of the American Academy of Political and Social Science, 406*, 94–106.

Murray, P. (1971). Blacks and the draft: A history of institutional racism. *Journal of Black Studies,* 2(1), 57–76.

Nteta, T. & Tarsi, M. (2015). Self-selection versus socialization revisited: Military service, racial resentment, and generational membership. *Armed Forces & Society, 42*(2), 362–385.

Office of the Under Secretary of Defense, Personnel and Readiness. (2015). *Population Representation in the Military Services: Fiscal Year 2014 Appendix D: Historical Data Tables. Table D-22: Non-Prior Service (NPS) Active Component Enlisted Accessions by Race with Civilian Comparison Group, FYs 2003–2014.* Published in 2015. [Oct. 16, 2016]. http://www.cna.org/research/pop-rep.

Patten, E. & Parker, K. (2011). Women in the U.S. military: Growing share, distinctive profile. *Pew Research Center Social & Demographic Trends.* Available at: http://www.pewsocialtrends.org/2011/12/22/ women-in-the-u-s-military-growing-share-distinctive-profile/

Pettit, B. & Western, B. (2004). Mass imprisonment and the life course: Race and class inequality in U.S. incarceration. *American Sociological Review, 69*(2), 151–69.

Phillips, C. (2011). Institutional racism and ethnic inequalities: An expanded multi-level framework. *Journal of Social Policy, 40*(1), 173–192.

Sampson, R. & Laub, J. (1996). Socioeconomic achievement in the life course of disadvantaged men: Military service as a turning point, circa 1940–1965. *American Sociological Review, 61*(3), 347–67.

Segal, M. (1986). The military and the family as greedy institutions. *Armed Forces & Society, 13*(1), 9–38.

Segal, D., Bachman, J., Freedman-Doan, P., & O'Malley, P. (1999). Propensity to serve in the U.S. military: Temporal trends and subgroup differences. *Armed Forces & Society, 25*(3), 407–27.

Segal, D.R. & Segal, M.W. (2005). Army recruitment goals endangered as percentage of African American enlistees declines. *Population Reference Bureau.* Available at: http://www.prb.org/Publications/Articles/2005/ArmyRecruitmentGoalsEndangeredasPercentofAfricanAmericanEnlisteesDeclines.aspx

Teachman, J. (2007). Race, military service, and marital timing: Evidence from the NLSY-79. *Demography,* 44, 389–404.

Teachman, J. & Tedrow, L. (2004). Wages, earnings, and occupational status: did World War II veterans receive a premium? *Social Science Research, 33*, 581–605.

————. (2007). Joining up: Did military service in the early all volunteer era affect subsequent civilian income? *Social Science Research, 36*, 1447–1474.

Terry, W. (1971). The angry blacks in the Army. Chapter in *Two, Three Many Vietnams,* edited by the editors of Ramparts, with B. Garrett and K. Barkley. San Francisco: Canfield Press.

U.S. Congressional Budget Office. (1989). *Social Representation in the U.S. Military.* Washington, D.C. Available at: https://www.cbo.gov/sites/default/files/101st-congress-1989–1990/reports/89-cbo-044.pdf

Young, W. (1982). *Minorities and the Military: A Cross-National Study in World Perspective.* Westport, CT: Greenwood Press.

Chapter 3

Rising Minority

Hispanics in the US Military

Karin De Angelis

As one of the largest and fastest growing minority groups in the United States, Hispanics are reshaping the major institutions of American life, including the military. The all-volunteer military now has more racial and ethnic minorities, more women, and more women who are racial and ethnic minorities, than it had under conscription. Hispanics, when compared to their proportional presence in the civilian labor force of comparable age, are underrepresented in the military, mainly because of their low high school graduation rates (Asch, Buck, Klerman, Kleykamp, & Loughran, 2009). However, when compared to the overall Hispanic population who meet enlistment standards, Hispanics are overrepresented in the American military and currently comprise 13.6 percent of the enlisted active duty force and 16.8 percent of new accessions (Office of Under Secretary of Defense, Personnel and Readiness, 2016; Sanchez, 2013). Their numbers will continue to rise as more Hispanics meet the educational and English language proficiency levels required to serve (Asch, Buck, Klerman, Kleykamp, & Loughran, 2009). This trend continues despite the engagement of the United States in two deployment-intensive conflicts beginning in 2001 until today.

The demographic shifts in the proportional presence of Hispanic service members have been documented by the Department of Defense in its annual reports on social representation in the military. These reports track who serves, in what capacity, and whether representation levels in the military are equitable with civilian comparison groups by race, ethnicity, sex, and education level. In both military and civilian demographic research, the term "Hispanic" represents individuals from over twenty Spanish-speaking countries.

From these data, it is clear that Hispanic men and women have greatly increased their representation across all military branches over time, with the greatest concentration in the sea services (i.e., the Navy and the Marine

Corps). The increased presence of Hispanics in the armed forces may lead to a military that represents the society it defends, leading to increased social legitimacy (Janowitz, 1960). However, there are also concerns regarding this demographic shift, as the gains in military representation are reflected in the enlisted force (83.4 percent of total military) but not the officer corps (16.6 percent of total military force) where only 6 percent of commissioned officers are Hispanic (Office of the Deputy Assistant Secretary of Defense, 2013; Office of Under Secretary of Defense, Personnel and Readiness, 2015).

Current trends suggest that the percentage of commissioned officers who are Hispanic will continue to increase. The service academies, for example, have increased the representation of Hispanics in each current class. The US Naval Academy's Class of 2019 was 12 percent Hispanic. The US Air Force Academy and the US Military Academy both reported that their Class of 2019 was 11 percent Hispanic (USAFA, 2016; USMA, 2016; USNA 2016).

In this chapter, I discuss the current trends in representation, in addition to the relevant historical events that have shaped them. I also focus on broader social forces, such as calls for equal citizenship and inclusion, as well as organizational policies and culture that shape the military experience of Hispanic service members currently. I conclude with recommendations for future research on Hispanics in the American military.

EMERGENCE AS A UNIQUE ETHNIC GROUP

Hispanics have a long, storied history in the American military (see Rosenfeld & Culbertson, 1992 and Pew Hispanic Center, 2003 for summaries). They have participated in every major American conflict beginning with the Revolutionary War where Spanish individuals, such as General Bernardo de Gálvez, governor of the Louisiana territories, and Captain Jorge Farragut, actively assisted the colonies in their war against the British. During the Civil War, approximately 9,900 Mexican-Americans, many of whom settled in the United States after the US-Mexican War ended in 1848, served in both Confederate and Union units (see Thompson, 2000, for a historical analysis of Hispanics during this time). One of the most renowned Hispanic sailors of the American Civil War, Admiral David Farragut, became the first Admiral of the US Navy after his brave leadership in the Battle of Mobile Bay (Rochin & Fernández, 2005).

The total mobilization required for World War I led to the increased service of Hispanics, but not without barriers. The population of the United States changed in the early 20th century with waves of immigrants coming from Europe, including Spain, Mexico, and Latin America, ready to serve; however, many of them did not speak English. Because of the language difference, Hispanics often were relegated to menial jobs and were not integrated with English-speaking service members. With the growing presence of immigrants in the American population, the percentage of Hispanics in the military increased steadily. However, the economic pressures of the Great Depression led politicians to deport approximately two million Hispanics of Mexican origin, including many who had served as draftees (Balderrama & Rodríguez, 2006).

Hispanics also served during World War II. Although precise records of military service by ethnicity are not available, an estimated 53,000 Puerto Ricans served in the 65th Infantry Regiment and 350,000 Mexican-Americans served in National Guard units from Texas, New Mexico, Arizona, and California. The New Mexican National Guard deployed to the Bataan Peninsula when the Japanese forces captured the area and forced them to endure the Bataan Death March. Twelve Hispanics earned the Medal of Honor during World War II. This record of service continued through the Korean War and the Vietnam War. The all-Puerto Rican 65th Infantry Regiment distinguished itself again in Pusan, Korea and earned a Presidential Unit Citation for valor. During the Vietnam War, Cuban Americans, whom by virtue of their small stature, distinguished themselves by disproportionately serving as "tunnel rats" responsible for clearing the underground tunnel system maintained by the Viet Cong (Mangold & Penycate, 1985). Nine Medals of Honor were awarded to Hispanics during the Korean War and fourteen were awarded during Vietnam.

Even with these decorations, a twelve-year investigation mandated by Congress and led by the Pentagon found systemic discrimination against minority veterans, including many Hispanics. Many Hispanics did not receive formal recognition of their achievements and valor, especially regarding the Medals of Honor, during World War II, the Korean War, and the Vietnam War. The Obama Administration corrected this deliberate exclusion and awarded an additional twenty-four Medals of Honor to veterans, most of whom had already died. This group is known as the Valor 24 (Smith, 2014). Overall, Hispanics have been awarded forty-two Medals of Honor, which is more than any other minority group (Mariscal, 2010).

Evidence of systemic discrimination also surfaced with the reintegration and support of Hispanic veterans, especially after World War II. At that time, existing veterans groups were segregated by race and ethnicity so Hispanic veterans, especially Mexican-Americans, had little recourse when they were denied benefits earned through the G.I. Bill of Rights of 1944. To counter this exclusion, Dr. Héctor García founded the American G.I. Forum, a congressionally supported civil rights organization, to lobby for equal rights for Hispanic veterans, including burial rights (motivated by the controversy surrounding the burial of Private Felix Longoria), voting and educational access, and Hispanic representation on draft boards (Allsup, 1982).

Private Felix Longoria, US Army, died while serving in the Philippines during World War II. Upon return of his body, Private Longoria's family wished to bury him in their local cemetery in Three Rivers, Texas. This cemetery had a whites and Mexican-only section; the funeral home director mandated that the family abide by this separate but unequal organization and also refused to allow them access to the cemetery chapel. The American G.I. Forum lobbied on the Longoria family's behalf and eventually secured Private Longoria's burial in Arlington National Cemetery. Historians assert that the controversy surrounding Private Longoria's burial contributed to the rise of Mexican-American activism throughout the United States (see Allsup, 1982 and Carroll, 2003 for detailed historical information.) Although veterans groups are now integrated, the American G.I. Forum continues today with chapters in fourteen states, Washington, D.C., and Puerto Rico.

Changes in how demographers categorize Hispanics as a racial and now ethnic group allow us to recognize the service members who have served since the beginning of the all-volunteer force (AVF), including the twenty-six Hispanic service members who died during Operations Desert Shield/Storm. Additional research, discussed below, is now available about today's Hispanic veterans and their actions in Afghanistan, Iraq, and around the globe, where 665 Hispanics have died while serving (DeBruyne & Leland, 2015).

HISPANIC: A BUREAUCRATIC DEFINITION

The term "Hispanic" is an administrative category initially created by the federal government to represent individuals from twenty Spanish-speaking nationalities as well as those who were early settlers in the American Southwest (Tienda & Mitchell, 2006). It includes people from a range of cultural backgrounds and immigrant statuses, including Puerto Ricans, Mexican-Americans, and Cuban-Americans, among others. Table 3.1 shows the ten largest Hispanic groups in the United States. The main reason why data on Hispanic service members are limited through the Vietnam War is that the Department of Defense did not track Hispanics as a separate ethnic group until the beginning of the AVF in 1973. Prior to these changes, when the military sought to complete research on Hispanic service members, it screened for Spanish surnames to identify research participants (Barton & Kinzer, 1977).

Likewise, the Census attempted to count Hispanics in the American population during the early part of the 20th century with little success. The big push came in 1970 with the Census long form, which was sent to one in six households. Because of a poorly worded question, this attempt underestimated the Hispanic population. The question was reworded and moved

Table 3.1   Percent of Largest Hispanic Groups in United States by Origin

Ethnic group	Percent
Mexicans	64.0
Puerto Ricans	9.0
Cubans	3.5
Salvadorans	3.5
Dominicans	3.3
Guatemalans	2.4
Colombians	1.9
Hondurans	1.5
Spaniards	1.4
Ecuadorians	1.3

Data from López, G. & Patten, E. (2015). The impact of slowing immigration: Foreign-born share falls among 14 largest US Hispanic origin groups. Washington, D.C.: Pew Research Center.

to the short form, which was sent to all households, leading to increased accuracy. The 2000 Census separated ethnicity, which was asked first, and race and gave respondents the option to self-identify as Latino/Hispanic. The 2010 Census had minor changes in wording in the hopes of increasing self-reporting and racial identification, with the option of further specifying race and country of origin (Passel, 2010). Changes in the measurement of the Hispanic population demonstrate its diversity by race and country of origin and the difficulty of using rigid bureaucratic categories. The intentional alignment of demographic data collection between the Department of Defense and the Census Bureau also allowed for comparisons between civilian and military populations, but it has taken time to standardize these measurements.

Because the term "Hispanic" privileges European-Spanish origins over those indigenous to Latin America, the term may be offensive to some who choose to use other categorizations, such as Latino(a), Chicano(a), Tejano(a), and/or Boricua. Each term has a different meaning and specifies different requirements for membership. The term "Latino" highlights ties to countries that were once under Roman rule, while the terms "Chicano" and "Tejano" refer to those Hispanics with roots in the American Southwest and Texas before those territories were gained by the United States as spoils of the US-Mexican War. "Boricua" is a term that refers to a Puerto Rican living in the United States. The diversity of terms used for official categorization and for individual self-identification demonstrate how the construction of who is a Hispanic changes over time and place as certain social forces shape definitions of ethnicity and group membership (Oboler, 1995). Current research suggests that American Hispanics prefer the term Hispanic over Latino by a margin of three to one, a preference that is especially concentrated on the East Coast (Tienda & Mitchell, 2006).

In addition to the difficulties in measuring Hispanics as a unified category, their motivations for service have not been examined to the same degree as white and African-American service members of both sexes (see Burk, 1995; Campbell, 1984; Moore, 1996 for work on women and African-Americans). Because of this research gap, the male Hispanic military experience often is theorized as a "nonwhite" experience within the white-black dichotomy that shapes much of the military's history with race, ethnicity, integration, and equity. Further, this research does not parse out experiences by country of origin. Dempsey and Shapiro's work (2009) is an exception. They find that Hispanic soldiers report similar reasons for joining the military as their white counterparts: service to country, economic stability, and educational benefits. Citizenship is not a major reason for service. Research about Hispanic women in the military is even more limited (see De Angelis, 2015 for current work). Hispanics also have received much less coverage from military equal opportunity programs, which emerged mainly in reaction to the poor race relations between white and African-American service members and rarely acknowledged the integration experiences of other racial and ethnic groups.

CURRENT TRENDS AND CONCERNS

Civilian Hispanics in the United States

At four times the rate of population growth for the white population, Hispanics are one of the largest and fastest growing minority groups in the America population today (Saenz, 2010). High fertility, steady immigration, and low mortality due to a relatively young age distribution are the main causes for this trend. Between the years 1980 and 2014, the Hispanic population in the United States grew from 14.8 million to 55.4 million, accounting for 56 percent of the population growth in the United States (Krogstad & López, 2015; Passel, Cohn, & López, 2011). Whereas in 1980 Hispanics accounted for 6.5 percent of the total US population, they now account for 17.3 percent (Stepler & Brown, 2016).

Hispanic women average three births each, compared to other minority groups and whites who average two, with the highest birth rate among women who are recent immigrants (Saenz, 2010). There also is a large difference in rates of international migration, with a net increase of almost five million (or 13.5 percent) of Hispanics from 2000 to 2009 versus a net increase of over one (1.3) million non-Hispanic whites (or 0.7 percent). Since 2009, rates of immigration have declined, particularly in regard to Mexican immigrants (Krogstad & López, 2015; Saenz, 2010). However, even with this decline, the population will continue to rise through births, meaning that a greater proportion of the Hispanic population will be American-born (Brown, 2014; Saenz, 2010). In fact, data from the Pew Hispanic Center (2011) show that births have surpassed immigration as the biggest driver of the Mexican-American population, with the population growing by over seven million (7.2) through births. Because of this growth, Hispanics are having a significant impact on all major American institutions, including the military.

In addition to their dramatic growth, Hispanics are also a very young population, making them an important source of the labor and taxable income needed to provide a social security net for the aging majority (Tienda & Mitchell, 2006). Whereas the white population is almost evenly split between children and the elderly, there are five times as many people under the age of fifteen than over the age of sixty-five in the Hispanic population (Saenz, 2010). Demographic projections suggest that Hispanics will comprise approximately 20 percent of the American population by 2025, with even greater numbers among fifteen- to nineteen-year-olds, who are a key military recruiting group. In 2010, the median age of the Hispanic population was twenty-five, compared to a median age of thirty for non-Hispanics overall, including thirty-two for African-Americans, twenty-five for Asians, and forty-one for whites (Pew Hispanic Center, 2011). By the year 2030, approximately 25 percent of the non-Hispanic white population will be at retirement age or older compared to just 10 percent of the Hispanic population (Tienda & Mitchell, 2006). Mexican-Americans are younger than the Hispanic population overall (Pew Hispanic Center, 2009).

Hispanics also are a highly diverse group, with different countries of origin, races, religions, socioeconomic positions, and citizenship statuses (Zambrana, 2011). The largest categories of Hispanics in the United States are Mexicans at 64 percent, followed distantly by Puerto Ricans at 9 percent, and Cubans at 3.5 percent (López & Patten, 2015; Motel & Patten, 2012). There are important disparities by socioeconomic status among groups within the broader Hispanic community. South Americans and Cubans tend to fare the best economically, while Mexicans, Central Americans, and Puerto Ricans tend to experience greater economic disadvantage. Hispanic representation in highly skilled occupations is below average; this is especially true for Mexican and Central Americans. Instead, they are concentrated in low-skilled, low-paid, highly unsecure jobs in the agriculture, service, and production industries that allow for low education and lack of English proficiency.

There are also great discrepancies within the Mexican-American population that fall along nativity lines; these differences became especially pronounced during the Great Recession. US-born Mexican-Americans have higher high school graduation rates (77 percent vs. 38.7 percent), higher median family incomes ($40,590 vs. $32,000) and lower poverty rates (24.2 percent vs. 26.2 percent) than foreign-born Mexicans. However, they also have higher unemployment rates at 13.1 percent versus 10.4 percent (Saenz, 2010). This may reflect migration trends, as immigrants had the option of returning to their native country during the recession while US-born Mexican-Americans were more limited in their ability to move for work. Hispanics, especially Mexicans, have fared poorly with structural economic changes that have increased the demand for high-skilled workers, especially those with higher education degrees and have had to contend with a decline in jobs because of the past recession (Kochhar, 2008).

Differences in the Hispanic population by country of origin also extend to levels and rates of educational attainment. Over the last few decades, Hispanics (as well as Native Americans) consistently have been the minority group with the highest high school dropout rates. In 2005, 33 percent of Hispanic high school students dropped out compared to 10 percent of African-Americans and 6 percent of whites. Among Hispanic subgroups, Central Americans (33 percent) and Mexican-Americans (25 percent) had the highest dropout rates and native born had lower rates (13 percent) than their foreign-born counterparts (38 percent) (KewalRamani, Gilbertson, Fox, & Provasnik, 2007). However, the rate of high school dropouts has dropped dramatically. In 2013, the rate was at 12 percent; researchers are still trying to account for this change (National Center for Education Statistics, 2013). The lack of a high school diploma is a major disqualifying factor for Hispanic youth interested in military service (Asch et al., 2009). Each of the service branches has different entrance standards, but overall there is a preference for high school graduates or for high-quality youth who have completed the General Educational Development test and scored relatively high on the Armed Forces Qualifying Test. Thus, the decline in high school dropout rates bodes well for greater numbers of Hispanic enlistments.

This positive trend also carries over to Hispanic enrollment in college, which also has increased. From 1993 to 2013, the number of Hispanics enrolled in college increased 201 percent, or over 728,000. This rate of growth exceeds that of African-Americans and whites whose rates increased 78 and 14 percent, respectively. Currently, Hispanics are the largest minority group on American college campuses; however, this increase is mainly in two-year programs rather than four-year programs (Krogstad, 2015; Tienda & Mitchell, 2006). Among Hispanics aged between twenty-five and twenty-nine years, only 15 percent have a bachelor's degree or higher; this is in stark contrast to the 20 percent of blacks, 40 percent of whites, and 60 percent of Asians from the same age bracket with four-year degrees or higher (Krogstad, 2015). Since four-year degrees are a prerequisite for officer commissioning, the number of Hispanic officers in the military will continue to be lower than other racial and ethnic groups until there is an increase in graduation rates at four-year colleges.

Trends in Military Service

The growing presence of Hispanics in the civilian population and their relative youthfulness make them a strategic recruiting pool for the military, especially as the enlistment behavior of other minority groups decline (Asch et al., 2009; Tienda & Mitchell, 2006). Additionally, Hispanic youth demonstrate higher propensity to serve in the military than whites (although a lower propensity than African-Americans) and have had proven success in both basic training and in their first term of enlistment (Asch et al., 2009; Segal, Bachman, Freedman-Doan, & O'Malley, 1999). As a result, military policymakers see the recruitment of Hispanics as a "win-win" situation for the military since it can focus on recruiting from a young population with great propensity to serve plus a history of success in the organization itself (Hattiangadi, Lee, & Quester, 2004).

Since the military builds its volunteer force through recruiting and retention, it is important to consider both total representation and accession numbers. Accessions are the number of individuals who enter into military service and show immediate changes in enlistment rates by service branch. All of the service branches report an increase in Hispanic accessions, with the Navy and the Marine Corps showing the greatest increase. Consequently, the percentage of Hispanics as a percentage of active duty personnel has increased steadily since 1977 (Figure 3.1). Current trends suggest that their numbers will continue to grow as more Hispanics meet the requirements for service. The percentage of Hispanics has increased in all service branches, with the exception of the Air Force, which experienced a steady increase until 2006, followed by a continuing decline through 2014. The sea services have experienced the largest increase, with the Navy and the Marine Corps alternating as the service branch with the highest percentage of Hispanic representation (Figure 3.2). Although the Navy reported a decline from 2003 to 2005, it experienced a large jump in active duty Hispanic service members from 8.3 percent in 2005 to 15 percent in 2007. As of 2015, 16.7 percent of enlisted sailors self-identified as Hispanic. Likewise, the Marine Corps has experienced steady growth in the percentage of Hispanic Marines, with 19.7 percent of the enlisted force identifying as such. In the Army, which has the greatest percentage of African-American service members, 14.8 percent of the enlisted force is Hispanic.

The increase in accessions and overall representation of Hispanic personnel is happening across service branches for both men and women. Hispanic women are now surpassing Hispanic men in accession percentages by gender across all service branches with the greatest difference in the Marine Corps. For the Marine Corps in Fiscal Year (FY) 2015, Hispanic women were 27.1 percent of female accessions while Hispanic men were 19.1 percent of male

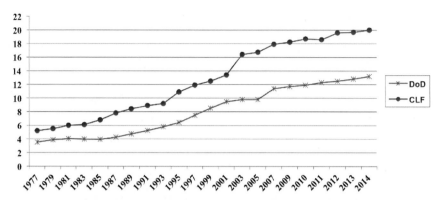

Figure 3.1   Hispanics as a Percentage of Active Duty Enlisted Personnel (DoD) with Civilian Labor Force (CLF) Aged 18–44, FYs 1977–2014. *Source*: Data from Department of Defense, Population Representation in the Military Services, Fiscal Year 2002–2014. Retrieved from: https://www.cna.org/research/pop-rep.

accessions (Table 3.2). These enlistment behaviors are especially interesting because they differ from those of African-Americans. Like Hispanic women, African-American women are a greater percentage of enlisted accessions compared to African-American men (Segal, Thanner, & Segal, 2007). However, African-American women have their highest representation in the Army and their highest accession numbers in the Navy, just like African-American men. African-American women also have their lowest accession numbers in the Marine Corps, also like African-American men. Thus, the enlistment and overall representation of Hispanic women in the Marine Corps is a unique social behavior for racial and ethnic minority groups in the military.

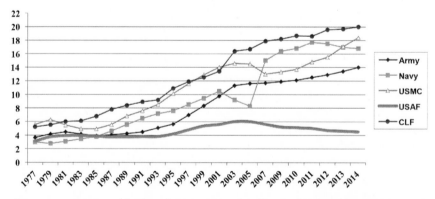

Figure 3.2   Percent of Hispanic Representation by Service Branch, FY1977–2014. *Source*: Data from Department of Defense, Population Representation in the Military Services, Fiscal Year 2002–2014 retrieved from: https://www.cna.org/research/pop-rep.

Currently, no sociological research exists that explains why Hispanics disproportionately join the sea services over the other services (Gifford, 2005). There is policy research on the sea services' success of recruiting Hispanics, which highlights their highly organized recruiting system, especially for the Marine Corps, and the ability of their recruiters and their media campaigns to connect with key influencers, such as parents and extended family members (Asch et al., 2009; Asch, Buck, Klerman, Kleykamp, & Loughran, 2005; Hattiangadi et al., 2004).

The US military has a large presence in several states with large Hispanic populations, especially California and Texas. California is home to three Army posts, ten Navy and Marine Corps installations, and seven Air Force bases, including the large Camp Pendleton (Marine Corps) and Naval Base San Diego (Department of Defense [DoD], 2011). Texas does not have the concentration of Navy and Marine Corps installations that California does; rather, it has a large Army and Air Force presence, with three large posts and seven bases, respectively (DoD, 2011).

Kleykamp (2006) found that military presence in the local community influences individual decisions to join the military and concluded that as military installations become more concentrated in rural, southern, and western parts of the country, an increasing percentage of recruits will come from these areas. This conclusion is important for considering the overall enlistment behaviors of Hispanics, because they are concentrated in these same areas of the country. However, we do not know if those Hispanics living in California disproportionately are attracted to the Navy and Marine Corps while those living in Texas disproportionately are drawn to the Army and Air Force. In

Table 3.2   **Percent Hispanic of Enlisted Accessions by Gender and Service Branch, FYs 2001–2014**

	Army		Navy		USMC		USAF		DoD	
	Men	Women	Men	Women	Men	Women	Men	Women	Men	Women
2001	11.1	10.9	12.5	13.3	14.4	16.9	6.8	7.4	11.4	11.1
2002	11.2	13.3	12.1	13.7	13.6	16	6.9	8.3	11.1	12.2
2003	10.3	12.7	12.8	15.4	14.4	17.6	7.8	9.2	11.2	12.7
2004	12.3	14.8	16.1	18	17.4	19.6	10.3	12.9	13.9	15.5
2005	11.7	14.4	15.7	18.4	16	19.2	10.6	12.2	13.6	15.5
2006	11.2	13.3	15.6	19.1	15.3	19.9	10.6	13	12.9	15.2
2007	11	13	16	19.1	15.9	21.6	10.5	12.7	13.1	15.3
2008	11.4	13.4	20.7	22.4	16.9	22.5	13.4	15.1	15	17
2009	11.5	12.2	22.2	23.7	16	21.7	15.6	17.2	15.4	17.6
2010	11.9	13.4	16.3	19.4	13.5	17.6	4.9	6.1	11.7	13
2011	12.3	13.7	17.2	20.5	14.4	19.6	4.6	6	12.1	13.6
2012	12.7	14	17	20.1	15.1	20.8	4.5	5.8	12.3	13.7
2013	13.2	14.7	16.5	19.4	16.6	23.3	4.4	5.7	12.6	14
2014	13.8	15.1	16.3	19.2	17.9	25.4	4.3	5.6	13	14.4

Data from Department of Defense, Population Representation in the Military Services, Fiscal Year 2002–2014. Retrieved from: https://www.cna.org/research/pop-rep.

other words, we do not know if Hispanics, and recruits more broadly, are selecting their service branch based on exposure to the military overall, or are tailoring their selection to service branches in their communities.

CONSEQUENCES OF MILITARY SERVICE

Due to their concentration in the Marine Corps—which focuses on ground combat—Hispanics, particularly the men, may be at a disproportionately higher risk of wartime casualty. Buzzell and Preston (2007) suggest that the rate of death in the Marine Corps is more than double that of other service branches, and in the case of the Air Force, the death rate for the Marine Corps is more than twenty-three times higher. The risk of injury or death may be exacerbated by the overrepresentation of Hispanic men in the combat occupational specialties, such as infantry, within the Marine Corps and Army. In FY 2009, which was the height of the conflicts in Iraq and Afghanistan, 20.8 percent of Hispanic men in the Marine Corps were in the combat arms compared to 12 percent of African-Americans and 28 percent of non-Hispanic white men (OSD, 2010). In contrast, African-American service members are more likely to serve in support positions and white service members are more likely to serve in technical positions, although they also have a substantial presence in the combat arms (OSD, 2010; Segal & Segal, 2004).

Although in the current battlefield there is less of a clear line separating the frontline from the rear, certain occupations still face higher casualty risk. In his study of combat casualties and race during the first year of the Iraq war, Gifford (2005) found that no racial or ethnic minority experienced disproportionate casualties. However, during periods of active aggressive fighting, Hispanic casualties were higher than their representation in ground combat units.

Building on Gifford's work, Buzzell and Preston (2007), whose work examines military deaths in Iraq from 2003 to 2006, argue that there is clear variation in risk of death for Hispanics. During this time period, they found that Hispanics had a death risk that was 18 percent higher than that of non-Hispanics, and that this distinction applied even outside of periods of active fighting. Buzzell and Preston do not explicitly link the increased death rate of Hispanics to their representation in the Marine Corps or Army; however, their analysis clearly demonstrates the risks associated with service in ground combat and the increased death rate experienced by Hispanics early in the Iraq War. Likewise, Gifford (2005) suggests that the social processes that sort Hispanics, as well as other racial and ethnic minorities, into certain service branches and occupations have not been studied in detail and that the Hispanic military experience is "underexamined and undertheorized" (p. 203).

In addition to increased risk of death on the battlefield, certain occupations, such as infantry, have less transferability into the civilian sector, making it difficult to transition from military service to the civilian job market. In her study on the effect of prior military service on hiring for entry-level work, Kleykamp (2009) finds that veterans with military experience in the combat arms do not experience a hiring advantage, regardless of race or ethnicity. Military service has been credited with providing a "bridging environment" for less-advantaged groups by providing access to and experience with certain skills that facilitate integration into civilian work environments (Browning, Lopreato, & Poston, 1973; Fredland & Little, 1985; Lopreato & Poston, 1977). Thus, Hispanic men, who are concentrated in the combat arms, may find that their military service provides less social and cultural capital when compared to veterans who served in technical or administrative specialties. This potentially makes the occupational bridge from military to civilian work more difficult.

CITIZENSHIP STATUS AND MILITARY SERVICE

There are important differences between Mexican-Americans compared to Puerto Ricans and Cubans by citizenship status and how group members are incorporated into the American population. Puerto Ricans, by virtue of Puerto Rico's status as an American commonwealth, automatically are citizens of the United States (Office of Insular Affairs, 2011) and thus do not have to use military service as a way of expediting citizenship. As citizens, they are free to live, work, and travel throughout the United States, although they may experience difficulties with language assimilation as Spanish is the official language of Puerto Rico. Cubans enjoy some of the most lenient policies regarding refugee and asylum status and have multiple avenues for legal migration and resettlement in the United States not available to other ethnic groups (Office of Cuban Affairs, 2005; Wasem, 2007).

Mexican-Americans are unique in that a sizeable proportion of their population is indigenous to the United States: that is, they trace their ancestry to the American Southwest and Texas. The American Southwest, formally part of Mexico, became part of the United States after Mexico's defeat in the 1846 US-Mexican War. Prior to the war's end, the United States also annexed Texas, which had previously seceded from Mexico as the independent Republic of Texas, and became part of the United States in 1845.

In addition to the Chicano and Tejano population, there also is a sizeable proportion of Mexican-Americans who are immigrants, or children of immigrants. Currently, Mexicans account for the largest proportion of immigrants, both documented and undocumented, in the United States. Mexicans who are legal permanent residents of the United States may choose military service as a pathway toward expedited citizenship, an option that Puerto Ricans and Cubans do not have to consider. Although some of their trends reflect the integration experiences of previous waves of minority groups there are several important distinctions that shape how Mexican-Americans experience military service. Approximately 35 percent of Mexican-Americans are foreign born, and among those about 18 percent are undocumented (González-Barrera & López, 2013). Undocumented immigrants may not serve in the military until they update their status to legal permanent resident; however, this requirement may change if immigration reforms, such as the once proposed DREAM Act, are passed (DREAM Act Portal, 2016; Mariscal, 2010).

For Hispanics who are noncitizens, military service has become a viable employment option, particularly for those seeking American citizenship. In recognition of the service of noncitizens as well as a recruiting tactic, the US government now expedites naturalization requests for noncitizen service members, a group that includes multiple nationalities, but claims a sizeable proportion of Hispanic immigrants (Hattiangadi, Quester, Lee, Lien, & MacLeod, 2005). Despite being noncitizens, legal permanent residents are eligible to serve in the American military, although they are not permitted in occupational specialties that require a security clearance and cannot be commissioned.

Although it is unknown how many are of Hispanic ethnicity, an estimated 35,000 noncitizens currently serve in the Active Component of the military and comprise 5 percent of Navy accessions, 3 percent of Army and Marine Corps accessions, and 2 percent of Air Force accessions (Hattiangadi et al., 2005; McIntosh & Sayala, 2011). In recognition of the service of noncitizens, as well as the potential to motivate an important recruitment pool, in 2002 President George W. Bush issued an executive order shortening the service requirement for expedited naturalization from three years of service to one day of service during wartime. He also declared the post-9/11 period as a "period of hostilities" (Hattiangadi et al., 2005; Lee & Wasem, 2003, p.1). This shortened timeline does not apply to service during peacetime, which requires noncitizens to serve in the military for at least one year (Lee & Wasem, 2003). All expedited naturalization requests for military service members are contingent upon successful completion of the initial enlistment contract under honorable conditions. Since the implementation of this plan, the US Citizenship and Immigration Services have naturalized more than 109,321 service members (US Citizenship and Immigration Services, 2015).

CONCLUSION

Hispanics are one of the largest and fastest growing minority groups in the United States. They also are a youthful population with a high propensity to serve, making them an important recruiting base. The recruitment of a volunteer military member during a time of war is a complex process that involves multiple intervening institutions, people, practical considerations, and subjective reasons. Past research demonstrates that the decision to join the military is based on multiple factors, such as exposure to the military lifestyle, rational calculation of pay and benefits, and individual sentiments of service and patriotism (Segal, et al., 1999). Although it is a combination of these factors which ultimately draws interested individuals into military service, certain factors may carry greater or lesser weight with different social groups. As a consequence, the demographic makeup of today's AVF does not mirror the American population directly but is a reflection of which individuals view military service as a suitable or beneficial activity in their life course and which do not. Of those individuals who consider military service, they must also meet the educational, physical, moral, and mental standards of enlistment.

Although the decision to join the military ultimately is an individual one, recruits may differ in their motivations because of constraints and opportunities specific to their social location, cultural preferences, by military policy that determines eligibility, and by military attempts to have a recruiting presence in a community (Asch et al., 2009; Segal et al., 1999). These guiding factors and their influence on the decision to join the military may vary by ascribed characteristics such as race, ethnicity, and gender. The decision to serve is also shaped by individual and group perceptions of service branch culture, mission, and opportunity and may be reflected in the racial, ethnic, and gender demographics of each service branch. When looking at trends in military representation, it is clear that Hispanics are increasing their numbers throughout the military, especially as more of them meet the educational and linguistic requirements for service. This trend holds for Hispanic women, who surpass Hispanic men in military representation in all service branches. It is also clear that Hispanic representation for both men and women is highest in the sea services.

Because of this trend, more scholars in the social sciences are studying Hispanic service members. However, their experiences are often qualified as falling somewhere between the white and African-American military experience, and rarely as something distinctly their own. Exploratory research suggests that Hispanic service members differ from other racial and ethnic groups in terms of propensity to serve, casualty rates, occupational selection, intergenerational military experiences, military families, retention behaviors, and motivations for service (see De Angelis, 2015; Dempsey & Shapiro, 2009; Gifford, 2005; Lutz, 2008; Segal et al., 1999). Future research on diversity and inclusion in the military should focus on the potentially unique Hispanic military experience, especially as they claim a greater share of the American population and consequently, the military population.

In particular, there are significant differences in enlistment behaviors among Hispanics, whites, and African-Americans by service branch that merit further comparison. Gravitation by Hispanics toward the Navy and Marine Corps could be due to a multitude of factors, including common values, geographic proximity, and/or network connections that we do not see with other racial and ethnic groups. Because Hispanic men are at greater risk for wartime casualty in the Marine Corps over the other services, it is also important to consider what drives them into this service. The Army, which traditionally has the largest proportion of African-Americans in its ranks, has not shown the same success in recruiting and retaining Hispanics and the Air Force has, by far, the least success. Additionally, the representation of Hispanic women in the Marine Corps is a unique trend that runs counter to previous analyses on women's military participation. This growth in representation is especially interesting since women in the Marine Corps do not have the option of serving in traditionally feminine fields, such as nursing, which is where a large number of military women are concentrated in the other services.

Future research also should further parse out Hispanics by country of origin, although this task will be difficult to accomplish because these data are not routinely collected by the Department of Defense. Because there is great diversity in the Hispanic community, including a multitude of different citizenship statuses and racial identities, there may be motivations and experiences unique to each group. Lutz (2008) has exploratory research that suggests that Central and South Americans may have the highest propensity to serve compared to other Hispanics. Mexican-Americans may be more inclined toward military service as a pathway toward equal citizenship because they do not hold the same statuses as Cubans or Puerto Ricans. Puerto Ricans, who tend to have greater racial diversity than other Hispanic groups, may have more in common with African-Americans than with Mexican-Americans when it comes to their military experiences.

As one of the largest and fastest growing minority group in the United States, Hispanics are reshaping the major institutions of American life, including the military. The increased service of Hispanics in the military is relevant for building and maintaining a volunteer force and for macrolevel concerns regarding legitimacy and social representation (Janowitz, 1960). As researchers of and leaders in the military, it is important that we take stock of this rising minority group in the United States.

REFERENCES

Allsup, C. (1982). *The American G.I. forum: Origins and evolution.* Austin: University of Texas Center for Mexican American Studies.

Asch, B., Buck, C., Klerman, J.A., Kleykamp, M., & Loughran, D.S. (2009). *Military enlistment of Hispanic youth.* Santa Monica, CA: RAND.

Asch, B., Buck, C., Klerman, J.A., Kleykamp, M., & Loughran, D.S. (2005). *What factors affect the military enlistment of Hispanic youth: A look at enlistment qualifications.* Santa Monica, CA: RAND.

Balderrama, F.E. & Rodríguez, R. (2006). *Decade of betrayal: Mexican repatriation in the 1930s.* Albuquerque, NM: University of New Mexico Press.

Barton, D. H. & Kinzer, N.S. (1977). *Preliminary research on American soldiers of Spanish-ethnic origin and heritage.* Alexandria, VA: Army Research Institute for the Behavioral and Social Sciences.

Brown, A. (2014). *U.S. Hispanic and Asian populations growing, but for different reasons.* Retrieved from http://www.pewresearch.org/fact-tank/2014/06/26/u-s-hispanic-and-asian-populations-growing-but-for-different-reasons/

Browning, H. L., Lopreato, S.C., & Poston, D.L. (1973). Income and veteran status variations among Mexican Americans, Blacks, and Anglos. *American Sociological Review, 38*(1), 74-85.

Burk, J. (1995). Citizenship status and military service: The quest for inclusion by minorities and conscientious objectors. *Armed Forces & Society, 21,* (4), 503–529.

Buzzell, E. & Preston, S.H. (2007). Mortality of American troops in the Iraq war. *Population and Development Review, 33,* (3), 555–566.

Campbell, D. (1984). *Women at war with America: Private lives in a patriotic era.* Cambridge: Cambridge University Press.

Carroll, P., & Limón, J.E. (2003). *Felix Longoria's wake: Bereavement, racism, and the rise of Mexican American activism.* Austin, TX: University of Texas Press.

De Angelis, K. (2015). The organizational experiences of Mexican American men and women in the US Marine Corps: The impact of structural presence. *Res Militaris,* Special Issue on Women in the Military Part 1. Available at: http://resmilitaris. net/index.php?ID=1021752

DeBruyne, N. & Leland, A. (2015). *American war and military operations casualties: Lists and statistics.* Washington, D.C., Congressional Research Service.

Department of Defense. (2011). *Military installations.* Retrieved from http://www.militaryinstallations.dod.mil/pls/psgprod/f?p=MI:CONTENT:0::::P4_INST_ID,P4_TAB:320008,SI

Dempsey, J.K. & Shapiro, R.Y. (2009). The Army's Hispanic future. *Armed Forces & Society 35,* 526–561.

DREAM Act Portal. Accessed on April 15, (2016). Available at http://dreamact.info/

Fredland, J. E, &. Little, R.D. (1985). Socioeconomic-status of World War II veterans by race: An empirical test of the bridging hypothesis. *Social Science Quarterly, 66,* (3), 533–551.

González-Barrera, A., & López, M.H. (2013). *A demographic portrait of Mexican-origin Hispanics in the United States.* Washington, D.C.: Pew Hispanic Center.

Gifford, B. (2005). Combat casualties and race: What can we learn from the 2003-2004 Iraq conflict? *Armed Forces & Society, 31,* 201–225.

Hattiangadi, A.U., Lee, G., & Quester, A.O. (2004). *Recruiting Hispanics: The Marine Corps experience.* Alexandria, VA: Center for Naval Analyses.

Hattiangadi, A. U., Quester, A.O., Lee, G., Lien, D.S., & MacLeod, I.D. (2005). *Non-Citizens in today's military: Final report.* Alexandria, VA: Center for Naval Analyses.

Janowitz, M. (1960). *The professional soldier: A social and political portrait.* New York: The Free Press.

KewalRamani, A., Gilbertson, L., Fox, M.A., & Provasnik, S. (2007). *Status and trends in the education of racial and ethnic minorities*. Washington, D.C.: U.S. Department of Education.

Kleykamp, M.A. (2009). A great place to start? The effect of prior military service on hiring. *Armed Forces & Society, 35*, 266–85.

.Kleykamp, M.A. (2006). College, jobs, or the military? Enlistment during a time of war. *Social Science Quarterly, 87*, 272–290.

Kochhar, R. (2008). *Latino labor report, 2008: Construction reverses job growth for Latinos*. Washington, D.C.: Pew Hispanic Center.

Krogstad, J. M. & López, M.H. (2015). Hispanic population reaches record 55 million, but growth has cooled. Pew Hispanic Center. Retrieved from http://www.pewresearch.org/fact-tank/2015/06/25/u-s-hispanic-population-growth-surge-cools/

Lee, M. M. & Wasem, R.E. (2003). *Expedited citizenship through service: Policy and issues*. Washington, D.C.: Congressional Research Service.

López, G. & Patten, E. (2015). *The impact of slowing immigration: Foreign-born share falls among 14 largest U.S. Hispanic origin groups*. Washington, D.C.: Pew Research Center.

Lopreato, S. C., & Poston, D. L. (1977). Differences in earnings and earnings ability between black veterans and nonveterans in the United States. *Social Science Quarterly, 57*, 750–766.

Lutz, A. (2008). Who joins the military?: A look at race, class, and immigration status. *Journal of Political and Military Sociology, 36*, 167–188.

Mangold, T. & Penycate, J. (1985). *The tunnels of Cu Chi: A harrowing account of America's tunnel rats in the underground battlefields of Vietnam*. New York: Berkley Books

Mariscal, J. (2010). Latin@s in the U.S. military. In N.E. Cantu & M.E. Franquiz (Eds.), *Inside the Latin@ experience* (pp. 37–50). New York: Palgrave MacMillan.

McIntosh, M.M & Sayala, S. (2011). *Non-citizens in the enlisted U.S. military: Executive summary*. Alexandria, VA: Center for Naval Analyses.

Moore, B. L. (1996). *To serve my country, to serve my race*. New York: New York University Press.

Motel, S. & Patten, E. (2012). *The 10 largest Hispanic origin groups: Characteristics, rankings, top counties*. Pew Hispanic Center, Retrieved from http://www.pewhispanic.org/2012/06/27/the-10-largest-hispanic-origin-groups-characteristics-rankings-top-counties/

National Center for Education Statistics. (2013). Retrieved from https://nces.ed.gov/fastfacts/display.asp?id=16

Oboler, S. (1995). *Ethnic labels, Latino lives*. Minneapolis, MN: University of Minnesota Press.

Office of Cuban Affairs. (2005). *Fact sheet: The Cuban Readjustment Act*. Retrieved from http://www.state.gov/www/regions/wha/cuba/cuba_adjustment_act.html

Office of the Deputy Assistant Secretary of Defense (Military Community and Family Policy). 2013 Demographics: Profile of the Military Community; Office of the Deputy Assistant Secretary of Defense; (2013).: Retrieved from (2016) http://download.militaryonesource.mil/12038/MOS/Reports/2013-Demographics-Report.pdf.

Office of Insular Affairs. (2011). Puerto Rico. Retrieved from http://www.doi.gov/oia/Islandpages/prpage.htm

Office of the Under Secretary of Defense, Personnel and Readiness. (2016). *Population representation in the armed services, FY2015.* Department of Defense: Arlington, VA.

———. (2015). *Population representation in the armed services, FY2014.* Department of Defense: Arlington, VA.

———. (2014). *Population representation in the armed services, FY2013.* Department of Defense: Arlington, VA.

———. (2013). *Population representation in the armed services, FY2012.* Department of Defense: Arlington, VA.

———. (2012). *Population representation in the armed services, FY2011.* Department of Defense: Arlington, VA.

———. (2011). *Population representation in the armed services, FY2010.* Department of Defense: Arlington, VA.

———. (2010). *Population representation in the armed services, FY2009.* Department of Defense: Arlington, VA.

———. (2009). *Population representation in the armed services, FY2008.* Department of Defense: Arlington, VA.

———. (2008). *Population representation in the armed services, FY2007.* Department of Defense: Arlington, VA.

———. (2007). *Population representation in the armed services, FY2006.* Department of Defense: Arlington, VA.

———. (2006). *Population representation in the armed services, FY2005.* Department of Defense: Arlington, VA.

———. (2005). *Population representation in the armed services, FY2004.* Department of Defense: Arlington, VA.

———. (2004). *Population representation in the armed services, FY 2003.* Department of Defense: Arlington, VA.

———. (2003). *Population representation in the armed services, FY2002.* Department of Defense: Arlington, VA.

———. (2002). *Population representation in the armed services, FY2001.* Department of Defense: Arlington, VA.

Passel, J. S. (2010). *Census history: Counting Hispanics.* Washington, D.C.: Pew Research Center.

Passel, J. S., Cohn, D., & López, M.H. (2011). Hispanics account for more than half of nation's growth in past decade. Pew Hispanic Center. Retrieved from http://www.pewhispanic.org/2011/03/24/hispanics-account-for-more-than-half-of-nations-growth-in-past-decade/

Pew Hispanic Center. (2011). The Mexican American boom: Births overtake immigration. *Fact Sheet,* July 14, Washington, D.C.

———. (2009). Hispanics of Mexican origin in the United States, 2007. *Fact Sheet,* September 16, Washington, D.C.

———. (2003). Hispanics in the Military. *Fact Sheet,* March 27, Washington, D.C.

Rochin, R.I. & Fernández, L. (2005). *U.S. Latino patriots: From the American Revolution to Iraq 2003.* Julian Samora Research Institute—Michigan State University Vol. e-book series. Retrieved from http://works.bepress.com/refugio_rochin/3/

Rosenfeld, P., & Culbertson, A.L. (1992). Hispanics in the military. In S.B. Knouse, P. Rosenfeld, & A. Culbertson (Eds.), *Hispanics in the workplace* (pp. 211–230). Newbury Park, CA: Sage Publications.

Saenz, R. (2010). Latinos in the United States 2010. *Population bulletin.* Population Reference Bureau, Washington, D.C.

Sanchez, E. L. (2013). U.S. military, a growing Latino army. *NBC Latino,* Retrieved from http://nbclatino.com/2013/01/01/u-s-military-a-growing-latino-army/

Segal, D.R., Bachman, J.G., Freedman-Doan, P., & O'Malley, P. (1999). Propensity to serve in the U.S. military: Temporal trends and subgroup differences. *Armed Forces & Society, 25,* 407–427.

Segal, D.R. & Segal, M.W. (2004). America's Military Population. *Population Bulletin, 59,* 4, 1–40.

Segal, M.W., Thanner, M.H., & Segal, D.R. (2007). Hispanic and African American men and women in the U.S. military: Trends in representation. *Race, Gender and Class, 14,* 48–62.

Smith, J. F. (2014). Medals of Honor go to 24 Army veterans who had been denied. *The New York Times,* March 18. Retrieved from http://www.nytimes.com/2014/03/19/us/politics/medals-of-honor-go-to-24-army-veterans-who-had-been-denied.html?_r=0

Stepler, R. & Brown, A. (2016). Statistical portrait of Hispanics in the United States. Pew Hispanic Center. Retrieved from http://www.pewhispanic.org/2016/04/19/statistical-portrait-of-hispanics-in-the-united-states-key-charts/

Tienda, M. & Mitchell, F. (Eds.). (2006). *Hispanics and the future of America.* Washington, D.C. The National Academies Press.

Thompson, J. (2000). *Vaqueros in Blue & Gray.* Austin, TX: State House Press.

United States Air Force Academy. (2016). *Demographic Profile of the Class of 2019.* HQ USAFA/A9N. Colorado Springs, CO.

United States Military Academy (2016). *Class of 2019 Welcome Brief.* Office of the Superintendent. West Point, NY.

United States Naval Academy (2016). *2019 Class Portrait.* Naval Academy Admissions. Annapolis, MD.

United States Citizenship and Immigration Services. (2015). *Fact Sheet: Naturalization through Military Service.* Washington, D.C.: Office of Communications

Wasem, R.E. (2007). Cuban Migration Policy and Issues. *CRS Report for Congress.* Library of Congress: Washington, D.C.

Zambrana, R.E. (2011). *Latinos in American society: Families and communities in transition.* Ithaca, NY: Cornell University Press.

Chapter 4

Fighting to Belong

Asian-American Military Service and American Citizenship

Deenesh Sohoni

The military has been recognized as one of the most crucial institutions in setting the parameters of national citizenship, and in helping facilitate the expansion of these boundaries to include racial minorities. Historically, it is during periods of war and strong external threat that notions of shared American identity become most salient. It is also during these periods that racial minorities can demonstrate their patriotism through military service, and thus make a claim for the full benefits of social membership (Bruscino, 2010).

As with other minority groups, military service has at times provided Asian-Americans the opportunity to prove themselves "true" Americans and deserving of all the legal rights of American citizenship. Yet frequently, pre-existing racialized stereotypes of Asian-Americans as "permanent foreigners," unable or unwilling to assimilate into American society, have led to discriminatory policies that constrained their participation in the military, as well as limited the benefits they received when they served.

This chapter contributes to research on diversity in the US military by studying the military participation of Asian-Americans. Specifically, this chapter provides a legal-historical analysis of how Asian foreign nationals used the military to prove their patriotism and their worthiness to receive US citizenship, and of how US-born Asian-Americans used the military to prove their loyalty and worth as citizens. In doing so, I highlight the critical role Asian-Americans played in challenging legal race-based barriers to US citizenship, as well as in contesting state sanctioned racial discrimination against its citizens. I conclude with how and why the history of Asian-American participation in the US military has continued relevance for contemporary public and legal debates regarding race, immigration and naturalization laws, military service, and American citizenship.

RACE, IMMIGRATION AND NATURALIZATION LAWS, AND MILITARY SERVICE

Scholars studying the relationship between race and citizenship have long emphasized the historical conflict between two dominant ideologies of national membership: first, civic citizenship based on a shared set of "American" values and beliefs; and second, ethnocultural membership rooted in Anglo-Saxon Protestant values, and a presumption of the innate superiority of "whites" (Calavita, 2005; Glenn, 2000; Kettner, 1978; Smith 1997; Sohoni & Vafa, 2010).

Glenn (2000, p. 2) traces the origins of the concept of civic membership to the founding of the United States, when colonial leaders tried to create a political rebuttal to the European feudal system, with its social hierarchies based on "differential legal and customary rights." Instead, they sought to establish a political system based on a social contract among members of free and equal status, such that those who willingly contributed to the well-being of the community were seen as deserving of its membership (Kettner, 1978). This ideology of equality and inclusion is enshrined in the language of the Declaration of Independence, which states, *"We hold these truths to be self-evident, that all men are created equal."*

The ideology of civic membership has also played an important role in shaping Americans' attitudes toward military participation. From early on in American history, there has been a strong belief that not only is military service a duty and right of citizenship but also that those who willingly fight on behalf of their country prove worthy of its citizenship (Jacobs & Hayes, 1981; Janowitz, 1976; Kettner, 1978). A contemporary example of this view can be found in the arguments that have been and are being put forth in support of the military pathway option of the DREAM Act.[1]

At the same time, there existed equally strong beliefs that viewed American national identity as rooted in a common European heritage and saw racial minorities, such as Native Americans and blacks, as unsuitable for the obligations and responsibilities of citizenship (Calavita, 2005; Glenn, 2000), and as a threat to the nature of America as a "white" nation (Smith, 1997). This ideology of racial differentiation and exclusion is found in the US Constitution,[2] and in the early legislative history of Congress, which passed the Naturalization Act of 1790, limiting the right to naturalize to free white citizens.

This ideology has also found strong legal support at other points in American history, as evidenced by the passage of restrictive immigration and naturalization policies often directed against non-European immigrants, and the differential treatment frequently afforded to white and nonwhite US citizens. These ethnocultural beliefs also influenced military participation through the norms and rules that governed who is eligible to serve in the military, and for those serving in the military, under what conditions.

Legal History of Asian Immigration and Citizenship

The period following the Civil War saw significant demographic and legal challenges to the existing US racial order. Immigrants from Asia first began to enter the United States in noticeable numbers, first from China and Japan, then from the Philippines, Korea, and India (see Table 4.1). Between 1860 and 1890, the Chinese ancestry population tripled from a little over 30,000 to over 100,000. With passage of the Chinese Exclusion Act of 1882, which barred Chinese immigrants from entering the United States, there was a shift to immigration from Japan as a way to meet US agricultural labor needs. As a result, the Japanese ancestry population in the United States went from a couple of thousand in 1890 to over 200,000 in 1920 (Hing, 1993). Similarly, when the Gentleman's Agreement of 1908 led to the informal restriction of Japanese immigrants, employers began recruiting immigrants from other Asian countries (and Asians residing in Hawaii for the mainland) (Hing, 1993).

Increased immigration from Asia occurred at the same time as large-scale growth in immigration from South, Central, and Eastern Europe, leading to greater hostility toward all these groups, and greater public support for more restrictive immigration policies (Daniels & Graham 2001; Sohoni, 2007).[3] Immigration from Asia also coincided with changes in the legal status of blacks at the end of the Civil War. The Naturalization Act of 1790 had originally restricted naturalization to "white persons," laying the foundations for a racially defined citizenship. In the aftermath of the Civil War, Congress passed legislation that gave new rights to blacks, particularly with respect

Table 4.1 Asian Ancestry Population, by Group and Decade

Decade ending	Chinese	Japanese	Filipino	Asian-Indian	Korean
1860	34,933[a]	xxx	xxx	xxx	xxx
1870	64,199[a]	xxx	xxx	xxx	xxx
1880	105,465[a]	xxx	xxx	xxx	xxx
1890	107,488[a]	xxx	xxx	xxx	xxx
1900	118,746	85,716	xxx	xxx	xxx
1910	94,414	152,745	2,767	5,424	5,008
1920	85,202	220,596	26,634	***	6,181
1930	102,159	278,743	108,424	3,130	8,332
1940	106,334	285,115	98,535	2,405	8,568
1950	150,005	326,379	122,707	***	7,030[b]
1960	237,292	464,332	176,310	12,296[c]	11,000[c]

xxx, not applicable.
***Missing data.
[a]Includes only Chinese living on the US mainland.
[b]Hawaiian population only.
[c]Includes only foreign-born population.
Source: Sohoni, D. (2007). Unsuitable suitors: Anti-miscegenation laws, naturalization laws, and the construction of Asian identities. Law and Society Review, 41: 587–618. Adapted from Hing, B. O. (1993). Making and remaking Asian America through immigration policy, 1850–1990. Stanford, CA: Stanford University Press.

to naturalization and citizenship. Specifically, the Civil Rights Act of 1866, stipulated that:

> Ch. 31. [a]ll persons born in the United States and not subject to any foreign power, excluding Indians not taxed, are hereby declared citizens of the United States; and such citizens, *of every race and color*, without regard to any previous condition of slavery or involuntary servitude . . . , shall have the same rights, in every State and Territory of the United States. (Emphasis added)

The 14th Amendment, and in particular its equal protection clause, further clarified the ability of states to create race-based legislation, by prohibiting states from denying "any person within its jurisdiction the equal protection of the laws."

Finally, in 1875, Congress passed the most progressive and comprehensive legislation regarding citizenship and naturalization. The Civil Rights Act of 1875 provided that

> Sec. 1. [i]t is the duty of government in its dealings with the people to mete out equal and exact justice for all, of whatever *nativity, race, color or persuasion, religious or political*; . . . That all persons within the jurisdiction of the United States of America shall be entitled to the full and equal enjoyment of the accommodations, advantages, facilities, and privileges of inns, public conveyances on land or water, theatres, and other places of public amusement; subject only to the conditions and limitations of law and applicable alike to *citizens of every race and color*, regardless of any previous condition of servitude (Emphasis added).

Civil Rights legislation appeared, in theory, to provide Asian immigrants an avenue to naturalize and gain citizenship. In fact, during debates regarding the wording of the Naturalization Act 1870, several Congressmen sought to remove the term "white" from naturalization laws altogether (Haney López, 1996). However, fear among representatives from Western states that the rapidly growing Chinese population would seek citizenship rights-led Congress to reject proposals to make naturalization statutes colorblind or to extend naturalization rights to Asian immigrants (Chang, 1999). As a result, the Naturalization Act of 1875 finally read:

> "The provisions of this title shall apply to aliens being free white persons, and to aliens of African nativity, and to persons of African descent."

For the judiciary, this left the problem of reconciling the conflict between Congressional Civil Rights legislation, which granted stronger protections to racial minorities, and immigration and naturalization laws, which continued to rely on racial categories in determining citizenship. For those of Asian ancestry, the judiciary's response was to distinguish between the "rights of citizens" and the "right to become a citizen" (Sohoni, 2007; Sohoni & Vafa, 2010).

The underpinnings of this legal distinction first arose when Chinese immigrants facing deportation from the United States challenged the Chinese Exclusion Act of 1882 based on its incompatibility with existing treaties between the United States and China. In two critical court cases, *Chae Chan Ping v. United States* (1889) and *Fong Yue Ting v. United States* (1893), the Supreme Court granted Congress nearly unrestricted power over immigration and naturalization through the "plenary power doctrine," which held that only the executive and legislative branches have the "sovereign power to regulate immigration, and that this power was beyond judicial review" (Chin, 1998).[4] Thus, while the Supreme Court would eventually rule in *United States v. Wong Kim Ark* that US-born Asians were guaranteed birthright (*jus soli*) citizenship, and in theory, protection from race-based discrimination, the Court continued to allow Congress to pass legislation based on racial status that served to limit Asian immigration and naturalization (Sohoni & Vafa, 2010).

With passage of the Immigration Act of 1917, which created the Asiatic Barred Zone, Congress extended the Chinese exclusion laws to include all other Asians groups (Hing, 1993).[5] Finally, in response to post–World War I anti-immigrant sentiment, Congress passed the Immigration Act of 1924 (Johnson-Reed Act). While primarily concerned with limiting immigration from Southern, Central, and Eastern European countries (through the use of national quotas), this Act also permanently excluded all "aliens ineligible for citizenship." Under the Naturalization Act of 1870 and the revisions in the Act of February 18, 1875, and with the noteworthy exception of Filipinos, this meant "Asians" (Hing, 1993).[6] The net result of these Congressional Acts was that until racial restrictions on naturalization were finally removed by the Immigration and Nationality Act of 1952, Asian immigrants were banned from entering the United States because they were ineligible for citizenship, and ineligible for citizenship because they were not white (or black).

However, the impact of these discriminatory laws affected not only foreign-born Asians, but also their US-born offspring. Specifically, the justifications used for prohibiting Asian immigrants—that they were incapable of assimilating, and "innately" unsuited for republican forms of government—suggested a "biological" component for cultural differences, and allowed for the creation of a racialized ethnicity that included a perception of the intrinsic foreignness of Asians that linked together foreign-born and US-born Asian-Americans (Saito, 1997). This linking of race and foreignness has repeatedly, during periods of strong external threat, allowed for some US citizens to be seen as still tied to their ancestral countries, and thus never truly "American" (Daniels, 2004; Stein, 2003).

Race and Military Service

Racial minorities living in the United States have long viewed military service as a means to challenge racial prejudices and stereotypes, and as an avenue to higher status within American society. For instance, during the Revolution- ary War, blacks fought on both sides of the war, hoping that loyalty to their respective sides would be rewarded by greater social and legal rights. Even after African-Americans acquired formal citizenship following the Civil War, black leaders continued to push military service as a way for blacks to prove their worth as citizens (Segal, 1989). Yet, as Astor (1998) notes, despite their willingness to serve, between independence and World War II, the use of African-Americans followed a clear pattern:

> At first, the authorities declined to enlist them. As the shortages of manpower became apparent, they were grudgingly enrolled, largely for menial work rather than combat duty and denied positions that might give them authority over white servicemen. With the passage of time the consumption of cannon fodder would grant some the right to bleed for their country. And when the shooting was over and the number of men under arms sharply reduced, they were the first to be dismissed (p. 14).

Like African-Americans, members of Asian groups also have had a long and complicated history of military service on behalf of the United States. While Asian ancestry individuals have served on behalf of the United States since at least the War of 1812 (Williams, 2005), it was not until the early 1900s that the first widespread use of Asians in the US military began (see Table 4.2). The forced opening of Japan in 1853 by Commodore Perry marked the start of US involvement in Asia. In 1898, the United States "annexed" the Philippines and Hawaii, and a year later started its "Open Door" policy in China (Okihiro, 2001, p. 25–26). The resulting increased pressure to protect US interests in Asia forced the military to seek local labor (most prominently Filipinos) to meet its personnel needs.

Whereas African-Americans faced intense levels of racism in their attempts to prove their worth as citizens, Asian aliens had to overcome racial- ized constructions that portrayed them as perpetual outsiders in order to prove themselves worthy of citizenship (Moore, 2003). Specifically, even as many Asian aliens willingly chose to serve in the US military, they faced race-based legal restrictions that made them ineligible for US citizenship. This distinc- tion would come, in time, to affect even how US-born Asian citizens were treated by the United States and its armed services, in particular, with respect to the experiences of Japanese-Americans during World War II. In the fol- lowing section, I discuss how the racial and nativity status of Asian foreign nationals and US-born Asian-American citizens affected their ability to serve their country and claim membership as Americans.

ASIAN-AMERICAN MILITARY SERVICE

Military Naturalization and Asian Citizenship[7]

In principle, only American citizens are eligible to serve in the US military; however, in practice, the United States has long relied on noncitizens to satisfying its military needs (Ford, 2001). During the Revolutionary War, George Washington relied heavily on German and Irish foreign nationals to supplement his forces, and even though Congress technically restricted the enlistment of aliens upon independence, these restrictions were typically suspended in times of military conflict (Ford, 2001). For example, during the Civil War, the Union Army enlisted European resident aliens, and even unofficially encouraged the recruitment of European immigrants with offers of free passage to the United States (Jacob & Hayes, 1981). In order to legitimize these practices, Congress passed the Act of July 17, 1862, which created "military naturalization" as a pathway to citizenship:

> Sec. 21. That any alien, of the age of twenty-one years and upwards, who has enlisted or shall enlist in the armies of the United States, . . . , may be admitted to become a citizen of the United States, . . . and that he shall not be required to prove more than one year's residence within the United States previous to his application to become such citizen.

With respect to citizenship, naturalization laws make aliens legally the same as US-born Americans (Kettner, 1978). Normally, the naturalization process requires a waiting period of several years, during which time aliens are expected to "become firmly attached to the well-being of the Republic" (Kettner, 1978, p. 243). This waiting period served to allow individual immigrants to demonstrate their loyalty and allegiance, qualities considered essential for constructing and maintaining national unity (Kettner, 1978). Military service was sufficient in demonstrating these characteristics, thus justifying the shorter waiting periods permitted by military naturalization.

Scholars note that for many European immigrants, military naturalization provided not only an accelerated pathway toward citizenship but also an important force in their "Americanization" (Ford, 2001; Jacob & Hayes, 1981; Kettner, 1978). For Asian aliens, however, the right to seek military naturalization placed into legal conflict the respective ideologies of civic and

Table 4.2: Estimates of Asian and Asian American Military Participation

Time Period	Military Participation: Context and Background	Estimated Numbers Serving
19th Century War of 1812 (1812-1815)	Accounts of Filipinos ("Manilamen") helping General Andrew Jackson defend New Orleans against the British under the command of Jean Baptise Lafitte.[1]	Unknown number of Filipinos.
Civil War (1861-1865)	Evidence that Chinese foreign nationals fought on both sides of the Civil War.[1]	≈50 Chinese
Spanish-American War (1898)	Evidence that Chinese and Japanese-Americans served aboard US warships in the Battle of Manila.[2]	Unknown number of Chinese and Japanese-Americans.
20th Century Philippine-American War (1899-1902)	President William McKinley signs Executive Order (1901) allowing the US Navy to enlist Filipinos as part of the insular force.[3]	≈500 Filipinos.
WWI (1914-1918)	Over 2.5 million Americans served in US Army, with around 18% being foreign born.[4]	≈5,700 Filipinos[5] and several thousand "other Asian."[4]
WWII (1939-1945)	Approximately 16 million Americans served in the US Armed Forces. The majority were US born due to the effects of restrictive immigration policies.[4] In the US, Filipinos originally were not allowed to enlist. Most Filipinos living in the Philippines mainly served in segregated units as part of the US Army— Philippine Scouts, Philippine Division. Chinese-Americans mainly served in integrated units, about 40% were foreign-born.[8] Japanese-Americans initially were denied the opportunity to serve. Most fought in the all-Japanese-American 100th Infantry Battalion and the 442nd Infantry Regiment—known collectively as the 442nd Regimental Combat Team.	In total, approximately 60,000 Asian Americans in the United States served. About 7,000 Filipino Americans residing in the United States served.[6] Between 142,000 and 400,000 Filipinos served in various capacities under or working with the US military.[7] Between 12,000 and 15,000 Chinese-Americans served.[9] Approximately 33,000 Japanese-Americans served.

1948	President Harry S. Truman Issues Executive Order 9981, abolishing racial discrimination in the US Armed Forces, which eventually ending segregation in the military.	
Korean and Vietnam Wars	Based on 1990 Census figures, the number of surviving Asian American veterans are:	32,559 for the Korean War.[8]88,052 for the Vietnam War.[8]
21st Century Current Forces	Today Asian Americans comprise 3.8% of the active duty population, a percentage similar to their representation in the general population.[10]	52,326 Asian Americans are serving on active duty.[10]

[1] Williams (2005). Citing speech given by David Chu, undersecretary of defense for personnel and readiness, at the DoD Asian-Pacific American Heritage Month luncheon on June 2, 2005.
[2] Japanese-American National Museum. "Japanese-Americans in America's Wars: A Chronology." http://www.janm.org/nrc/resources/militarych/ (Last accessed 3/5/2016).
[3] Bureau of Naval Personnel (1976).
[4] Bruscino (2010).
[5] Kramer (2006).
[6] Lee (2015).
[7] Frank (2005).
[8] US Department of Veterans Affairs (1998).
[9] Wong (2005).
[10] US Department of Defense (2013).

ethnocultural membership and put the courts in the position of resolving the contradiction between military naturalization legislation, which granted all aliens who served in the military the right to naturalize, and more general naturalization laws that limited citizenship to whites and blacks (Sohoni & Vafa, 2010).

In the first three cases that appeared before the federal courts, judges sought to deny that legislation allowing military naturalization was incompatible with existing race-based policies prohibiting Asian aliens the right to naturalize. Rather than debate the constitutionality of race-based naturalization laws, the courts followed the precedent established by earlier Supreme Court cases, that decisions regarding who should be able to enter the country and who could become a citizen were matters of "national interest" and thus strictly the domain of the legislative and administrative branches of government.

For example, in 1908, the District Court in Washington ruled that Buntaro Kumagai, a Japanese alien who had served honorably in the US Army, was ineligible for citizenship (*In re Buntaro Kumagai*). In presenting the court's opinion, Judge Hanford argued that the Constitution clearly delineated the roles of Congress and the courts with respect to naturalization, and thus distinguished between those born in the United States, who had the right to citizenship "without distinction to race or color," and aliens, who could only claim the privilege of becoming citizens under the provisions of laws enacted by Congress (p. 923).

Thus, rather than address the question of whether military naturalization laws provided a challenge to the ideology of race-based citizenship, Judge Hanford shifted the legal issue to whether Congress had intended military naturalization to provide an exception to laws limiting naturalization to whites and blacks. In presenting the court's ruling, Judge Hanford held that because both the Act of July 17, 1862, which had authorized military naturalization, and the (Naturalization) Act of February 18, 1875, which limited naturalization to whites and blacks, had been incorporated into succeeding immigration and naturalization laws, Congress must have intended military naturalization to give way to the broader framework of race-based naturalization.

In the following two years, the District Court in New York (*In re Knight*, 1909), and the Court of Appeals for the Fourth Circuit (*Bessho v. United States*, 1910), reached very similar decisions regarding military naturalization for foreign-born Asians. In the first case, Knight, whose father was English, and whose mother was half-Chinese and half-Japanese, argued that his service in the US Navy entitled him to naturalize under the Act of July 26, 1894, which specified that "any alien" who had served in the US Navy "shall be admitted to become a citizen of the United States."[8] As in the case of *In re Buntaro Kumagai*, the court ruled that race-based naturalization laws took precedence over military naturalization. In justifying the court's opinion,

Judge Chatfield argued that Congress must have known that members of other races would serve in the US Army and Navy, and thus by *not* specifying which racial groups were eligible for military naturalization, Congress had meant to limit military naturalization to whites and blacks, the only groups allowed to naturalize based on the more general immigration and naturalization laws.[9] Similarly, in *In re Bessho*, the court ruled against a Japanese petitioner who had served in the US Navy, arguing that because Congress failed to specifically repeal section 2169 of the Revised Statutes limiting naturalization to whites and blacks,[10] it must have intended race to matter in questions of citizenship.

The net result of these cases was that despite Congressional legislation that appeared to grant US citizenship to any alien who served in the military, and the willingness of the US military to allow them to serve, Asian aliens who had fought on behalf of the United States were denied its citizenship (Sohoni & Vafa, 2010). Furthermore, these rulings served to reinforce the dominance of ethnocultural views of US citizenship, as well as the right of Congress to make and use immigration and naturalization laws to ensure the demographic and ideological dominance of whites. As Judge Hanford noted in *In re Buntaro Kumagai* "the use of the words 'white persons' indicates the intention of Congress to maintain a line of demarcation [*sic*] between races, and to extend the privilege of naturalization only to those of that race which is predominant in this country." (p. 924)

However, these legal justifications for excluding Asian-Americans from citizenship soon came under pressure due to the unique legal situation of Filipinos and the Philippines. Particularly critical for judicial proceedings was the legal status of Filipinos as "nonalien/noncitizens" owing allegiance to the United States, and the need to attract foreign labor to meet military needs in Asia. Under the Treaty of Paris (1898), which ended the Spanish-American War, the United States gained control of the Philippines from Spain. When Filipino rebels continued their struggle for independence against the United States,[11] the US government responded by establishing the Philippine Scouts, units of Filipino-enlisted men led by US Army officers, to help quell the rebellion. The United States' eventual victory forced Filipino leaders to accept US sovereignty, and the new territorial government under US stewardship (Cabotaje, 1999).[12] In the years leading up to World War I, the US Navy began recruiting Filipinos to fill its most menial positions (such as stewards and mess men) and meet its growing manpower needs (Segal, 1989). Between 1903 and 1914, the number of Filipinos serving in the US Navy grew from nine individuals to about six thousand (Espiritu, 1995).

When Filipinos first tried to use their military service as a means to seek US citizenship, the federal courts used the same legal arguments that they had used against the naturalization of foreign-born Chinese-Americans and

Japanese-Americans. For instance, in 1912, the District Court in Pennsylvania denied Alverto, a citizen of the Philippines, who at the time had been serving in the US Navy for seven years, his petition to become a US citizen (*In re Alverto*, 1912). Citing the precedent established in the three previously described cases, Judge Thompson argued "however commendable" Alverto's naval service, Congress had only intended to extend naturalization by service to those "who were of the white or African races" (p. 690). Judge Thompson further argued that since the Philippines was a protectorate of the United States, Filipinos were technically not "aliens" and thus ineligible to naturalize.

At the beginning of World War I, Congress passed the Act of June 30, 1914, granting citizenship to aliens who served for four years in the US Navy or Marine Corps. As with previous military naturalization legislation, Congress neglected to specify racial eligibility or restrictions. However, Congress did add that military naturalization was restricted to aliens who were eligible for citizenship under existing law. In 1916, the District Court of Massachusetts used the unique legal status of the Philippines to support the right of Filipinos living in the United States to seek citizenship. In *In re Mallari*, Judge Morton argued that since the (Naturalization) Act of June 29, 1906 authorized admission to citizenship for "all persons not citizens who owe permanent allegiance to the United States" (p. 417), that Mallari would be eligible to naturalize given his status as a resident of the Philippines.[13]

A year later, however, two federal courts reached strongly contrasting decisions regarding the military naturalization of Filipinos. In *In re Rallos* (1917), the District Court of the Eastern District of New York denied Rallos, a half-Spanish, half Filipino, who had served in the US Navy, US citizenship. Judge Chatfield argued that because Filipinos were not legally aliens, they could not naturalize. He further argued that granting Filipinos military naturalization would defeat the purpose of existing immigration and naturalization laws, which limited naturalization to whites. However, in the same year, in *In re Bautista*, the District Court of Northern California granted a Filipino's petition for citizenship. The court argued that because Section 30 of the Naturalization Act of June 29, 1906 authorized "the admission to citizenship of *all persons not citizens who owed permanent allegiance* to the United States" (p. 767). Congress must have intended to allow Filipinos and Puerto Ricans the opportunity to naturalize. However, unlike the opinion in *In re Mallari*, Judge Morrow argued that this did not mean that all Filipinos were eligible, but only those with necessary qualifications—which in the case of Bautista, was his naval service. Furthermore, Judge Morrow noted that it would not make sense to deny Bautista citizenship, since this "would defeat the purpose of the act to encourage enlistment." (p. 769)

During World War I, and largely in response to the US Navy's personnel demands in Asia, Congress passed the Act of May 9, 1918, which for the first time specified that "Filipinos" and "Porto Ricans" who served in the US military were eligible to naturalize. However, the Act also stated that "any alien" who had enlisted or planned to enlist in the US Army, Navy, Marine Corps, and Coast Guard was eligible to naturalize, while simultaneously concluding that the Act should not be seen as repealing or enlarging section 2169 of the Revised Statutes, thus leaving the status of members of other Asian groups unclear.

To further complicate matters, Congress passed the Act of June 19, 1919, which made "[a]ny person of foreign birth" eligible for naturalization if they served in the US military during World War I. The vagueness of Congressional legislation with respect to non-Filipino Asians led some federal and state court judges to grant citizenship to Asian servicemen (Salyer, 2004). Yet, it is important to note that these were primarily administrative decisions made at the height of wartime patriotism and did not substantively or symbolically challenge the primacy of race-based citizenship (Sohoni & Vafa, 2010).

Once World War I ended however, the judiciary was again forced to interpret the conflicting legislative messages regarding military and race-based naturalization. In the case of *In re Para* (1919), the District Court for the Southern District of New York denied two aliens, one of South American Indian ancestry and one of Japanese ancestry, the right to naturalize despite their service in the US Navy during World War I. In supporting its opinion, the court argued that "any alien" in the Act of May 9, 1918, was limited to whites and blacks, *and* to Filipinos and Puerto Ricans, who had been spelled out in the language of the legislation (p. 643–644).

The joint cases of *In re En Sk Song* and *In re Mascaranas*, in 1921, would further clarify this legal distinction between Filipinos/Puerto Ricans and other Asian groups. Specifically, in these cases, the District Court for the Southern District of California ruled that even though both Song (a Korean) and Macaranas (a Filipino) had engaged in military service for the United States, only Mascaranas was eligible for citizenship under the Act of May 9, 1918. At the same time, Judge Bledsoe noted that these legislative acts lacked the uniformity expected of naturalization law, and the problematic nature of denying citizenship to someone who had "bared his breast to the bayonet of the enemy." (p. 25–26)

In total, between the end of World War I and 1925, federal and state courts repeatedly and consistently interpreted congressional intent in this manner, culminating in the Supreme Court decision in *Toyota v. United States* (1925) where the Court upheld the District Court of Massachusetts's decision to vacate an order allowing a Japanese alien to naturalize based on his military service (Sohoni & Vafa, 2010). Specifically, the Supreme Court ruled that the Act of May 9, 1918 did not provide a challenge to the long history of "national policy to maintain the distinction of color and race" because Congress had only intended to make an exception for Filipinos and Puerto Ricans who had *served in the military* (p. 412).[14]

Despite the Act of June 24, 1935,[15] which allowed Asian-American World War I veterans previously ineligible for citizenship to naturalize, it was not until World War II that Congress finally dismantled the racial restrictions that prevented Asians from citizenship (Sohoni & Vafa, 2010). On December 17, 1943, Congress overturned the Chinese Exclusion Acts, allowing Chinese aliens to naturalize. Three years later, Congress passed legislation making Filipinos and Asian-Indians eligible for citizenship.[16,17] This process culminated with the passage of the Immigration and Nationality Act of 1952, whereby Congress made all races eligible for citizenship, thereby also eliminating race as a bar to immigration (Sohoni & Vafa, 2010). However, it is important to note that the primary motivation behind the repeal of these race-based discriminatory policies against Asians was less about improving the status of Asian aliens within the United States, and more about symbolically rewarding our war-time Asian allies, and responding to the needs of Cold War politics (Hing, 1993).

Patriotism and the Constitution

The legal conflict between civic-based and ethnocultural-based ideologies of US membership, described above for foreign-born Asian-Americans, also affected US-born Asian-Americans. For US-born Asian-Americans, this discord is best captured by the contrasting experiences of Japanese-Americans and members of other Asian-American groups during World War II.

For US-born Japanese-Americans, their fate as "Americans" became intrinsically tied to relations between the United States and Japan. In the years leading up to World War II, the United States expected and was preparing for a conflict with Japan in the Pacific, with the primary surprise being the speed and success of the Japanese attack on US Naval Forces at Pearl Harbor on December 7, 1941 (Daniels, 2004). Before the Japanese attack on Pearl Harbor, US-born Japanese-Americans were treated similar to other US citizens with respect to military service. In preparation for the impending war, President Roosevelt had signed into law the Selective Training and Service Act of 1940, the first peacetime military draft in US history. Critically, this law was one of the first to contain a nondiscrimination clause:

> Sec. 4. (a) *Provided*, that in the selection and training of men under this Act, and in the interpretation and execution of the provisions of this Act, there shall be no discrimination on account of race or color.

Over the next year, more than 3,000 US-born Japanese-Americans were inducted into the armed forces by the Selective Service System, with many other US-born Japanese-Americans enlisting with National Guard units

(Daniels, 2004). In fact, many of the first responders that provided aid after Pearl Harbor and helped secure the coastline against potential Japanese landing were Japanese-American members of the Hawaiian National Guard (Crost, 1994). However, after the attack, and in direct violation of the nondiscrimination clause of the 1940 statute, many military commanders began discharging Japanese-Americans, and local draft boards stopped drafting them (Daniels, 2004). Soon after, the Selective Service System illegally sent out a directive to draft boards requiring them to classify all Japanese-Americans, regardless of their citizenship status, as 4-C, a category normally reserved for enemy aliens (Daniels, 2004).

This grouping of foreign-born Japanese-Americans (Issei) and US-born Japanese-Americans (Nisei) would continue when President Franklin D. Roosevelt issued Executive Order 9066 on February 19, 1942. Despite multiple reports indicating that the majority of Japanese-Americans were likely to prove loyal to the United States, and that mass incarceration was unnecessary, President Roosevelt issued the Order by which nearly 120,000 Japanese-Americans living on the West Coast were forcibly relocated to internment camps, irrespective of their citizenship status (Daniels, 2004; Lee, 2015).[18] This treatment was in sharp contrast to the treatment of German-Americans and Italian-Americans, who despite originating from countries that were also at war with the United States, only saw a select number of foreign-born members placed into confinement, and only after each was examined individually (Daniels, 2004).

In summarizing the various groups responsible for the wartime internment of Japanese-Americans, Daniels (2004, p. 46) has concluded:

> A deteriorating military situation created the opportunity for American racists to get their views accepted by the national leadership. The Constitution was treated as a scrap of paper not only by McCloy, Stimson, and Roosevelt but also by the entire Congress, which approved and implemented everything done to the Japanese Americans, and by the Supreme Court of the United States, which in December 1944, nearly three years after the fact, in effect sanctioned the incarceration of the Japanese Americans.

By early 1943, however, with an attack by Japan no longer considered likely, the War Relocation Authority began to explore options for the release of "loyal" detainees, one of which was to make them available for the draft.[19] The majority of the Nisei would end up fighting in segregated units—the 442nd Regimental Combat Team and the 100th Infantry Battalion[20]—in Europe, while a smaller number of Japanese-Americans were recruited to serve as translators for the Military Intelligence Service (MIS) in the Pacific Theatre (Croft, 1994). As has been well-documented, the 442nd become one of the most decorated combat units in World War II (McCaffrey, 2013); less chronicled, but equally importantly, Japanese-Americans in the MIS proved critical in translating captured documents, monitoring radio traffic, and interrogating prisoners (Crost, 1994; Daniels, 2004).

Even more neglected has been the valuable contributions made by US-born Japanese-American (Nisei) women to the war effort. As has been detailed by Moore (2003), a large number of Nisei women volunteered for the Women's Army Auxiliary Corps (WAAC)/Women's Army Corp (WAC) with the US Army—serving in such capacities as clerical workers, typists, and nurses.[21] Critically, the WAC's need for qualified women to fill these roles, and the voluntary nature of military service for women, enabled Nisei women to resist attempts to create segregated companies (Moore, 2003).

In contrast to Japanese-Americans, who had to overcome government hostility to prove their worth as citizens, members of other Asian ethnic groups, such as Chinese-, Filipino-, Korean-, and South Asian Americans found themselves actively supported by the US government in their efforts to prove themselves worthy Americans. Specifically, members of these groups, who previously had been the frequent target of racial prejudice and discrimination, now found themselves classified as "good Asians" due to their homelands' statuses as wartime allies of the United States or as enemies of Japan (Lee, 2015).

One illustration of the impact of this changed status can be found in the government-supported media campaign intended to change public stereotypes regarding Chinese-Americans, from "inassimilable" to "law-abiding, peace-loving, courteous people living quietly among us," and to teach Americans how to differentiate between "good" and "bad" "Orientals," rather than viewing them as indistinguishable (Lee, 2015, p. 254). (In)famously, as part of this campaign, on December 22, 1941, both *Time* and *Life* magazine would run stories with pictures to help readers distinguish between their Chinese "friends" and enemy "Japs" (Lee, 2015, p. 254).

It was within this changed social context, that members of other Asian-American ethnic groups joined the US military. For many, serving in the US military allowed them to help their countries of origin, as well as prove their loyalty to America. Overall, about 12,000–15,000 Chinese-Americans would enlist in the US military, serving in both integrated units and all-Chinese units (such as the Fourteenth Air Service Group [ASG]) (Wong, 2005). Likewise, Filipino-Americans, after initially being declared ineligible to serve due to their legal status as "US nationals," soon began to enroll in large numbers once Roosevelt changed the draft law. In California, nearly 16,000 Filipino-Americans registered their names for the draft, and more than 7,000 Filipino-Americans would go on to serve in the segregated 1st Filipino Infantry Regiment and the 2nd Filipino Infantry Regiments. While numerically smaller, other Asian-American ethnic groups also provided soldiers for the United States war effort (Lee, 2015).

Without taking away the significance of the military service provided by Asian-Americans toward US war efforts, and the pride this patriotism engendered within their respective communities, it is important to note that the changed status of other Asian-American groups within American society was fundamentally a result of international policy concerns related to the war (i.e., not being seen as "racist" by war-time allies) and was based on their members' respective ethnic identification, rather than on their US-born members being suddenly seen as more American. Thus, like US-born Japanese-Americans, US-born members of other Asian-American groups still found their ethnicity more important than their nativity status in terms of how they were viewed and depicted by the dominant white society.

ASIAN-AMERICAN SERVICE TODAY

It would be easy to present the history of Asian-American military service as a story of a racial minority group successfully fighting to overcome societal prejudice and discrimination, and the slow but inexorable victory of civic citizenship over ethnocultural citizenship. However, while elements of such a narrative exist, the history presented here points to a much more complicated story. Rather, the history of Asian-American military service demonstrates the resilience of racial ideologies for "American citizenship" despite strong instrumental pressures toward the inclusion of minorities. Specifically, it shows that despite the willingness of Asian-Americans to fight for their country and the general acceptance of Asian-Americans into its ranks by the military, that this has rarely had an immediate or direct effect on the legal or social status of Asian-Americans within broader American society.

As detailed in this chapter, during periods of armed conflict, Congress frequently passed vague and inconsistent legislation that appeared to allow Asian nationals serving in the US military the right to naturalize, but this legislation was typically repealed when the need for surplus manpower ended. Similarly, despite the opportunity provided by military naturalization cases to establish egalitarian, civic-based definitions of citizenship, the judiciary chose to interpret congressional legislation in ways that limited the ability of Asian aliens to naturalize, thus reinforcing ethnocultural views of citizenship (Sohoni & Vafa, 2010). Likewise, for US-born Asian-Americans, ethnic status appears to have been more important than nativity status with respect to being accepted as Americans—both in the case of US-born Japanese-Americans, who were interned despite their US citizenship (and also initially forbidden to serve), and in the case of other US-born Asian-Americans, who found their status in the US improved because they looked like (and were seen as representing) America's Asian allies.

Furthermore, despite the patriotism exhibited by Asian-American and other minority soldiers during World War II, in the immediate aftermath of the War, the US Armed Services continued or returned to their previous policies of segregation and exclusion (Bruscino, 2010). In fact, it was only due to the active efforts of Civil Rights leaders, and the support of political leaders like President Harry S. Truman, who in 1948 issued Executive Order 9981, ordering the desegregation of the US military, that the military started on their way toward integration (Bruscino, 2010).[22]

Today, Asian-Americans have made great strides in terms of military participation. Once underrepresented as a percentage of the US population, they now comprise around 4 percent of the active duty military in the United States, a percentage similar to their overall representation among the military service age-eligible population (US Department of Defense, 2013). Asian-Americans have also served as high-ranking officers in all branches of the US Armed Forces, including most prominently General Eric K. Shinseki, the former Secretary of Veteran Affairs, who was the first Asian-American four-star general, and who served as the 34th Chief of Staff of the Army (US Army, 2016). In addition, the number of Asian-Americans entering the service academies has steadily increased over the past five years, and they now make up a greater percentage of the US Military Academy at West Point and the US Naval Academy (7.0 percent and 7.1 percent in the Class of 2017, respectively) than their percentage of the US student-age population (Ang, 2014).

Despite these gains, there is still some evidence that Asian-Americans continue to face prejudice and discrimination in the service based on their presumed "foreignness," as suggested by a study of Asian-American Vietnam veterans—who reported facing discrimination for "looking like the enemy" (Chao, 1999), and as seen in the case of Danny Chen, a born and raised New Yorker, who committed suicide after reportedly facing physical abuse and racial slurs about his Chinese heritage from other men in his unit (Hajela, 2012). Similarly, despite the fact that nearly 50,000 US soldiers have been granted permanent beard exemptions for medical reasons, it took the threat of a lawsuit against the US Department of Defense for Sikh Americans to receive religious accommodations that would allow them to serve with turbans and beards in accordance with their faith (Wang, 2016).

Furthermore, the legal legacy underlying the historical treatment of Asian-Americans still endures. While legislation like the McCarran-Walter Act of 1952 and the Immigration and Nationality Act Amendments of 1965[23] have officially put an end to the use of race and ethnicity in immigration and naturalization laws, and while the judiciary has become more willing to place judicial constraints on the most blatant forms of racial and ethnic discrimination, the courts have still not fully repudiated the principles, established in *Chae Chan Ping* (1889) and *Fong Yue Ting* (1893), that Congress has the right to determine what constitutes "national interests" in immigration and naturalization policies (Chin, 1998; Sohoni & Vafa, 2010).

Therefore, even though race-based immigration and naturalization laws are no longer legally acceptable, this does not mean that there have been no attempts to exclude broad categories of immigrants, especially during times of economic uncertainty and with concerns regarding national security. Whereas in the past racial/ethnic markers were used to deny citizenship to certain immigrant groups, today we see a transition to secondary characteristic. For example, emphasis on the criminality and illegality of Mexicans immigrants has helped create a perception of them as a threat, a threat with racial overtones, and one requiring harsher immigration policies as well as a greater acceptance of the discriminatory monitoring of US-born Hispanics (Sohoni & Sohoni, 2014).

Moreover, the relationship among military naturalization, race, citizenship, and the nature of American identity continues to play out today with new immigrant groups. In the past decade and a half, the House and Senate have repeatedly failed in attempts to pass the DREAM Act, which would have provided undocumented minors an opportunity to gain legal status by serving in the US military or attending college (Olivas, 2009).[24] Attempts like the DREAM Act, which would allow citizenship for "high-quality" undocumented immigrants through military service, are again likely to raise legal issues regarding naturalization and citizenship that the courts will need to face. Given the history of judicial deference that the courts have given to Congress with respect to immigration and naturalization, it is quite possible that the courts could permit Congress to pass racially, ethnically, or religiously discriminatory legislation, such as a version of the DREAM Act, that does not allow undocumented minors from Middle Eastern countries the same rights as other undocumented minors (Sohoni & Vafa, 2010).

Finally, as Daniels (2004, pp. 115–121) warns in the epilogue to the revised version of his book on the Japanese internment, it is unclear whether in a post-9/11 climate, that "race prejudice, war hysteria, and a failure of political leadership," might lead to discriminatory policies against both foreign and US-born Arab Americans if there are heightened concerns of terrorist attacks. These concerns appeared during the 2016 Presidential Election, suggesting the potential for foreign- and native-born members of certain ethnic and religious groups to become linked in the public's consciousness (Diamond, 2015). Daniels (2004) notes that *Korematsu v. United States* (1944), the landmark Supreme Court case that tested the constitutionality of Executive Order 9066, and held that military necessity could justify the imprisoning of US citizens based on racial criteria, has not been officially overturned.[25]

The example of the Japanese-Americans experience during World War II provides a powerful reminder that people from all backgrounds can provide outstanding service to their country in the armed forces, and the continued need to be vigilant against racist and nativist immigration and naturalization policies.

NOTES

1. The Development, Relief, and Education of Alien Minors ("DREAM") Act, first introduced in 2001 by Dick Durbin (D-IL) and Orrin Hatch (R-UT) as Senate Bill 1291 (107th Congress), would allow for aliens brought to the United States as children an opportunity to "earn" their citizenship by meeting certain education requirements or through service in the US military.

2. For instance, the infamous 3/5th Compromise in Article 1, Sec. 2 of the US Constitution, which treated "slaves" (not directly stated) as 3/5 of a person for apportioning seats in the House.

3. Critically, Daniels and Graham (2001) note that Asian immigrants constituted only a small fraction of total immigrants during this period. For example, in the 1900 Census, only 1.2 percent of the foreign-born originated from Asia, compared to nearly 85.0 percent from European countries.

4. In *Chae Chan Ping v. United States* (1889), also known as the Chinese Exclusion Case, the Supreme Court upheld a part of the Chinese Exclusion Act (1888) that Chinese "aliens" could be excluded from the United States, even though they were US residents who possessed government-issued papers assuring their return; while in *Fong Yue Ting v. United States* (1893), the Supreme Court ruled that an "alien" could be deported strictly based on their race.

5. The zone covered most of Asia, including the islands of the Pacific. China and Japan were not included as the Chinese Exclusion Act (1888) and the Gentleman's Agreement (1908) already restricted immigrants from these countries.

6. Since the Philippines were a protectorate of the United States, Filipinos could enter the United States as noncitizen nationals.

7. The following section draws on my earlier work with a colleague, which gives a more detailed account of this process (Sohoni & Vafa, 2010).

8. Ch. 165, 28 Stat. 123, 124 cited in *In re Knight*, 171 F. at 300.

9. Judge Chatfield also discussed what percentage of "Mongolian" blood would disqualify someone from being classified as "white." Drawing on an earlier federal case, *In re Camille*, 6 F. 256 (1880), Judge Chatfield argued that Knight could not be considered white, as "a person, one-half white and one-half of some other race, belongs to neither of those races, but is literally a half-breed."

10. Section 2169 of the Revised Statutes, Amended in 1875, U.S. Comp. St. 1901, p. 1333.

11. The Philippine-American War, 1898–1902

12. Congress would incorporate the Philippine Scouts into the regular US Army regiments in World War II (Act of Feb. 2, 1901, §36, 31 Stat. 748), see (Cabotaje, 1999).

13. Ironically, the court ruled that Mallari was ineligible for citizenship for procedural reasons, as he had used the Act of July 26, 1894 relating to military naturalization, rather than the (Naturalization) Act of June 29, 1906, which used the term "owe permanent allegiance."

14. See also *De La Ysla v. United States* (1935) and *United States v. Javier* (1927), which further clarified that Filipinos seeking to naturalize had to do so based on their military service.

15. As detailed by Salyer (2004), Asian veterans of World War I were able to win the support of the traditionally nativist American Legion to pressure Congress to allow for their naturalization. However, five years later, Congress passed the Nationality Act of October 14, 1940, which again restricted citizenship to whites, those of African descent, and Filipinos who had served in the military, again blocking off naturalization for members of other Asian groups.

16. Act of Dec. 17, 1943, Ch. 344, 57 Stat. 600 ("The Chinese Repealer" or Magnuson Act). The Filipino and Indian Naturalization Act (Ch. 534, 60 Stat. 416).

17. Ironically, in the same year that Congress removed the racial bars that had prevented Filipinos who had not served in the military naturalizing, it also passed the Rescission Acts of 1946, 60 Stat. 14 (1946) and 60 Stat. 223 (1946), taking away veterans benefits for those who had not served directly under the US military (i.e., the Filipino Army, recognized guerilla groups, and members of the New Philippine Scouts). Among the benefits denied to these veterans was the right to military naturalization (Cabotaje, 1999).

18. Two-thirds of those interned were US citizens.

19. To determine "loyalty," the government designed a questionnaire that tested the "American-ness" vs. "Japanese-ness" of detainees. These included the two controversial questions: Q 27, which asked all draft-age males if they were "Willing to serve in the armed forces of the United States on combat duty, wherever ordered?" and Q28, which asked all others if they would be willing to "swear allegiance to the United States of America . . . and forswear any form of allegiance or obedience to the Japanese emperor . . ." that many Japanese-Americans (particularly Issei) found difficult to answer (Lee, 2015).

20. The 100th Infantry Battalion was primarily made up of Japanese-Americans from Hawaii, many who had previously been in the Hawaiian National Guard (Crost, 1994). After suffering heavy losses in Italy, they joined the 442nd Regimental Combat Team.

21. After contentious debate in Congress, on May 15, 1942, President Roosevelt signed Public Law 77–554, creating the Women's Army Auxiliary Corps (WAAC). The goal of the WAAC was to free servicemen from clerical positions to serve in combat. Originally, as the WAAC, while women received military pay, food, housing, and medical care, they did not have military status nor receive pensions. This auxiliary status was challenged, and on July 1, 1943, after being approved by the House and Senate, President Roosevelt signed Public Law 78–110 creating the Women's Army Corp (WAC) as part of the US Army (Moore, 2003).

22. In response to the recommendations by several boards and committees that found that segregation in the armed forces was both inefficient and morally indefensible, President Truman passed Executive Order 9981 on July 26, 1948, which

abolished racial discrimination in the U.S. Armed Forces and eventually led to the end of segregation in the services (Bruscino, 2010).

23. The 1965 Immigration and Nationality Act (also known as the Hart-Celler Act) ended the national origins quota system that had favored immigrants from Northern and Western Europe.

24. Since 2001, when it was first introduced in the Senate, there have been over twenty attempts to pass variants of this bill.

25. In 2011, the Justice Department acknowledged it had been in error in prosecuting the case, and that it had hidden relevant information that US-born Japanese were not likely to be a threat to national security.

REFERENCES

Ang, L. (2014). Chinese cadets numbers rise in US military academies. *China Daily USA*. (August 7, 2014). Retrieved from http://usa.chinadaily.com.cn/epaper/2014–08/07/content_18265759.htm. Astor, G. (1998). *The right to fight: A history of African Americans in the military*. Navato, CA: Presidio Press.

Bruscino, T. A. Jr. (2010). Minorities in the military. In Bradford, James C. *A Companion to American Military History*. 2. Hoboken, N.J.: Wiley-Blackwell.

Bureau of Naval Personnel. (1976). *Filipinos in the United States Navy*. Report available at Naval History and Heritage Command. Retrieved from.http://www.history.navy.mil/browse-by-topic/diversity/asians-and-pacific-islanders-in-the-navy/filipinos-in-the-united-states-navy.html

Cabotaje, M. A. (1999). Equity denied: Historical and legal analyses in support of the extension of U.S. veterans' benefits to Filipino World War II veterans. *Asian Law Journal*. 6: 67–97.

Calavita, K. (2005). Law, citizenship, and the construction of (some) immigrant others. *Law and Social Inquiry*, *30*: 401–420.

Chang, R. S. (1999). *Disoriented: Asian Americans, law, and the nation state*. NY: New York University Press.

Chao, J. (1999). *Asian American vets can't forget Vietnam War racism*. San Francisco: Chronicle. Retrieved from http://www.sfgate.com/news/article/Asian-American-vets-can-t-forget-Vietnam-War-3090545.php

Chin, G. J. (1998). Segregation's last stronghold: Race discrimination and the constitutional law of immigration. *UCLA Law Review*, *46*: 1–74.

Crost, L. (1994). *Honor by fire: Japanese Americans at war in Europe and the Pacific*. Novato, CA: Presidio Press.

Daniels, R. (2004). *Prisoners without trial: Japanese Americans in World War II*. Revised Edition. New York: Hill & Wang.

Daniels, R., & Graham, O. L. (2001). *Debating American immigration, 1882–Present*. Lanham, MD: Rowman & Littlefield.

Diamond, J. (2015). *Donald Trump: Ban all Muslim travel to U.S.* Retrieved from http://www.cnn.com/2015/12/07/politics/donald-trump-muslim-ban-immigration/

Espiritu, Y. (1995). *Filipino American lives*. Philadelphia, PA: Temple University Press.

Ford, Nancy G. (2001). *Americans All: Foreign-born Soldiers in World War I.* College Station, TX: Texas A & M University Press.

Frank, S. (2005). *Filipinos in America.* Minneapolis, MN: Lerner Publications.

Glenn, E. (2000). Citizenship and inequality: Historical and global perspectives, *Social Problems, 47*: 1–20.

Hajela, D. (2012). Asian American soldier's suicide called a 'wake-up call' for the military. *Washington Post.* Retrieved from https://www.washingtonpost.com/politics/asian-american-soldiers-suicide-called-a-wake-up-call-for-the-military/2012/02/19/gIQA7Ke4QR_story.html.

Haney Lopez, I. (1996). *White by law.* New York: NY University Press.

Hing, B. O. (1993). *Making and remaking Asian America through immigration policy, 1850–1990.* Stanford, CA: Stanford University Press.

Hoeffel, E. M., Rastogi, S., Kim, M. O., & Shahid, H. (2012). *The Asian population: 2010: 2010: Census Briefs.* U.S. Census Bureau. Retrieved from https://www.census.gov/prod/cen2010/briefs/c2010br-11.pdf

Jacobs, J, & L. Hayes. (1981). Aliens in the U.S. Armed Forces: A historico-legal analysis. *Armed Forces and Society, 7*: 187–208.

Janowitz, Morris. (1976). Military institutions and citizenship in western societies. *Armed Forces and Society, 2*: 185–204.

Kettner, J. (1978). *The development of American citizenship, 1608–1870.* Chapel Hill: The University of North Carolina Press.

Kramer, P. A. (2006). *The blood of government: Race, empire, the United States and the Philippines.* Chapel Hill: University of North Carolina Press.

Lee, E. (2015). *The making of Asian America: A history.* New York: Simon and Schuster.

McCaffrey, J. M. (2013). *Going for broke: Japanese American soldiers in the war against Nazi Germany.* Norman: University of Oklahoma Press.

Moore, B. L. (2003). *Serving Our Country: Japanese American women in the military during World War II.* Piscataway N.J.: Rutgers University Press.

Okihiro, G. Y. (2001). *Common ground: Reimagining American history.* Princeton: Princeton University Press.

Olivas, M. A. (2009). The political economy of the Dream Act and the legislative process: A case study of comprehensive immigration reform. *Wayne Law Review. 55*: 1759–1810.

Saito, N. T. (1997). Alien and non-alien alike: Citizenship, 'foreignness,' and racial hierarchy in American law. *Oregon Law Review, 76*: 261–345.

Salyer, L. E. (2004). Baptism by fire: race, military service, and U.S. citizenship policy, 1918–1935. *The Journal of American History, 91*: 847–876.

Segal, D. (1989). *Recruiting for Uncle Sam.* Lawrence, KS: University of Kansas Press.

Smith, R. M. (1997). *Civic ideals.* New Haven, CT: Yale University Press.

Sohoni, D. (2007). Unsuitable suitors: Anti-miscegenation laws, naturalization laws, and the construction of Asian identities. *Law and Society Review, 41*: 587–618.

Sohoni, D. & Vafa, A. (2010). The fight to be American: Military naturalization and Asian citizenship. *Asian American Law Journal, 17*: 119–151.

Sohoni, D & Sohoni, T. (2014). Perceptions of immigrant criminality: Crime and social boundaries. *The Sociological Quarterly. 55*: 49–71.

Stein, E. (2003). Construction of an enemy. *Monthly Review. 55*: 125–129. Retrieved from http://monthlyreview.org/2003/07/01/construction-of-an-enemy/

U.S. Army. (2016). *Profiles-Asian Pacific Americans in the United States Army.* Retrieved from http://www.army.mil/asianpacificamericans/profiles/

U.S. Department of Defense. (2013). *Demographics: Profile of the military community.* Retrieved from http://download.militaryonesource.mil/12038/MOS/Reports/2013-Demographics-Report.pdf

U.S. Department of Veterans Affairs. (1998). *A report on Asian Pacific Islander veterans.* Readjustment Counseling Service.

Williams, R. (2005). DoD's Personnel chief gives Asian-Pacific American history lesson. *DoD News.* Retrieved from http://archive.defense.gov/news/newsarticle.aspx?id=16498

Wang, F. K.H. (2016). Army grants accommodations to 3 Sikh-American soldiers to serve with turbans, beards. *NBC News.* Retrieved from http://www.nbcnews.com/news/asian-america/army-grants-accommodations-3-sikh-american-soldiers-serve-turbans-beards-n554881

Wong, K. S. (2005). *Americans first: Chinese Americans and the Second World War.* Cambridge: Harvard University Press.

CASES CITED

Chae Chan Ping v. United States, 130 U.S. 581 (1889).

De La Ysla v. United States, 77 F.2d 988 (9th Cir. 1935).

Fong Yue Ting v. United States, 149 U.S. 698 (1893).

In re Alverto, 198 F. 688 (E.D. Pa. 1912).

In re Bautista, 245 F. 765 (N.D. Cal. 1917).

In re Buntaro Kumagai, 163 F. 922 (D.C. 1908).

In re Camille, 6 F. 256 (C.C. 1880).

In re En Sk Song, In re Mascaranas, 271 F. 23 (S.D. Cal. 1921).

In re Knight, 171 F. 299 (E.D.N.Y. 1909).

In re Mallari, 239 F. 416 (D. Mass. 1916).

In re Para (1919), 269 F. 643 (S.D.N.Y. 1919).

In re Rallos, 241 F. 686 (E.D.N.Y. 1917).

Korematsu v. United States, 323 U.S. 214 (1944).

Toyota v. United States, 268 U.S. 402 (1925).

United States v. Wong Kim Ark, 169 U.S. 649 (1898).

United States v. Javier, 22 F.2d 879 (D.C. Cir. 1927).

STATUTES AND CONSTITUTIONAL AMENDMENTS CITED

Act of July 17, 1862, Ch. 200, 12 Stat. 594.

Act of June 19, 1919, Ch. 24, 41 Stat. 222.

Act of June 24, 1935, 49 Stat.

Act of June 30, 1914, Ch. 130, 38 Stat. 392.

Act of May 9, 1918, Ch. 69, 40 Stat. 542.

Chinese Exclusion Act, Ch. 126, 22 Stat. 58 (1882).

Civil Rights Act of 1866, 14 Stat. 27–30, enacted April 9, 1866.

Civil Rights Act of 1875, 18 Stat. 335–337, enacted March 1, 1875.

Immigration Act of 1917, Public Law 301, 39 Stat. 874, enacted February 15, 1917.

Immigration Act of 1924 (Johnson-Reed Act), Public Law 68–139, 43 Stat. 153, enacted May 26, 1924.

Immigration and Nationality Act of 1952 (McCarran–Walter Act), Public Law 82–414, 66 Stat. 163, enacted June 27, 1952.

Immigration and Nationality Act of 1965 (Hart-Celler Act), Public Law 89–236, 79 Stat. 911, enacted June 30, 1968.

Nationality Act of 1940, 54 Stat. 1137, enacted October 14, 1940.

Naturalization Act of 1790, Ch. 3, 1 Stat. 318, enacted March 26, 1790.

Naturalization Act of 1870, Ch. 255, §7, 16 Stat. 256, enacted July 14, 1870.

Naturalization Act of 1875, Ch. 80, 18 Stat. 318 (R.S., 2169, pg. 382), enacted February 18, 1875.

Naturalization Act of 1906, 34 Stat. 596, enacted June 29, 1906.

Selective Training and Service Act of 1940 (Burke-Wadsworth Act), 54 Stat. 885, enacted September 16, 1940.

Treaty of Paris, 30 Stat. 1754 (1898).

U.S. Const. Amend. XIV, Passed June 13, 1866, Ratified July 9, 1868.

Chapter 5

Native American "Warriors" in the US Armed Forces

William C. Meadows

This chapter briefly examines American-Indian/Native American participation in the US Armed Forces, focusing on service from the Civil War to the present. Included is a survey of the background of Native military service, numbers and factors of participation, the unique legal status and cultural relationship of Natives with the United States, unique military contributions, Native military cultural practices, and future prospects for Native service in the US Armed Forces. Section headings will use English translations of the more common collective names Native Americans developed for enemy populations. Many Native American band and tribal ethnonyms and personal names are based on phenotype, physical body characteristics or conditions, dress, hairstyles, and material culture forms. As descriptions of a physical object or state of being, they are used as reference terms of a matter of fact with no inherent offensive association (USMC, 1945, pp. 2; Viola, 2008; Meadows, 2013, pp. 7, 2015). While some of these forms may appear unusual to non-Indians, they must be viewed with cultural relativism or in the native context to fully understand them. The basis for these names will be included in endnotes with each section.

Whereas Euro-American warfare often centers on political and geographical objectives, Native American warfare also involves a wide range of personal, communal, and religious aspects. Many Native forms of song, dance, graphic art, clothing and regalia, fraternal and sororal organizations, social status and rank, personal medicine, talismans, and even personal and family surnames are derived from military service. Many Natives view contemporary military service through older tribal traditions related to warfare, using the term "warrior" to describe and refer to veterans, past and present. Natives have long blended aboriginal tribal concepts of warfare with US Armed Forces service, thereby creating newer syncretic traditions (Holm,

1996, pp. 23, 30–65, 100–102; Meadows, 1999, 2010) of military service while retaining many traditional native cultural forms. As the US military incorporates the concept of "warrior spirit" as a part of the larger soldier ethos, the lengthy historical and cultural prominence of "warrior" status in many Native American societies provides an important preconditioning element that has long facilitated Native American service and syncretism in the US Armed Forces.

NATIVE AMERICANS IN THE US MILITARY

In addition to intertribal conflicts, that were often exacerbated and sometimes caused by European intrusions, Native peoples have been involved in every war in American history. Until the end of the Civil War and despite attempts to remain neutral in Euro-American conflicts, Native Americans often found themselves caught between opposing European powers; French, British, Spanish, Colonial, American, and during the Civil War North (Union) and South (Confederate). In North America, the French and Indian War (1756–1763) focused on the colonial conflicts between England and France and their respective Indian allies for control of the fur trade, opposing tribes, and the continent. During the Revolutionary War, George Washington informed the Continental Congress that Indians could "be made of excellent use as scouts and light troops" (Viola, 2008, p.19) and in 1776 Congress authorized him to enlist 2,000 men. Eventually, of the 250,000 men who served under Washington in the Revolutionary War, around 5,500 were Natives (Viola, 2008).

Indians have fought in every major American campaign, from serving on both sides of the American Revolution at the Battle of Oriskany Creek in 1777 to the present conflicts in the Middle East. Four of the six Iroquois tribal divisions fought with the British, while the Oneida and Tuscarora joined the Patriot cause. During the War of 1812, Cherokee and Choctaw were pivotal in Andrew Jackson's victories in the American south, only to be betrayed by him when he forced their removal to Indian Territory (now Oklahoma) in the 1830s, including removing the Cherokee against the Supreme Court's rulings. In the Seminole Wars of the 1830s and 1840s, Creek, Delaware, and some Seminole troops fought in support of the United States against the Seminole people. Seminole forces often stymied US Forces in the Florida swamps, resulting in some Seminoles being allowed to remain in Florida to this day (Holm, 1996; Viola, 2008)

The first Native American to attend the US Military Academy at West Point was David Moniac (sometimes pronounced Manac), a Muskogee-Creek from Montgomery, Alabama, who entered the academy at the age of fifteen years and eight months in 1817. Following the start of the Second Seminole War in

December 1935, Moniac returned to active military service as a captain in the Mounted Creek Volunteers. He was killed during fighting at Withlacoochee River and was buried with full military honors on January 15, 1837, near the present Florida National Cemetery at Bushnell, Florida. Following Moniac, ninety-two American Indians have graduated from West Point (Crain, n.d.).

The Civil War

Despite lacking US Citizenship, over 20,000 American Indians fought in the Civil War, including over 4,000 with the Union, and over 15,000 with the Confederacy forming at least four entirely Indian regiments. Natives served on land and sea, from privates to commissioned and noncommissioned officers. Ely Parker (Tonawanda Seneca) rose to the rank of Brevetted Brigadier General and while serving under General Ulysses S. Grant drafted the surrender documents signed by General Robert E. Lee at Appomattox. Stand Watie (Cherokee) was the last Confederate general to surrender, nearly two months after Lee (Hauptman, 1995; Sutton & Latscher, 2013; Viola, 2008).

The largest concentration of American-Indians participated in engagements in Indian Territory and the borders of Arkansas and Missouri. Small units of northern tribes tended to enlist with the Union, remaining as small tribal clusters in numerous divisions throughout the war. Nearly 150 Ottawa and Ojibwa, including a few Delaware, Huron, Oneida, and Potawatomi, served as sharpshooters in Company K, 1st Michigan Sharpshooters. Small contingents of Seneca served in Company D, 132nd New York State Volunteers, popularly called the "Tuscarora Company," while other Seneca served in the 14th Heavy Artillery. A number of Oneida in the 3rd and 14th Wisconsin Volunteers and Menominee in Company K, 37th Regiment, served in integrated army units and in naval blockading vessels. A few Pequot served in the 31st US Colored Infantry and other units. In 1862, 170 of 201 Delaware men of service age voluntarily enlisted, becoming Union scouts and home guards that participated in numerous battles in Indian Territory (Hauptman, 1995; Viola, 2008; Sutton & Latschar, 2013).

Southern tribes from the Carolinas to Indian Territory enlisted primarily with the Confederacy. The majority came from North Carolina, Mississippi, and Indian Territory, and served in their own separate companies such as the 1st and 2nd Cherokee Mounted Rifles, Catawba infantry in the Army of Northern Virginia, and Creek and Cherokee regiments in Indian Territory. Eastern Band Cherokee served in William Holland Thomas' famed Confederate Legion of Cherokee Indians and Highlanders from 1862 to 1865. Resenting past harsh treatment and opposing classification as "free persons of color," others assisted the Union. The Pamunkey of Virginia worked as river pilots for General George McClellan's Army of the Potomac in the Peninsula

Campaign of 1862, while the Lumbee of North Carolina became guerillas who fought Confederate Home Guards in the swamp country of North Carolina during Sherman's Carolina Campaign in 1865. With the Union abandonment of Indian Territory and its treaty and annuity obligations in May 1861, the Confederacy made a concerted effort to recruit American-Indians. By that fall, groups of Cherokee, Chickasaw, Choctaw, Creek, and Seminole had signed treaties with the Confederacy, while others from these tribes organized military companies as home guards, often attempting to protect or regain their homes and lands (Hauptman, 1995; Viola, 2008; Sutton & Latschar, 2013).

Relocating most Indians east of the Mississippi River to Indian Territory, the Indian Removal Act of 1830 created numerous divisions within Indian nations. After reestablishing thriving communities in Indian Territory, tribes were further divided over issues of slavery and secession. Reinvigorating these earlier factions, the Civil War resulted in members of numerous tribes fighting against one another and widespread destruction and death from raids and fighting in eastern Indian Territory. Seeking refuge in Kansas and Texas, others received little aid and endured continual raids and hardships. The reassignment and withdrawal of Union soldiers from western areas broke treaty provisions to protect friendly Indian groups and often resulted in a lack of law and order. US Army efforts to pacify western tribes during the Civil War resulted in several massacres and major displacements of Dakota, Shoshone, Navajo, Apache, and Cheyenne, Arapaho, and white traders located under a peace agreement at Sand Creek and flying American and white flags (Hauptman, 1995; Sutton & Latschar, 2013).

Natives fought in the war for varied reasons including past alliances, treaty obligations, to validate tribal status and leadership, adventure, income to relieve poverty, enlistments of tribal peers, disputes over slavery, and dependency on Anglo political structures through Bureau of Indian Affairs services. Another primary motivation to serve was the hope of obtaining a larger land base or that remaining tribal lands would be protected from further white encroachment, and that they would receive better treatment after the war from either the US or Confederate government. However, most tribes had their dreams dashed, continuing to loose tribal lands and autonomy with the formation of Oklahoma Territory and later the state of Oklahoma. Delaware that served on both Confederate and Union sides were forced to relocate to southern Cherokee lands in Indian Territory and even to become citizens of the Cherokee Nation (Hauptman, 1995; Sutton & Latscher 2013; Viola, 2008).

Wolves For the Blue Coats—Indian Scouts[1]

Following post-Civil War cutbacks in spending, troop numbers, and troop reassignments for Reconstruction projects, limited numbers of troops were left to man ongoing conflicts with Indians in the American West. American ideals of Manifest Destiny and pressure to open up new lands for Euro-American settlement intensified efforts to finish clearing the Plains of Indians. The martial and equestrian image of the Indian was already well ingrained in the American psyche, and needing individuals familiar with the western geography and tribes, Congressional approval for an Indian scouting corps was passed in 1866. Pro-assimilation supporters in the Indian service and civic groups embraced the program, believing it would provide Indians with employment, an outlet for their martial skills, accelerate the settlement of nonreservation Indians, and further assimilate Indians into American culture. Between 1866 and 1890 members of several tribes (Apache, Crow, Cheyenne, Lakota, Pawnee, Shoshone, etc.) served as scouts, some informally and others organized later as official units. Scouts also served as combat troops, in helping to bring in resistant bands of their own and other tribes, and in roles both with and independent of Anglo troops (Dunlay, 1982; Meadows, 2015). Between 1864 and 1877 the Pawnee Indian Scout unit under Major Frank J. North provided invaluable scouting and combat service to the US Army during the height of the Plains Indian wars (Dunlay, 1982; Tate, 1986; Van de Logt, 2010).

Based on the success of East Indian troops in the British military in India, on March 8, 1891, the US Secretary of War directed the recruitment of fifty-five Native Americans into regular army units west of the Mississippi; in each Troop L of the first eight US Cavalry Regiments, and in Company I in several infantry regiments (Britten, 1997). Although not required, English was taught as a part of the program and Indians, including noncommissioned officers, were often paid less than non-Indian enlistments. As regular enlisted cavalry in a noncombat era, Troop L members served as police, guards, messengers, hunted game, and assisted with cattle-drives and other duties at local military posts and Indian reservations. Although issues related to differential treatment and pay and cultural differences in military ideology led some company leaders to lose faith in the program, others reported excellent results. Under Captain Hugh L. Scott, Troop L at Fort Sill, Oklahoma Territory was viewed by many, including the War Department, as the most successful. Demonstrating the larger value of the program to those in his company, Scott (1928) reported excellence in military service, skills, loyalty, increased community social prominence, saving money, and the purchase of homes at the end of their tenure. Between March 1891 and June 1897, 1,071 Indian served in the Army's Indian Scout program (Meadows 2015, pp. 57–65).

Spanish American War

Although efforts to raise all-Indian military units continued, Native American soldiers were typically treated as individuals and integrated into white units after 1897 (White 1968). In 1898 Captain Leonard Wood, with Theodore Roosevelt as second in command, was authorized to raise a regiment of cowboy and mounted riflemen. Drawing volunteers from Arizona, New Mexico, Indian, and Oklahoma Territories, they organized the First Volunteer Cavalry Regiment who became better known as the "Rough Riders." Native American recruits came primarily from Indian and Oklahoma territories, with smaller numbers from New Mexico and Arizona territories. Many Natives served as advance guards and scouts in the action in Cuba; with some both wounded and killed in action. Although the native role in the Spanish American War is little known, Roosevelt commended several instances of his Native American troop's bravery and service (Roosevelt, 1899; Britten, 1997; Viola, 2008).

Native American troops saw action in the Western Pacific during the Filipino Revolution (1898–1902) and the Boxer Rebellion in China (1900). While the enlistment of Indian scouts other than Apaches had declined by the early 1900s, several Apache and Oklahoma Indians were recruited and used by Brigadier-General John Pershing during the 1916 punitive expedition against Pancho Villa in Mexico (Britten 1997, pp. 36–37, 103).

Fighting the Metal Hats—World War I[2]

Prior to the United States entering the war in 1917, several hundred Indians from northern reservations showed their willingness to fight by crossing the border to enlist in the Canadian Army between 1915 and 1917 (Winegard, 2012). While some Indians had received US citizenship through allotment via the Dawes Act of 1887 or individual tribal treaties, approximately one-third of all American Indians did not possess US citizenship and thus, "took a military oath to defend the Constitution of the United States without possessing any rights under it" (Bennett & Holm, 2008, p. 10). Despite uncertainty regarding their citizenship status, many volunteered for military service while others were drafted. While focusing on assimilating Indians into mainstream Anglo-American culture, government-run Indian boarding schools, such as Carlisle, Haskell, and Phoenix, ran military style, regimented programs that preconditioned many Indians for military service and were heavily recruited from. World War I marked the first time that Natives served as regular combat troops rather than as auxiliary units attached to non-Indian units. Over 17,300 Indian men registered for selective service and more than 12,000 served in the war (Britten, 1997; Krouse, 2007).

It has long been stated that American Indian servicemen have represented a greater percentage of their total population than any other race or ethnic group in every 20th-century American war (Collier, 1942; Neuberger, 1942a, 1942b; Bernstein, 1991; Britten, 1997; Townsend, 2000). This premise may have begun with a December 1918 statement by Commissioner of Indian

Affairs Cato Sells who wrote, "Considering the large number of old and infirm Indian and others not acceptable under the draft, leaving about 33,000 of military eligibility, I regard their representation of 9,000 in camp and actual warfare as furnishing a ratio to population unsurpassed, if equaled, by any other race or nation" (NARA, 1918, p.4). Britten (1997) cites 12,000–12,500 or around 25 percent of the adult male Indian population, Chambers (1997) over 12,500, and Barsh (1991) up to 15,000 or 30 percent. This is remarkable as the Native American population had reached its nadir in 1900 at just over 237,000 from the effects of disease, colonization, warfare, boarding schools, and a century and a half of US Federal Indian policy.

Natives joined for varied personal and tribal reasons including tribal and family warrior traditions, tribal and American patriotism, duty, to gain status in their tribal communities, employment opportunities, to escape the harsh environment of reservations, to gain full rights and better treatment for Indian peoples from the government, travel and adventure, and levels of education, acculturation, and geography. In sum, there was no single Indian response to enlistment or service in the war. Natives served with distinction and were widely lauded by commanding officers, including General John Pershing. On the home front, Indians contributed through agricultural and livestock production, off-reservation work in war industries, and women contributing large amounts to Liberty Bond and war saving stamp drives and Red Cross service (Britten, 1997; Krouse, 2002).

By Word War I "the idea that Indians possessed special inherent propensities for warfare and scouting was firmly entrenched in the American psyche" (Holm, 1996, p.89). Some attributed these alleged skills to biology rather than culture, assuming Indians had a better sense of direction, could see better at night, were more stealthy, and could detect the enemy better than non-Indians. Known as the "Indian Scout Syndrome," these beliefs resulted in Indian soldiers often being assigned a disproportionate number of dangerous scouting, patrol, messenger, and sniper assignments, which led to a significantly higher casualty rate than among other American Expeditionary Forces (AEF) soldiers. Yet the tendency of Indian soldiers to accept whatever task they were assigned with little or no complaint, to volunteer for dangerous tasks, and a willingness to fight also contributed to this image. Officers frequently noted Indian performance in terms of endurance, running ability, and resourcefulness, and their use in large number for particular tasks suggests they performed these objectives well. A mutually reinforcing dialectic between non-Indian beliefs and Indian responses appears to have developed in that non-Indians perceived Indians to have enhanced martial abilities leading them to assign Indians to dangerous tasks (the syndrome), which increased their risk of injury or death. The overall Native willingness to accept and perform these assignments, endure hardships, and not complain, simultaneously fed non-Indian beliefs while reinforcing traditional warrior values, traditions, and bringing status in tribal communities (warrior culture). Ironically, while the government and the Bureau of Indian Affairs encouraged and intended military service as a means to civilize Indians by mixing with non-Indians, the armed forces emphasized using their perceived natural warrior instincts as Indians (Holm, 1996; Britten, 1997; Krouse, 2007).

Approximately 5 percent of all Indians in World War I were killed in action or wounded, compared to a 1 percent casualty rate for the entire AEF, with some tribes suffering casualty rates of 10–14 percent of their servicemen (Barsh, 1991). Other indications of Indian patriotism were the individual tribal declarations of war against Germany by the Oneida and Onondaga and the fact that several Indian veterans expressed a desire for more action and that the war would have lasted longer (Britten, 1997; Krouse, 2007)! The overwhelming positive testimony of Indian military abilities by military officers (US Congress, 1920; Britten, 1997) only reinforced Anglo-American views of nearly superhuman abilities and the Indian Scout Syndrome and led to more requests for forming all-Indian units. These well established beliefs would continue in future conflicts.

Throughout 1919, many tribes held honor, military society, and Scalp and Victory Dances, powwows, feasts, purification rites, and other ceremonies to honor and ritually cleanse returning Indian veterans. Some individuals were given new Indian names based on their service or were asked to name children based on their wartime experiences. In several tribes new songs were composed about the war, many during ceremonies to honor and welcome home veterans. One genre of these songs, often referencing the American Flag and tribal veterans' service, became known as "Flag Songs" and continue today as tribal equivalents to the National Anthem. Some tribes also initiated veterans into traditional men's warrior and dance societies, and formed Indian chapters of American Legion and Veterans of Foreign Wars posts (Densmore, 1919; Britten, 1990; Meadows, 1999), several of which continue to the present such as the Stephen Youngdeer Post 143, in Cherokee, North Carolina.

Although the Bureau of Indian Affairs had been attempting to suppress Native cultural practices for years, the performance of traditional ceremonies in association with American patriotism was so widespread and seen as embracing American values by the general public that the Bureau of Indian Affairs (BIA) finally acquiesced in their attempts to end them. The cultural revivals spurred by military service in World War I helped keep numerous traditions alive for another generation and long enough for culturally protective legislation to manifest in the 1930s (Britten, 1997; Meadows, 1999).

In 1919, Indian veterans of World War I who still lacked citizenship were offered that status under H.R. 5007, but only if they applied for it in what constituted a complex bureaucratic process. Many did not apply due to the travel, financial constraints, and complexity involved. In 1924 the Indian Citizenship Act finally bestowed US citizenship to all American Indians (Britten, 1990; Krouse, 2007).

The war provided valuable skills in learning English, mechanical trades, and greater firsthand exposure to how mainstream American and European societies worked and thought. Regardless of citizenship status, in the military Indians had been treated as equals for the first time, which helped heighten Indian political awareness and agency. The war also helped "de-villainize and de-mythologize" popular misconceptions on both sides, provided natives with a means to regain warrior status while highlighting their service and domestic wartime contributions, and helped foster numerous Pan-Indian political and cultural forms. However, despite widespread praise of native military service, government cutbacks in Indian health care and education, and increased pressures to sell and lease their lands to non-Indians followed. Military service increased interactions with non-Indians and helped to maintain aspects of native culture, as well as fostering an increase in purpose, discipline, and pride that allowed veterans to become a catalyst for change in government relations and native civil rights (Britten, 1997; Krouse, 2007).

Fighting the Metal Hats and the Small-Eyed People—World War II[3]

Although Nazi propaganda predicted an "Indian uprising" if asked to fight against the Axis (Neuberger, 1942b; Townsend, 2000), the Germans were quickly disappointed as Native Americans again demonstrated widespread armed forces support and voluntary enlistment for World War II. Nearly 4,000 men were already in the US Armed Forces prior to Pearl Harbor, and by October 1942 had increased to 10,000. More than 24,000 reservation and another 20,000 off-reservation Indians served in the armed forces during World War II (Bennett & Holm, 2008), representing more than 10 percent of the entire Native population. Native Americans in general enlisted at a ratio of one and a half times that of draftees, and Plains Indian volunteers surpassed inductees by a two to one margin. Native participation again exceeded any American ethnic group, including whites. Over one-third of all able-bodied Native men aged eighteen to fifty served, with up to 70 percent in some tribes (Collier, 1942; Bernstein, 1991; Townsend, 2000). As Commissioner Collier (1942) noted, this number "represents a larger proportion than any other element of our population" (p.29). Neuberger (1942a) reported that, "Army officials declare that had the percentage of volunteers been as high in the rest of the country as among the Indians, there would have been no need for Selective Service" (p.79). Nearly one-fifth of the 45th Division was Native, as were large segments of the 158th Regimental Combat Team, the

163rd Infantry Regiment, and other units. Natives also served in specialized roles as code talkers, and fifteen of the 138 elite Alamo Scouts were Native Americans (Indian Country Today 2011c).

Natives also contributed through providing natural resources, reservation lands, agricultural productions, war bond drives, and large scale work in urban war industries. Although Native Americans were not segregated in the military during World War II (which allowed them to experience American culture on a broader level than the reservation), they were still spoken of, and in some ways treated differently than whites, especially in terms of service. The continued beliefs that all Indians were "chiefs" and possessed natural martial skills furthered the Indian Scout Syndrome, with native people drawing some of the deadliest wartime assignments (Neuberger, 1942a; Bennett & Holm, 2008).

Excluding Purple Heart medals, Native Americans in the Army garnered over two hundred citations and medals including three Congressional Medals of Honor in the 45th Division. Over one hundred similar awards were awarded in the Army Air Corps. Major-General Clarence Tinker (Osage), the first Native general since the Civil War, personally led the American attack on Midway, where he was killed in action. Rear Admiral Joseph J. Clark (Cherokee), the first Native to receive an appointment to the US Naval Academy at Annapolis, served throughout the Pacific Theater. Ira Hayes (Pima) was immortalized in the photo of Marines raising the second flag on Mt. Suribachi during the fight for Iwo Jima, then ordered to return to the States where he participated in war bonds drives to bolster national morale. A total of 550 Natives were killed in the war including over 100 Sioux (Bernstein, 1991; Bennett &Holm, 2008). As the first time large numbers of Native servicemen fought in Asia, Natives serving in the Pacific frequently noted the similarities between American Indian and Asian phenotypes. While some struggled internally with this situation, there is no indication that it inhibited their service.

More important than decorations for heroism, however, individuals regained traditional forms of male status as warriors, on their own terms and on a large scale. Analogizing modern military service with traditional warfare, tribal elders once again viewed veterans as warriors and no greater traditional honor could be had. As World War II and Korean War veteran Atwater Onco (Kiowa) related in 1997 (Meadows, 2010):

> It was just like they used to. Because the warrior, the soldier boys that went into service, were just class, and were treated like they were going on a Kiowa war party years ago . . . And that's how they upheld not only World War II, but all the wars: Vietnam, Korea, Desert Storm, and other wars and conflicts. Every Kiowa that goes . . . the Kiowa people uplift the veteran, overall they think highly of the veterans and the person, especially during wartime, that goes to war. It's just

in us, in our Kiowa blood, to really think a lot of that person that fights for us, a warrior . . . . Overall, the Kiowa people are like that, they really respect their men that go to service to fight for the country.

Many tribes held prewar ceremonies to pray for and bless individuals prior to going overseas such as Native American Church meetings, sweat lodge and Sun Dance ceremonies, Christian Church meetings, and Navajo Blessingway Ceremonies. Many tribes also provided veterans with small medicine bundles containing sacred items including corn pollen, arrowheads, feathers, earth paint, peyote, and other botanicals that serve as sources of spiritual protection and power. Native soldiers wore these items similar to how Protestant, Catholic, and Jewish servicemen wore Christian crosses, Saints medals, and the Star of David. Many Native soldiers also observed daily practices involving prayers, songs, and the use of these protective religious medicines. Many Native communities also provided postwar celebrations such as powwows, honor dances, and giveaways to welcome individuals back into the community, as well as cleansing ceremonies to facilitate their social, psychological, and spiritual reincorporation into the community. Veterans who underwent Navajo Enemy Way, Cherokee Going To Water, Native American Church meetings, cedaring ceremonies, initiations into warrior and dance societies, and similar cleansing rites have attested to their help in readjusting to their postwar communities (Holm, 1996; Meadows, 1999; 2010; Clevenger, 2010; NEH, 2014).

Native women's auxiliary groups formed to undertake fundraising, send care packages to servicemen overseas, honor incoming and outgoing veterans with dances, and visit wounded veterans in hospitals. These organizations held dances with songs in their native languages bearing lyrics of a patriotic nature, describing the sacrifice of servicemen and referencing the importance of the US Flag. Many of these organizations, such as tribal chapters of the American War Mothers (N. Cheyenne, Kiowa, Osage, Oto, Pawnee, Comanche), The Carnegie Victory Club (Kiowa), The Stecker Purple Heart Club (Kiowa), and the Apache Service Club (Plains Apache), remain active to the present (Meadows 1999, pp. 127–132, 2010, pp. 330–361). In many communities, women's dance shawls are commonly decorated with the name, unit designations, insignia, and military ribbons of their male relatives' military service, that continually honor their service at dances.

Despite a widely lauded service record in World War II, many Indians continued to experience discrimination upon returning home. In some states, Indians were still prohibited from purchasing alcoholic beverages, and Indians in New Mexico, Arizona, and part of Utah, including returning Native veterans, were denied voting rights until 1948. The widespread exposure of Natives to other parts of the world and work experience in urban war industries prompted the US government to view this as evidence of assimilation and seek new policies furthering this trend. In 1946, the US government introduced the Indian Claims Commission to settle outstanding issues over questionable US acquisitions of Indian lands, and the Relocation Program that encouraged Indians to relocate from reservation and rural communities to urban areas. Maintaining that reservations would no longer be needed, whereby the US government could then terminate treaties with tribes and "get out of the Indian business," the Termination Program of 1950 began evaluating the cultural retention of tribes. Upon determining that groups were assimilated enough to no longer need the provisions legally promised to them in treaties, the US government began terminating the legal treaty status of some tribes. Although termination was eventually stalled and reversed, it helped to stimulate a revival of traditional Indian culture and activities including martial-related traditions. Many Native veterans of World War II pursued education through the G.I. Bill and a wide range of careers, becoming community cultural and governmental leaders and a driving force in the resurgence of Native pride, culture, and civil rights (Holm, 1996; Meadows, 1999).

Fighting the Short Wolf Men—Korea and Vietnam[4]

Approximately 10,000 Native Americans served in the Korean War, with 194 killed in action. Many Native veterans of World War II reenlisted for service in Korea. Four individuals received the Congressional Medal of Honor including Sgt. Woodrow Keeble (Sisseton-Wahpeton Sioux) who also earned five Purple Hearts, two bronze Stars, a Silver Star, and the Distinguished Service Cross. Vice Admiral Joseph J. Clark (Cherokee) was a commander of the Navy's Seventh Fleet. Yet despite commendable military service, non-Indian racism toward Indians continued in some parts of America. When SFC John Rice (Winnebago) was killed in action in Korea and denied burial in his native Sioux City, Iowa because of his race, President Truman arranged for him to be buried in Arlington National Cemetery with full military honors (Viola, 2008). The Korean War only reinforced the general Native cultural patterns and revivals associated with honoring veterans and regaining martial status in tribal communities that occurred with World War II. The large-scale increase of new Native veterans from 1941 to 1953, their reacquisition of "warrior status," increased Indian cultural awareness and pride, and the impacts of termination were major factors in the revival of several Southern Plains military and dance societies from 1957 through the 1980s. These include the Kiowa Gourd Clan in 1957, Kiowa Black Legs Society, Plains Apache Manatidie Society, Comanche Tuhwi and Little Ponies Societies, and numerous tribal and intertribal Indian veteran's organizations such as the Comanche Indian Veterans Association, and the Comanche War Scouts (Meadows, 1999; 2010).

Between 1960 and 1973 over 42,000 Native veterans served in the Vietnam War (1966–1975), with 230 killed in action, most between 1966 and 1973. Many others entered service but did not serve overseas. Comprising less than 1 percent of the entire US population, Natives represented more than 2 percent of all US troops in Vietnam (Holm, 1996). Native American Vietnam veteran Tom Holm's (1996) survey of 170 Native Vietnam veterans found that nearly 80 percent of them enlisted voluntarily, many volunteering for service in elite units such as Special Forces, Force Recon, Airborne, Rangers, and Special Ops groups. Thirty-one percent of them received wounds in action. Natives experienced the continuation of the Indian Scout Syndrome, noting that officers often selected them for hazardous duties such as walking point, scouts, tunnel rats, nighttime listening posts, Army LLRP (Long Range Reconnaissance Patrol, later 75 Ranger Regiment), and Marine Force Recon Battalions due to race over other characteristics. Indians were also heavily recruited for Special Operations Group Reconnaissance or Hunter-Killer Units (Holm, 1996).

Vietnam veterans grew up in an era of popular culture that glorified war and had provided a prosperous and secure postwar life for many non-Indians. While the larger political controversies associated with America's role in the war and mixed support for the war and its veterans at home complicated readjustment to civilian life, many American-Indians serving in Vietnam experienced additional complications. While their military service was a shared experience, Korean and Vietnam veterans did not receive the collective national welcome home or the accolades that World War I and II veterans did. Throughout the war it became increasingly apparent that blacks, Latinos, and Native Americans continued to live in communities controlled by outsiders, held lower paying occupations, and had less access to education and the dominant political system. Native servicemen continued recognizing similarities between American Indian and Asian phenotypes, the conditions of Indian reservations to the lives of Vietnamese peasants, both as largely nonindustrialized "tribal" peoples, and the colonial history that both groups experienced. From these developments, the Indian Civil Rights Movement of the late 1960s and 1970s, increasing tribal government, dissatisfaction with treaty violations, and the lack of mainstream American support, some Native veterans began to question their purpose in Vietnam; were they simply helping the whites do to another group what had been done to them? A Creek-Cherokee veteran stated (Holm, 1996), "Why was I fighting to uphold a US treaty commitment halfway around the world when the United States was violating its treaty commitments to my own people and about 300 other

Indian nations? . . . I was fighting the wrong people, pure and simple, and I've never gotten over it" (p.175).

Native servicemen were also troubled by non-Indian officers continually referring to enemy territory as "Indian Country" (Holm, 1996). Natives increasingly began to feel a sense of betrayal from the US government and found themselves returning to a "war at home" in the form of domestic colonial abuse through segregation, unequal rights, an ongoing pro-assimilation education system, and the United States not upholding its treaties with Indians. Holm characterized the experience of one's personal values and philosophical beliefs becoming at odds with the operant realties they are encountering as "cognitive dissonance." Adopting practices similar to the black Civil Rights Movement, many Vietnam veterans became politically active, pursuing national and tribal policy changes toward the current era of decreased federal control and increased Indian self-rule known as Self Determination (Holm, 1996).

Like other Vietnam veterans, Native veterans experienced disdain from the non-Indian American public, being called "baby killer," "war monger," and spat upon (Holm, 1996). Within Native communities however, veterans received virtually unconditional acceptance in their tribal communities who focused on honoring their veterans through powwows, dinners, induction into veteran's societies, naming ceremonies, prayer and other religious ceremonies that provided spiritual and social cleansing, acceptance, and community reintegration. Rather than focusing on the larger international and national political aspects of wars, the *hows* and *whys*, Native people continue to view military service not as a political statement or endorsement but primarily as a continuation of defending their people and land (Holm, 1996; Meadows, 1999).

While Native American veterans also suffer from Post Traumatic Stress Disorder (PTSD), Holm's (1986, 1996) work with 170 Native American Vietnam veterans found that Native veterans whose tribes provide prewar blessing ceremonies and postcombat cleansing and social ceremonies exhibit better rates of readjustment to civilian life. While some of these ceremonies have been lost or stripped away through US government suppression, many still remain. As Holm (1996) described, "The importance of tribal community, of healing a troubled kinsman, and of absorbing war-related trauma within the society in order to gain harmony within the group outweighs almost any other political consideration" (p.195). Often recovery is as much a social and cultural process as individual and psychological. One Kiowa Vietnam veteran related to me that he did not cope well with PTSD, his mixed-blood status, or readjustment back into the community until he was inducted into the Kiowa Black Legs Warrior Society and experienced the support and camaraderie of other veterans (Meadows, 2010). Several Native Vietnam-era veterans associations have been formed.

Fighting the Curved Knives—Desert Storm, Iraq, and Afghanistan[5]

Native Americans continued to serve in record numbers throughout the Desert Storm, Iraq, and Afghanistan campaigns. During Desert Storm, I (Meadows,1999) documented an almost constant progression of send-offs and homecoming dances sponsored by Southern Plains Women's societies and the honoring and induction of returning veterans into traditional dance and warrior societies. In December 2005, nearly 20,000 Native Americans and Alaskan Natives were serving in the US Armed Forces. Reminiscent of the Indian Scout Syndrome and prompted by the ease with which Taliban, al Qaeda, and other fighters slipped in and out of Afghanistan and Iraq, in early 2007 the Pentagon sent the Shadow Wolves, an elite group of well-trained Native American marksmen and trackers, to teach their skills to the police forces of nearby Tajikistan and Uzbekistan. Originally formed in the 1970s to assist Drug Enforcement Agency officials tracking drug smugglers across the Tohono O'odham Tribal Reservation near Tucson, Arizona, the unit is composed of members from several tribes, many who developed skills hunting game and tracking livestock as youth. Membership is reported to require one-quarter Indian descent (Viola, 2008).

In 2004, Native Americans from the 120th Engineer Combat Battalion, a National Guard unit based in Okmulgee, Oklahoma, with approximately 20 percent Native service personnel, held a powwow at the Al Taqaddum Air Base near Fallujah (Viola, 2008). In 2008, other Natives in a New Mexico unit held a "Native American Appreciation Month" celebration in Saddam Hussein's main palace of Al Faw at Camp Victory, Iraq (Clevenger, 2010).

NATIVE WORDS, NATIVE WARRIORS—CODE TALKERS

One of the most unique Native contributions in the US military is that of the code talkers, Native Americans used to send military messages in their native languages to foil enemy listeners. In both world wars, American forces suffered from the ability of German and Japanese forces to break US military codes. Although beginning with small groups of Eastern Band Cherokee, Choctaw, Comanche, and others during World War I as an impromptu tactic to counter German interception and breaking of American communications, this strategy was later expanded. Prior to World War II small groups of Comanche, Chippewa-Oneida, and Meskwaki, and in 1943 a group of Hopi, were recruited by the Army and developed codes in their languages. In 1942, the Marine Corps began recruiting and training Navajo, which became the largest code-talking program, providing a crucial advantage in every campaign from Guadalcanal through the occupation of Japan. While these groups each developed specialized military vocabulary within their respective languages, essentially creating a code within a code (Type 1 Code Talking), members of at least thirty other groups sent messages in their everyday native language for similar purposes (Type 2 Code Talking). Code Talkers provided fast, secure, real-time communications that was faster than existing encryption and decryption technology. None were ever broken by the enemy.

Legislation in 2000 for the Navajo, and in 2008 for members of other tribes, awarded Congressional Gold and Silver Medals for their service, the only such medals awarded to Native Americans to date. Ironically, most of these Indian men who served in both world wars went through government run Indian boarding schools that sought to eradicate Indian languages and cultures. Fortunately, these men were not only able to maintain their languages but gracious enough to share them for the United State's benefit as code talkers in both world wars. The code talkers have become icons and a part of the National narrative of the world wars (Meadows, 2002, 2007, 2009, 2011, 2016).

STRONG HEARTED WOMEN—NATIVE WOMEN VETERANS

Although much less known, Native women have long made military contributions. Four Lakota Roman Catholic sisters from Fort Berthold Reservation, South Dakota, served in the Spanish American War. Sister Anthony died from disease in Cuba and was buried with full military honors. Fourteen women served in the Army Nurse Corps during World War I, two serving overseas. Nearly 800 Native women served in World War II in the Women's Army Corps (WACs), the Women Accepted for Voluntary Emergency Service (WAVEs), the Women's Air Force Service Pilots (WASP), and the Marine Corps Women's Reserve (Bellefaire 2006). Their service continued through Korea, Vietnam, and to the present with many acquiring officer rank and choosing military service as a career choice. Darlene Yellowcloud (Lakota) joined the Army because so many of the men in her family had served. Her grandfather, Bear Saves Life, was killed in action in France during World War I and her father, brothers, brothers-in-law, uncles, and cousins were all veterans. Darlene served in Korea as a Specialist 4th Class (Bellefaire, 2006).

Beginning in World War II, the Alaska Territorial Guard (ATG), more commonly known as the Eskimo Scouts, and their wives patrolled the western coastline of Alaska and the islands between Alaska and Russia from June 1942 to March 1947. Around 6,389 Alaskan Natives from 107 communities, including at least twenty-seven women, served as unpaid volunteers during World War II. Members patrolled coastlines, shot down Japanese air ballons bearing bombs and radio listening equipment, rescued downed airmen, and other logistical, supply, and defense duties. As many as 20,000 Native

Alaskans may have contributed to the overall war effort of the ATG. Members were primarily those too young or too old to be drafted and ranged in age from twelve to eighty. These scouts are the only National Guard unit holding a continuous active duty mission. In 2000 all ATG members were granted US veteran status and honorable discharges by law. Natives continue to serve in the Alaska National Guard. In 1976, women were admitted as official members and began receiving pay, benefits, and recognition for their service which includes patrolling ice flows in the Bering Strait, monitoring movements on the tundra, and performing arctic search and rescue efforts. In 1980, at least sixty Native Alaskan women were serving as Eskimo Scouts (Marston, 1969; Bellefaire, 2006).

On March 23, 2003, the third day of Operation Iraqi Freedom, a convoy of the 507th Army Maintenance Company, a support unit of clerks, repairmen, and cooks, made a wrong turn in the desert. Intending to continue to a support position in the desert the turn brought them into the city of Nasiriyah. They were soon surrounded and attacked by Iraqi soldiers and Fedyeen paramilitary forces armed with AK-47s, mortars, and rocket-propelled-grenades (RPG). Pfc. Lori Piestewa (Hopi), with nine other troops in the Humvee she drove, accelerated and evaded heavy fire until their vehicle was struck by an RPG sending it into the back of a disabled tractor trailer. Three individuals were killed, while Piestewa, Shoshana Johnson, and Jessica Lynch were all wounded, but survived. The seven survivors were all captured. Piestewa later died at an Iraqi hospital from head injuries sustained in the attack. Jessica Lynch was rescued by US Special Forces from the Iraqi hospital. The 507th suffered eleven soldiers killed in action and nine wounded that day. As the first American woman to die in the war, and the first Native American women to die in combat on foreign soil, Piestewa quickly became an iconic symbol of Native women's courage and military service and a catalyst for numerous beneficial awards, community projects, and athletic events. She was posthumously promoted to the rank of Specialist. After a five-year effort, Arizona's controversially named "Squaw Peak" was renamed "Piestewa Peak" in her honor in 2008 (Rolling Stone, 2004; Bennett & Holm, 2008; Indian Country Today, 2011a). As her brother Wayland explained, "My parents have been visiting tribes all over the nation since Lori's death and Piestewa Peak is a symbol of honor and pride among all Indian peoples" (Rolling Stone, 2004). In March of 2001, 2,726 Native women were serving in the armed forces, including the Coast Guard (Dollarhide, 2002). By January 2013, over 5,000 Native women were serving in Iraq and Afghanistan (Schilling, 2013).

The inclusion of women veterans in tribal veteran's groups varies. In some traditional warrior and dance societies women veterans are frequently honored at public ceremonies but not allowed to become members. In more modern forms such as tribal veterans associations, and American Legion or

VFW Posts, women are typically full members. In several tribes women are now a regular part of the color guard at public functions.

In 2010 Sgt. Mitchelene BigMan (Crow) and two other Native women veterans designed jingle-dress style regalia in red, white, and blue, with designs and patches representing the US Flag, their unit, rank, combat, and the Iraqi Freedom patch. Their appearance prompted others to suggest they join the honor guard. They later formed the Native American Women Warriors (NAWW), becomming a very popular all-Native, female veteran color guard at Native powwows and events. Regional chapters are currently forming to meet the high volume of demands for appearances, and other Native women's veterans color guards have formed such as the Sister Nation Color Guard (Schilling, 2013; 2014). Native women's organizations have long served as auxiliaries to men's veterans societies (Meadows, 1999; 2010); however, with the increasing number of Native women in military service, it seems likely that at some point Native women will begin to form their own veteran's organizations, functions, and rituals. As Native women in the US military increase their contributions merit greater documentation and recognition.

FUTURE TRENDS

Native Americans will continue to contribute to the level of diversity in the US Armed Forces; including individuals from a wide array of federally recognized (566) and nonrecognized tribal nations, more Native women entering military service, and the continuing importance, role, and social status of veterans and military service in Native cultures and communities. Past trends suggest that Natives will also likely continue to seek service in specialized combat units. Due to the continued cultural importance of veterans in contemporary Native American communities, extensive kinship networks, well-developed tribal traditions of honoring veterans, limited economic opportunities in many communities, and educational opportunities, military service continues to offer Native Americans a number of cultural and economic opportunities. A Minority Veterans report (NCVAS 2013) estimates that Native Americans will continue to represent over 1 percent of the US military until 2040. Native American participation in the US armed services is only limited by its relative small numbers with only 3.1 million people. As of 2014, American Indians and Alaskan Natives represented 18,139 of 1,326,237 or just over 1 percent of the total US Armed Forces (DOD-MCFP, 2014). As demonstrated in Table 5.1, in relation to their overall population, Native Americans continue to provide one of the highest rates of voluntary enlistment of any ethnic group in the US Armed Forces.

Native American groups have long emphasized the qualities of protecting one's people and homeland, strength, personal courage, integrity, honor, pride, physical and spiritual toughness, and wisdom in their warrior traditions. The focus on these qualities in the contemporary armed forces facilitated a syncretism of the two systems, whereby Native Americans have continued to provide military service while simultaneously using that service to maintain many of their own cultural traditions. Despite numerous injustices, broken treaties, enforced ward-ship, denial of US citizenship and voting rights, and varied forms of discrimination, Native Americans continue to demonstrate exemplary service in the US Armed Forces and efforts to maintain past treaty obligations.

Of all minority groups in the US Armed Forces, American-Indian veterans have long represented the highest percentage of their total population at almost 9 percent (8.8 percent), with over 150,000 Native American veterans from 566 tribes residing in the United States. Of Native Americans in uniform, 48 percent reported serving in combat, and 49 percent on active duty are between the ages of seventeen and twenty-four (Ahtone, 2014). Currently, honorably discharged Native Americans represent 0.6 of the total US Armed Forces. Despite high participation and combat levels, Natives remain the most underserved population of US veterans, in part due to the rural nature of many communities and great distance to Veteran Administration facilities. As of 2013 Native American-Alaskan Native veterans maintained the highest rate of poverty (15.8 percent), uninsured status (12.3 percent), and the lowest per-capita income ($25,990), lowest employment rate (43.7 percent),

Table 5.1 Native American Participation in United States Conflicts, 20th–21st Centuries

Conflict	Number served	Total native population
–	–	237,196 (1900)
–	–	265,683 (1910)
World War I	12,000	244,437 (1920)
–	–	332,397 (1930)
World War II	44,000	333,969 (1940)
Korea	10,000	343,410 (1950)
Vietnam	42,000	551,669 (1960)*
–	–	827,268 (1970)
–	–	1,420,400 (1980)
Desert Storm	–	1,959,234 (1990)
Iraq/Afghan	–	4,119,000 (2000)
		5,200,000 (2010)**

*Alaska Natives included since 1960 (Shoemaker 1999:4; Norris et al. 2012).
** 2.9 million Native American/Alaskan Native alone; 2.3 million descend from one or the other races.
Data from Shoemaker, N. (1999). American Indian population recovery in the Twentieth Century. University of New Mexico Press, Albuquerque and Norris, T., Vines, P.L. & Hoeffel, E.M. (2012). The American Indian and Alaska Native Population: 2010 Census Briefs. http://www.census.gov/prod/cen2010/briefs/c2010br=10.ppf. Accessed December 19, 2015.

and lowest labor force participation rate (48.3 percent) of all US veterans (NCVAS, 2015).

Examining military participation rates of whites, blacks, and Hispanics, across race-ethnicity, immigrant generation, and socioeconomic status, Lutz (2008) found that significant disparities exist only by socioeconomic status. Her research shows that the all-volunteer US Armed Forces continues to exhibit an overrepresentation by working and middle classes. Although Native Americans were not examined by Lutz and in most studies of minority veterans (Armour, 1996; Gimbel & Booth, 1996), their lower socioeconomic status is a likely factor in participation rates, albeit uniquely enhanced by the strong warrior tradition (ethnicity) in many Native American cultures. While numbers of officers are increasing, lower education rates and job skills of the working class and poor appear to channel many Natives to lower echelon military positions. Future research on Native placement in the armed forces, whether Natives are overrepresented in combat arms, the extent of postdischarge education and veteran preference in jobs, and whether recent enlistments are motivated by a means to achieve improved socioeconomic status through subsequent civilian occupations is needed.

In 2006, 1.6 percent of all active duty forces in the US military (Army, Navy, Marines, Air Force, Coast Guard) were American Indian or Native Alaskan, with the greatest number and proportion comprising almost 4 percent of the Navy (DEOMI, 2006, p. 2). As shown in Table 5.2, a recent survey (Lutz, 2008) of military service in 1980–1981, 1990, and 2000 shows a marked increase in Native participation during the First Gulf War (August 2, 1990 to February 28, 1991), followed by a slight decline by 2000, yet an overall increase over a twenty-year span.

The persistence of the Indian Scout Syndrome and disproportionately drawing some of the deadliest wartime tasks spans from World War I through at least Vietnam, and for many Indians became accepted as a normal consequence of American-Indian military service (Holm, 1996; Bennett & Holm, 2008). In 2011, the US military used the code name "Geronimo" for Osama Bin Laden during the raid that killed the al-Qaida leader, with the message "Geronimo EKIA" (enemy killed in action) relayed to the White House. Controversy erupted as many Natives respect Geronimo for fighting many battles and facing his enemy, while viewing Bin Laden as a murdering terrorist who hid from his enemy (2011b). This event and the continued use of lables such as "chief" for all Indians, and "Indian Country" for enemy held territory, indicate that non-Indians still have much to learn about their native comrades and cultures.

Although high rates of Native American military service continue for a variety of reasons, including financial benefits, this trend does not solely represent accommodation and assimilation to American culture. As

Table 5.2   Relative Participation of Native Americans in the US Armed Services

	1980–1981	*1990*	*2000*
% of Native Americans in the civilian population	0.7%	0.8%	0.8%
% of Native Americans in the military	0.7%	1.2%	1.0%

Data from Lutz, A. (2008). Who joins the military?: A look at race, class, and immigration status. *Journal of Political and Military Sociology* 36(2):167–188.

demonstrated in numerous cultural forms associated with military service, Natives have long used syncretism to preserve, continue, and indigenize modern military service with traditional culture values and practices. Religious ceremonies bless individuals prior to combat while reinforcing the knowledge that individuals are not alone in combat and are supported by those at home. Postwar rituals often serve to spiritually cleanse the individual by helping to cast off the horrors and pain of war, while reincorporating individuals back into their home communities with unconditional support, acceptance, and traditional forms of honoring. Many Native groups expect returning individuals to contribute to the community by assuming community and leadership roles. This process continues in numerous Native ceremonies and traditions (induction into veteran's societies, pow-wows, give-aways, naming ceremonies, art, flag, veteran's and memorial songs, etc.) directly based on aspects of military service in the US Armed Forces. The popular form of the revived Kiowa Gourd Dance has diffused to become a Pan-Indian form of honoring Native veterans (Meadows, 1999; 2010). Native veteran's songs with lyrics continue to be composed as recently as the Iraq and Afghanistan campaigns.

As members of federally recognized (treaty-based) tribes and US citizens, Native Americans continue to defend their remaining lands and peoples, and those of the larger United States. No other minority has this unique form of duel citizenship and military service in the United States. Military honor and patriotism are not only a cultural ethos in many native communities, but with the continuation of honoring outgoing and returning Native veterans through community celebrations and rituals, constitute cultural events throughout the year. Native peoples continue to analogize modern military service in the US Armed Forces with earlier warrior traditions. As Southern Cheyenne veteran Bill Cody Ayon (Clevenger, 2010), described:

> I was brought up and given language, customs, and songs that honor those who have given their service to America's military, to my tribe, and to all indigenous

people. It is with this background that I follow the military road—like my father, my uncles, and my ancestors before me. To serve my family, my tribe, and my country is the greatest honor of all. Tradition has mandated this for me—from the echoes of warriors from the Little Bighorn to Iwo Jima to the streets of Baghdad. I thank them for their sacrifice.

On December 2, 2011, The National Museum of the American Indian in Washington, D.C. sponsored *Our Warrior Spirit: Native Americans in the US Military*, an overview of American-Indian military service including several native veterans. The event was broadcast as a live webcast at www.american-indian.si.edu/ webcasts. The warrior concept or ethos has long existed in the US Armed Forces such as the well-known Marine Corps concept of *Espirit de Corps*. The pyramidal structure of the Marine Corps Battle Drill Guide System (USMC, 1988) contains a section labeled "Basic Warrior Training Packages." Book One of the manual is "Basic Warrior Training." Similarly the Army has used the concept of "warrior ethos" in its Field Manual 22–100 (Conner Jr., 1999, p. 46). However since the 1980s a considerable body of literature has appeared, much of it from combat arms officers and noncommissioned officers, addressing the decline of the warrior spirit or ethos and leadership in the US military with the shift to military operations on urban terrain (MOUT), an increased focus on technological advances and skills, an all-volunteer military, impacts of political correctness, and calling for the need to raise or revive the warrior spirit or ethos in military troops. Although some programs have been developed to do so, the issue remains (Baucom, 1985; Conner Jr., 1999; Loeb, 2003; Stroszzi-Heckler, 2007; Knight, 2014). While a full discussion of this subject is beyond the scope of this chapter, it is important to consider that Native American cultures with their qualitatively different martial ethos might provide a model to enhance such a reinvigoration of ethos in the modern military. With the continuation of a warrior ethos, the exemplary record of Native American military service should continue as a significant factor in both the US Armed Forces and individual Native cultures and communities.

NOTES

1. In Plains Indian Sign Language "Wolves" is the common sign for scouts, and relates to their frequent wearing of wolf hides for diguises and to the immitation of this animal in scouting. As members of many tribes began serving as scouts for the US Army following the Civil War, they became known as "Wolves for the Blue Coats" (Dunlay 1982; Viola, 2008; Meadows 2013, 2015).

2. Iron Hats is the name that many Native American groups used to refer to the Germans based on their unique type of pointed metal helmets known as pickelhaub.

3. Native American names were formed for many of the major countries involved in World War II. The name of Iron Hats continued for Germans. The Kiowa called the Japanese Jáfòlsyàndàu (Small Eye Opening People, lit. Small Insect Eyed People. In Kiowa the J represents a soft "t" sound, the f a soft "p" sound), while the Navajo Code Talkers used the name Beh-na-ali-tsoisi (Slant Eyed) for the Japanese. Having very narrow eyes, a Kiowa man named Sam Toppah had a personal name based on the same name root. Tribes widely referred to the Chinese as Braided Hair from their queue, the Australians as Rolled Hats. The Pawnee were widely known in many languages and in sign language as "Wolf People" from the practice of their scouts wearing wolf hides and imitating their behavior (USMC, 1945:2; Viola, 2008; Meadows, 2013, 2015).

4. The Koreans and Vietnamese were referred to in some Native American languages by the name Wolf People (Viola, 2008). The Pawnee were widely known in Plains Indian Sign Language and in many spoken languages by the name "Wolf People" in reference to their scouts wearing wolf hides as disguises (Meadows, 2013, 2015).

5. This a Native American name in reference to the scimitar and other curved swords common to many Middle Eastern cultures.

REFERENCES

Ahtone, T. (2014). The Native American veteran: *Finding my place here.* Downloaded from Aljazerra.com/2014/native-veterans/finding-my-place/. Accessed February 1, 2016.

Armour, D.J. (1996). Race and gender in the U.S. Military. *Armed Forces & Society 23*(1): 7–27.

Barsh, R.L. (1991). American Indians in the Great War. *Ethnohistory 38*: 76–303.

Baucom, D.R. (1985). The professional soldier and the warrior spirit. *Strategic Review 13*(4): 7–66.

Bellefaire, J. (2006). *Native American women veterans. Women in military service for America memorial foundation, inc.* The Women's Memorial Washington D.C. http://womensmemorial.org/Education/NAHM.html. Accessed February 11, 2016.

Bennett, P & Holm, T. (2008). Indians in the military. Pp. 10–18 in *Handbook of North American Indians*, Vol. 2. Garrick A. Bailey vol. ed. Washington, D.C.: Smithsonian Institution Press.

Bernstein, A.R. (1991). *Americans Indians and World War II: Toward a new era in Indian affairs.* Norman, OK: University of Oklahoma Press.

Britten, T. (1997). *American Indians in World War I: At war and at home.* Alburuerque, NM: University of New Mexico Press.

Chambers, J.W. (1987*). To raise an Army: The draft comes to modern America.* New York: The Free.

Clevenger, S. (2010). *America's first warriors: Native Americans and Iraq.* Santa Fe, NM: Museum of New Mexico Press.

Collier, J. (1942). The Indian in a wartime nation. *Annals of the American Academy of Political and Social Science 223*(September): 29–35.

Conner, W.M. (1999). Developing the warrior spirit in ranger training. *Infantry* (May-August): 45–47.

Crain, D.A. n.d. *Native Peoples at West Point: Past, Present, and Future.* West-Point.org.http://www.west-point.org/family/ai-grads/DebCrainArticle.html. Accessed June 21, 2016.

Densmore, F. (1934). The songs of Indian soldiers during the World War. *Musical Quarterly 20*:419–425.

DEOMI (Defense Equal Opportunity Management Institute). (2006). Annual demographic profile of the Department of Defense and US Coast Guard FY 2006. *Defense Equal Opportunity Management Institute.* Patrick Air Force Base, Florida.

DOD-MCFP (Department of Defense, Military Community and Family Policy). (2014). *2014 Demographics: Profile of the military community.* Office of the Deputy Assistant Seretary of Defense. Washington, D.C.

Dollarhide, M. (2002). Native American women vets seek recognition. *Women's eNews.* Women's eNews. http://womensnews.org/2002/05/native-american-women-vets-seek-recognition.html. Accessed February 11, 2016.

Dunlay, T.W. (1982*). Wolves for the blue soldiers: Indian scouts and auxiliaries with the United States Army, 1860–90.* Lincoln, NE: University of Nebraska Press.

Gimbel, C. & Booth, A. (1996). Who fought in Vietnam. *Social Forces 74*(4): 1137–1157.

Hauptman, L.M. (1995). *Between two fires: American Indians in the Civil War.* New York: Free Press.

Holm, T. (1984). Stereotypes, state elites, and the military use of American Indian troops. *Plural Societies 15*: 265–282.

Holm, T. (1986). Culture, ceremonialism, and stress: American Indian veterans and the Vietnam War. *Armed Forces & Society 12*(2): 237–251.

Holm, T. (1996). *Strong hearts, wounded souls; Native American veterans of the Vietnam War.* Austin, TX: University of Texas Press.

Indian Country Today. (2011a). Remembering Lori Ann Piestewa: Hopi woman warrior. Story by Patty Jo King. April 13. http://indiancountrytodaymedianetwork. com/2011/04/13/remembering-lori-ann-piestewa-hopi-woman-warrior-27896. Accessed June 24, 2016.

Indian Country Today. (2011b). Indian country responds to Geronimo, bin Laden connection. May 4. http:// indiancountrytodaymedianetwork.com/2011/05/04/ indian-country-responds-geronimo-bin-laden-connection-32251. Accessed April 4, 2016.

Indian Country Today. (2011c). Remembering the Alamo scouts: Many Native Americans fought in World War II. May 27. Story by Michelle Tirado. http://indi-ancountrytodaymedianetwork.com/2011/05/27/remembering-alamo-scouts-many-american-indians-fought-world-war-ii-35011. Accessed September 9, 2016.

Knight, A.J. (2014). Retaining the warrior spirit. *Military Review.* September-October: 88–100.

Krouse, S.A. (2007). *North American Indians in the Great War.* University of Nebraska Press, Lincoln.

Loeb, V. (2003). Army plans steps to heighten 'warrior ethos; Leaders view many soldiers as too specialized. *Washington Post.* September 8.

Lutz, A. (2008). Who joins the military?: A look at race, class, and immigration status. *Journal of Political and Military Sociology 36*(2):167–188.

Marston, M. (1969). *Men of the tundra: Alaska Eskimos at war.* New York: October House.

Meadows, W.C. (1999). *Kiowa, Apache, and Comanche military societies.* Austin, TX: University of Texas Press.

Meadows, W.C. (2002). *The Comanche Code Talkers of World War II.* Austin, TX: University of Texas Press.

Meadows, W.C. (2007). North American Indian code talkers: Current events and research. In P.W. Lackenbauer, C. Mantle, & R. S. Sheffield (Ed.s), *Aboriginal peoples and military participation: Canadian and international perspectives* (pp. 161–214). Kingston, ON: Canadian Defense Academy Press.

Meadows, W.C. (2009). They had a chance to talk to one another: The role of incidence in Native American code talking. *Ethnohistory 56*(2): 269–284.

Meadows, W.C. (2010). *Kiowa military societies: Ethnohistory and ritual.* Norman, OK: University of Oklahoma Press.

Meadows, W.C. (2011). Honoring Native American code talkers: The road to the Code Talkers Recognition Act of 2008. *American Indian culture and research journal 35*(3):3–36.

Meadows, W.C. (2013). Kiowa Ethnonymy of Other Populations. *Plains Anthropologist 58*(226):5–30.

Meadows, W.C. (2015). Through *Indian* sign language: The Fort Sill Ledgers of Hugh L. Scott and Iseeo, 1889–1897. Norman, OK: University of Oklahoma Press.

Meadows, W.C. (2016). An honor long overdue: The 2013 Congressional Gold and Silver Medal ceremonies in honor of Native American Code Talkers. *American Indian Culture and Research Journal 40*(2):91–121.

NARA. (National Archives Records Administration). (1918). The Indian's war activities. 22 pp. December 1. Records of the Bureau of Indian Affairs, Division of Information. Records Relating to Indians in World War I and World War II. RG-75, Box I, World War I Folder. Washington, D.C.

NCVAS. (2013). Minority veterans: 2011. United States Department of Veterans Affairs. August. http://www.va.gov/vetdata/docs/specialreports/minority_veterans_2015.pdf. Accessed February 15, 2016.

NCVAS. (2015). 2013 Minority veterans report. United States Department of Veterans Affairs. August. http://www.va.gov/vetdata/docs/specialreports/minority_veterans_2015.pdf. Accessed February 15, 2016.

NEH. (National Endowment for the Humanities). (2014). *Healing the warrior's heart.* Taki Telondis, Director. 60 minutes. Washington, D.C.

Neuberger, R.L. (1942a). On the warpath. *Saturday Evening Post 215* (October 24):79.

Neuberger, R.L. (1942b). The American Indian enlists. *Asia and the Americas 42* (November):628–630.

Norris, T., Vines, P.L. & Hoeffel, E.M. (2012). *The American Indian and Alaska Native Population: 2010* Census Briefs. http://www.census.gov/prod/cen2010/briefs/c2010br=10.ppf. Accessed December 19, 2015.

Rolling Stone. (2004). A wrong turn in the desert. Story by Osha Gray Davidson. May 27. http://www.oshadavidson.com/Piestewa.htm. Accessed June 24, 2016.

Roosevelt, T. (1899). *The Rough Riders.* Charles Scribner's Sons, New York.

Schilling, V. (2013). Native American women warriors celebrate inauguration while raising awareness for native female veterans. *Indian Country Today.* January 21.

Schilling, V. (2014). Warriors at heart: Some of the native women who served in the military. *Indian Country Today.* April 3.

Scott, H.L. (1928). *Some memories of a soldier.* New York: Century Company.

Shoemaker, N. (1999). *American Indian population recovery in the Twentieth Century.* University of New Mexico Press, Albuquerque.

Strozzi-Heckler, R. (2007). *In search of the warrior spirit: Teaching awareness disciplines to the Green Berets.* Fourth Edition. Blue Snake Books. Berekely, CA.

Sutton, R. & Latschar. J.A. (Eds). (2013). *American Indians and the Civil War.* National Park Service, U.S. Department of the Interior. Eastern National Publishers. Fort Washington, Pennsylvania.

Tate, M. (1986). From scout to Doughboy: The national debate over integrating American Indians into the military, 1891–1918. *Western Historical Quarterly* 17:417–437.

Townsend, KW. (2000). World War II and the American Indian. Albuquerque, NM: University of New Mexico Press.

U.S. Congress. (1920). *Army reorganization: Hearings before the committee on military affairs, House of Representatives.* Sixty-sixth Congress, First and Second Sessions on H.R. 8287, H.R. 8068, H.R. 7925, H.R. 9970. September 29, 1919 to February 5, 1920. Vol. II. Government Printing House. Washington, D.C.

USMC. (United States Marine Corps). (1945). *Navajo Code Talker dictionary.* Revised June 15. Declassified DOD DIR 5200.9 Marine Corps Historical Division, Historical Reference Branch. Quantico, Va.

USMC. (United States Marine Corps). (1988). Battle drill guide. Individual training standards (ITS) system cccupational Field 03, Infantry. Marine Corps Institute. Marine Barracks. Washington, D.C.

Van de Logt, M. (2010). *War party in blue: Pawnee scouts in the U.S. Army.* Norman, OK: University of Oklahoma Press.

Viola, H.J. (2008). *Warriors in uniform: The legacy of American Indian heroism.* Washington, D.C.: National Geographic.

White, W.B. (1968). *The military and the melting pot: The American Army and military groups, 1865–1894.* Ph.D. dissertation. University of Wisconsin.

Winegard, T.G. (2012). *For king and kanata: Canadian Indians and the First World War.* Winnipeg: University of Manitoba Press.

Part II

SEXUALITY, GENDER, AND RELIGIOUS MINORITIES IN THE MILITARY

Chapter 6

Women and the US Military

Progress and Challenges

Janice H. Laurence

Though the military remains a primarily masculine domain, in the almost 250 years of US history, women have increased their participation in the profession of arms as well as in the overall workforce and American society. In fact, as of 2016, women are no longer barred from combat roles in the US military. Yet, the debate regarding women's access to the military continues (National Center for Veterans Analysis and Statistics, 2011). Personnel policy still struggles with the representation, roles, and acceptance of women in the US military.

HISTORICAL HIGHLIGHTS

In the United States, women have fought and died in every war since the American Revolution (Segal, 1989). Early on, women were on the battlefield either in sanctioned support roles (e.g., water bearers, cooks, or laundresses) or as fighters by masquerading as men. Women were called upon to serve primarily as nurses when needed and then sent home at the end of hostilities. Women were not only demobilized but they served in auxiliary status—with no rank, no benefits, and lower pay than "real," male soldiers. It was not until 1943, during World War II that women were given full (yet still unequal) military status (Segal, 1989). Women served as nurses and in other support roles until the end of the war, when again most were sent home (National Center for Veterans Analysis and Statistics, 2011). It was not until 1948 with the passage of the Armed Services Integration Act that women were made a permanent part of the military, albeit in limited numbers (2 percent of enlisted members and 10 percent of officers) and ranks until 1967 (Kamarck, 2015). The success of the all-volunteer force (AVF), beginning in 1973, is credited in large part to the increase of women in the military. Without a draft to press men into service, women have been gaining ground. Despite numerical progress, complete integration remains a challenge. Rules and policies regarding women have evolved over the decades of the AVF. Although restricted from ground combat, women gained access to combat aircraft and vessels in 1990s. (Submarines remained off limits to women until 2010.) But, the so-called "risk rule" adopted in 1988 prevented them from being collocated with non-combat units or missions if the risks of exposure to direct combat, hostile fire, or capture were equal to or greater than the risks in the combat units they supported (Kamarck, 2015). The risk rule was replaced with the Direct Ground Combat and Assignment Rule in 1994, which excluded women from direct ground combat units below brigade level.

Formal sidelining of women from direct ground combat did not prevent casualties among US military women. As of October 2015, 161 women have died and over 1,000 have been wounded in action while serving in Iraq and Afghanistan. Women have also been held as POWs and have received commendations for engaging the enemy. Given the nature of today's warfare and because women are needed and are contributing mightily to our national defense, the Direct Combat Exclusion Rule was rescinded in 2013 with a January 1, 2016 implementation deadline following a review of occupational standards and assignment policies.

REPRESENTATION AND ROLES

Increasingly, women are serving the United States as soldiers, sailors, marines, and airmen. Women comprise 15 percent of enlisted members and officers on active duty (Department of Defense [DoD], 2016). Their contributions are no longer restricted to nursing and administration but extend to supply, mechanics, electronics, and intelligence. In addition to their overall level of representation, women have gained solid ground in all fields except infantry, armor, artillery, and submarines. Although ground combat and other restrictions have been lifted, a lengthy implementation process is expected (DoD, 2015). But even before combat jobs were officially opened, women have been in the fight. They serve as pilots or aircrew on combat aircraft—fighter jets and attack helicopters—they patrol streets as MPs with standard issue rifles and command units. Even those who serve in maintenance companies or as medics are in the midst of a war zone. The asymmetric or nonlinear battlefield is everywhere—boundaries are blurred; the front line disappeared and now so has the distinct battlefield. There are no more fair fights. And in this setting, human resources—people and their skills are vital. Women in uniform are still rare relative to their population proportions, but compared to

Table 6.1.   Representation by Sex within the Active Duty Military (Fiscal Year 2014)

Service by sex	Enlisted		Officer Corps	
	Accessions*	Active duty	Accessions*	Active duty
Army				
Male	83.8	86.8	78.7	82.1
Female	16.2	13.2	21.3	15.8
Navy				
Male	76.9	82.0	77.7	84.8
Female	23.1	18.0	22.3	17.9
Marine Corps				
Male	89.3	92.3	88.7	82.7
Female	10.7	7.7	11.3	17.3
Air Force				
Male	80.2	81.3	72.7	80.1
Female	19.8	18.7	27.3	19.9
Total DoD				
Male	82.5	85.2	77.7	82.6
Female	17.5	14.8	22.3	17.4
Civilian Workforce**				
Male	50.1	53.5	44.2	48.4
Female	49.9	46.5	55.8	51.6

*Entering recruits are referred to as "accessions."
**Civilian comparison groups are defined as follows: Enlisted (Accessions = 18–23-year-olds; Active Force = 18–44-year-old workforce) Officers (Accessions = 21–35-year-old college graduates; active component = 21–49-year-old college graduates in the civilian workforce).
Data from DoD. (2016). Population Representation in the Military Services: Fiscal Year 2014 Summary Report. Washington, DC: Office of the Under Secretary of Defense, Personnel and Readiness. Published in 2016. Accessed May 18, 2016. http://www.cna.org/research/pop-rep.

the 2 percent cap imposed under the draft era, they represent significant *manpower*. Personnel readiness, both in terms of quantity and quality, depends upon men *and* women.

In Fiscal Year (FY) 2014, the US military services enlisted 138,902 new recruits and commissioned 15,094 second lieutenants (or ensigns in the Navy) to refresh active duty strength figures at 1,090,939 enlisted members and 216,084 officers, respectively (DoD, 2016). The representation levels of women among the service newcomers and total active duty force are shown in Table 6.1.

Among enlisted accessions (as entering recruits are called) women had the lowest representation level, 11 percent, in the Marine Corps and the highest level, 23 percent, in the Navy. At just under 8 percent, the Marine Corps again had the smallest percentage of women among active duty enlisted members. The Air Force had the highest percentage of women at almost 19 percent. For the officer corps, the Marine Corps continued the distinction of having the lowest female representation level, 11 percent, among newly

Table 6.2. Representation by Sex within the Active Duty Military by Occupational Area (Fiscal Year 2014)

	Enlisted Force					
	Army			*DoD*		
Occupational area	*Male*	*Female*	*Total*	*Male*	*Female*	*Total*
Infantry, gun crews & seamanship	22.7	1.5	18.5	14.6	3.5	12.4
Electronic equipment repair	6.0	4.4	5.7	9.7	6.7	9.1
Communications & intelligence	10.3	5.9	9.5	8.8	7.8	8.6
Medical & dental	8.1	14.7	9.4	7.9	14.0	9.1
Other allied specialties	3.2	4.2	3.4	2.3	2.2	2.3
Functional support & administration	17.9	42.3	22.6	15.5	32.3	18.9
Electronic/ mechanical Equipment repair	14.2	6.9	12.8	21.0	13.2	19.4
Craftsmen	3.0	2.2	2.9	3.7	2.6	3.5
Service & supply	14.2	17.9	14.9	12.5	13.8	12.8
Nonoccupational*	.4	.1	.3	4.0	3.9	4.0
	Officer Corps					
	Army			*DoD*		
Occupational Area	*Male*	*Female*	*Total*	*Male*	*Female*	*Total*
General officers & executives	0.4	0.1	0.4	0.5	0.2	0.4
Tactical operations	36.3	5.2	30.7	41.2	12.6	36.2
Intelligence	6.7	7.3	6.8	6.1	7.1	6.3
Engineering & maintenance	14.8	12.5	14.4	12.7	8.7	12.0
Scientists & professionals	8.4	5.9	8.0	6.5	6.1	6.5
Health care	15.5	42.9	20.4	13.0	41.2	18.0
Administration	6.7	13.4	7.9	5.1	9.9	6.0
Supply, procurement, & allied	9.9	11.9	10.3	8.2	9.0	8.4
Nonoccupational*	1.3	.8	1.2	6.7	5.2	6.4

*Includes patients, students, those with unassigned duties, and unknowns
Data from DoD. (2016). Population Representation in the Military Services: Fiscal Year 2014 Summary Report. Washington, DC: Office of the Under Secretary of Defense, Personnel and Readiness. Published in 2016. Accessed May 18, 2016. http://www.cna.org/research/pop-rep.

commissioned officers. At 27 percent, the Air Force had the highest percentage of women among officer accessions. The Air Force also had the highest
percentage of women among all officers on active duty (20 percent), whereas
the Army had the lowest percentage of women at just under 16 percent. Compared to appropriate civilian benchmarks, women are underrepresented in the
enlisted and officer ranks.

In addition to one's status as an officer or enlisted member, job or career
field assignment is an important consideration. Table 6.2 shows the occupational group distributions of enlistees and officers by sex. Whereas men serve
in military jobs characterized as combat (e.g., infantry, tactical operations,
and equipment repair), women serve in service and support roles (e.g., administrative and health care jobs). Among enlisted men in the Army, 23 percent
were in the infantry, while the corresponding percentage for women was less
than 2 percent. Functional support and administration jobs had the highest
percentage of Army women at 42 percent, whereas only 18 percent of Army
men were in such jobs. In the officer corps, 36 percent of Army men were in
tactical operations in contrast to only 5 percent of women. The reverse unbal-
ance occurs in health care, where 43 percent of female Army officers but only
15 percent of male Army officers were assigned.

Assignment differences are more than an interesting tidbit of military
trivia—they are an important factor for career progression! Men in tactical

**Table 6.3   Percentage Distribution of Male Enlisted Military Personnel by Occupational
Category Over Time**

PRIVATE Occupational category	Civil War	World War II	1992	2014
White collar	0.9	25.2	43.9	42.5
Technical[a]	0.2	11.6	29.7	30.9
Clerical	0.7	13.6	14.2	11.6
Blue collar	99.1	74.7	56.1	57.5
Craftsmen[b]	0.6	25.9	27.8	26.4
Service & supply	5.3	14.8	9.0	11.6
General military	93.2	34.0	19.3	19.5

[a]Includes electronic equipment repairers, communications and intelligence specialists, medical and dental
  specialists, and other technical and allied specialists.
[b]Includes electrical and mechanical equipment repairers and craftsmen.
Source for Civil War and WWII: Eitelberg, M.J. (1988, April). Manpower for military occupations.
  Washington, DC: Office of the Assistant Secretary of Defense (Force Management and Personnel).
Source for 1992: DoD. (1993). Population Representation in the Military Services, Fiscal Year 1992.
  Washington, DC: Office of the Assistant Secretary of Defense (Force Management and Personnel).
Source for 2014: DoD. (2016). Population Representation in the Military Services: Fiscal Year 2014
  Summary Report. Washington, DC: Office of the Under Secretary of Defense, Personnel and Readiness.
  Published in 2016. Accessed May 18, 2016. http://www.cna.org/research/pop-rep.

operations are promoted faster and farther than women, who historically have been excluded from tactical operations (DoD, 2015; Harrell & Miller, 1997; Hosek et al., 2001). About one in six enlisted members could be classified as purely combat job incumbents or in general military skills whereas one in four served in high-tech jobs in electronic equipment repair, communications and intelligence, or as other allied specialists. Even combat jobs have become more technologically complex and relatively less labor intensive over the years—and more manpower has been added behind the combat scenes.

Although most US military jobs are in the blue-collar category (infantry, gun crews, and seamanship; electrical and mechanical equipment repairers; and craftsmen), white-collar positions (electronic equipment repairers; communications and intelligence specialists; medical and dental specialists; other technical and allied specialists; and administration) are almost as plentiful. Table 6.3 presents snapshots of the occupational distribution of male enlisted personnel over the years. Clearly, the military employs proportionately fewer of its workers in general military skills today compared to the Civil War or even the World War II era. Although most enlisted military jobs continue to be in the blue-collar category, white-collar technical jobs have swelled.

In addition to the traditional combat and seamanship roles, the military enlisted workforce comprises technicians, clerks, administrative associates, mechanics, computer specialists, high-tech equipment operators and repairers, health care specialists, and a host of other "blue collar" employees. The most populous jobs in the military are those in electrical equipment repair, with about one in five of the service workers engaged in such occupational pursuits as aircraft, automobile, and engine mechanics, ordnance mechanics, line installers or fixing radio, radar, and sonar equipment. Around one out of six military workers are employed in administration as stock and inventory clerks, shipping and receiving clerks, dispatchers, and the like.

Counterinsurgency and stability operations in Iraq and Afghanistan over the past decade led to new roles for military women. The Lioness program counted on female soldiers and Marines to search local women at control points in Iraq. Subsequently, Female Engagement Teams (FETs) provided for more persistent engagement with Afghan women. FETs were expanded into Cultural Support Teams (CSTs) in 2011 and proved vital to understanding the local culture and especially for interacting with women in the villages where Special Operations Forces were deployed. Women in such positions are pulled from their regular jobs to visit and search local population women; to distribute humanitarian supplies; and to provide a culturally sensitive yet persistent presence with this important segment of the local population. Like other women in combat support roles (e.g., drivers, interpreters, military police), these women serve in volatile combat environments yet receive little ground combat training (Katt, 2014; Nicolas, 2015). It is notable that while

CSTs were attached to Special Operations Forces in support roles, three women, all US Military Academy (USMA) graduates, completed Ranger school in 2015 (Tan, 2015).

JOB PERFORMANCE AND BARRIERS

Representation is important but it is a deficient indicator of progress. Although there is agreement that women are vital to sustaining force levels and maintaining readiness, resistance to women's full participation in US national defense remains. Critics of military women and their expanding roles claim that there has been an erosion of military culture. Their arguments are couched in inflammatory rhetoric. Aside from questioning their physical and emotional fitness, women are feared to undercut cohesion and commitment and compromise good order and discipline. In other words, women are weaker than men in terms of upper body strength. What-is-more, it is argued that the presence of women disrupts male bonding and women distract men with their sexual wiles (French, 2015). It is also argued that pregnancy detracts from readiness and the ability to quickly deploy (Harrell & Miller, 1997). However, although pregnancy renders one nondeployable, so too do other gender-neutral factors, such as physical injuries (Congressional Commission, 1999). Furthermore, pregnancy is not rampant or common. Instead of focusing energy on decrying women for their contributions to the facts of life, why not come up with practical policies to deal with this temporary condition? All too often, female patriots have suffered the indignity of having their competency for and commitment to the profession of arms unfairly questioned. Equal opportunity and fairness for women is also important to the health and vitality of the military organization.

Physical Standards Controversy

Are there bona fide occupational qualifications that override gender inequities? This line of inquiry has escaped honest inquiry. Brains and brawn still have face validity, but surely with an environment as complex as the military, a full spectrum of expertise is required. Performance in any setting, and perhaps especially in the military, has many elements. These elements can be organized into the following categories: (a) knowledge, (b) skills, and (c) motivation (Campbell, McCloy, Oppler, & Sager, 1993). All too often, one performance component—physical strength—is singled out and discussed as if it were the only determinant. Admittedly, the average man has greater upper body strength than the average woman. However, upper body strength is not the only physical facet let alone the only skill that determines performance—physical or otherwise. Different absolute measures (e.g., running speed and distance) applied to men and women may equate to equal fitness levels.

One of the conditions for opening combat to women is the validation and implementation of gender-neutral occupational or performance outcome standards. Controversy swirls around such occupational standards with some claiming they are artificially high while others warn that any change could impact military readiness (Eden, 2015; Kamarck, 2015). Occupational standards should be "job related (based on the actual, regular, and recurring duties) . . . and measure individual, not average, performance" (DoD, 2015, p. iii). Furthermore, in addition to proper occupational standards, leadership must establish a supportive climate (Cone, 2016).

People who argue against women in the infantry point to the need for upper body strength, speed, stamina, and agility in the trenches. After all, those in the infantry under conventional land combat rather than counterinsurgency operations have dealt with heavy equipment, marches under load, and transporting of casualties (Rice, 2015). One important counter to the detrimental effects of the physical disparity between men and women is that occupations are designed around men. If the military was designed around women, men would encounter problems upon integration (Friedl, 2016). Proper fitting gear along with modernized equipment, tactics, techniques, and procedures would better utilize the strengths and contributions of men *and* women (DoD, 2015; Friedl, 2016; Salhani, 2015). Further leveraging technology (including "human factors" designs for women) should also be considered in the performance equation. An Air Force legend is that women were seen as unfit as Air Force mechanics because they were not able to haul a tool chest until a woman solved this problem by putting the tool chest on wheels!

It is important to recognize that there are performance challenges and advantages for both men and women. There is more to performance than absolute strength. And even strength can be improved through proper conditioning and training. From a series of in-depth interviews with military officers, Cohn (2000) argues that outcries over physical training (PT) standards differences by gender mask underlying anger and hostility toward women. Complaints about gender-normed PT standards are an institutionally acceptable way of claiming that women are inferior and do not belong in "his" organization. Adapting standards, policies, and equipment are seen as preferential treatment of women. There is anger and a resistance to changing the male organization (Cohn, 2000; Eichler, 2014). Negative reactions to the encroachment of women are not new but echo the findings of gender (not sexual) harassment detailed by Miller (1997). Although men are dominant and more powerful, they act as the oppressed group, blaming their limited opportunities on women. Rather than directly protesting, military men, and especially white officers, disparage women through gossip, rumors, indirect threats, constant scrutiny, and sabotage. Men resist women's authority and suggest that their power is illegitimately obtained (Miller, 1997).

Retention

Women are less likely to reach higher ranks and retention of women is lower than the rates for men (DoD, 2016; Hosek et al., 2001). Instead of responding to this fact with corrective action (as would accompany a similar retention downward spiral among men), women are marginalized further and the vicious cycle in retention patterns continues (Segal, Lane, & Fisher, 2015). It is time to attend to the underlying issues such as quality of life, family exigencies, training, assignment, mentoring, organizational climate, fair treatment, attitudes, expectations, and career progression. The US military must assimilate and accommodate the growing and vital diversity among its members, rather than yearning for the days when single young men were conscripted for a two-year term. Increasing gender diversity and capitalizing on women's leadership skills could well increase retention and enhance performance. In addition to competing family obligations and limited career progression, sexual aggression and an overall toxic social environment (Dichter & True, 2015; Hosek et al., 2001; Miner-Rubino, Settles, & Stewart, 2009; Segal, Smith, Segal, & Canuso, 2016) discourage women and so they leave service earlier than planned. Productivity tends to be higher when people enjoy their work and if they feel valued and competent (DiSilverio, 2003).

Marginality

Although trends in occupational distributions by subgroup are often noted (along with some progress toward better balance), potential differences in task assignment even within the same job or occupational specialty have not been systematically explored. One question of great import is: do men and women in the same job—actually do the same job? Formal focus group discussions with officers and enlisted personnel suggest that women and minorities are often moved into peripheral or collateral duties and activities. Women and minority officers are often placed in recruiting, Reserve Officer Training Corp (ROTC), and equal opportunity billets that tend not to be career enhancing to say the least (see Hosek et al., 2001). Enlisted women are often asked to do paperwork even when formal job titles are in technical fields such as electronics (Laurence, Wright, Keys, & Giambo, 1999). It requires no stretch of the imagination to posit that such task differences affect ratings of performance in the formally designated job. Without the opportunity to practice job skills, they may atrophy, thus impeding proficiency in a relative or absolute sense.

Family Stress

The odds are also against women in the military because they have a greater family role. One hint that the military places greater stress on women is in terms of family pattern differences between the genders. Given that for women, family life is often incompatible with military service obligations, men in the US military are more likely to be married then women. Whereas 54 percent of enlisted men are married, only 44 percent of women are married. The corresponding percentages for active duty officers are 72 percent and 53 percent, respectively. Most of the married women in the military are married to military men (DoD, 2016).

Cohesion

What about cohesion? After all, organizational effectiveness depends on more than task performance. Morale is important and can be affected—in a positive or negative manner—by change. The integration of women is one such "change" that can affect cohesion. Research has demonstrated that women's performance and attitudes are enhanced in integrated training settings (Mottern, Foster, Brady, & Marshall-Mies, 1997). Men's performance is not adversely affected by the presence of women in units. Furthermore, research shows that good leadership mitigates negative morale reactions by men to the coassignment of women (Harrell & Miller, 1997). Gender integration facilitates teamwork and cohesion, and reduces isolation and marginalization (Army Research Institute, 1977; Harrell & Miller, 1997). Data suggest that not only the equal opportunity climate but also overall organizational effectiveness are more favorable in units with higher levels of gender integration (Dansby, Laurence, & Wetzel, 1999). Opening more units to women in the mid-1990s had negligible effects on readiness, cohesion, and morale (DoD, 2015; Harrell, Beckett, Chien, & Sollinger, 2002).

Some critics claim that rather than praising and emulating the behavior of leaders who foster positive and cohesive gender interactions, leaders have given in to political correctness and the feminist agenda (Segal et al., 2016). It is bad for morale to follow this rhetoric because it leads to lower retention and less readiness (Hosek et al., 2001).

Women have valuable skills including interpersonal skills and management abilities that add to the medley of performance. For example, studies have found that leadership styles typical of women (i.e., interactive and transformational) are more suited for coalitions and cross-cultural competencies. Among business, industry, and police executives, for instance, women have been shown to outperform men on leadership traits (DiSilverio, 2003). Note that women's style tends to be participatory not indecisive. Such a relational style of leadership would facilitate cohesion and effectiveness of teams—which is certainly conducive to leading the new generation of soldiers (Ender et al., 2014).

The Defense Advisory Committee on Women in the Services (DACOWITS) reports that women in the military have the desire and ability to serve in combat. They love their jobs and the military lifestyle and appreciate the benefits. Yet, they feel stifled with regard to career advancement and perceive a lack of support from leadership and the overall climate (DoD, 2015). A review of DACOWITS site visit reports from 1995, 1997, and 2001 revealed that career constraints, marginalization, isolation, inattention to medical and child care needs can be expected to exact a psychological toll on performance and commitment. What-is-more, such military women report a bombardment of microaggressions that would certainly be expected to have a negative effect on retention. Quality of service—meaningful work and career satisfaction—outweighed pecuniary considerations (Laurence & Estrada, 2003). Most recent DACOWITS findings echo previous observations (DoD, 2015).

THE MILITARY CULTURE: FROM ISOLATION TO SEXUAL AGGRESSION

Sexual aggression has been shown to be a continuing problem that plagues the full participation of women in the US military (Cheney, Booth, & Turner, 2015). A hypermasculine military culture not only perpetuates sexual harassment and assault but also socially isolates those who report such crimes (Abrahms, 2016; DoD, 2015). Sexual aggression includes harassment and assault. Insufficient or deficient responses to such aggression represent a form of institutional betrayal, violating the trust within this "total institution, one in which the institution takes on a larger role in people's lives than other work environments" (Smith & Freyd, 2014). Many aspects of the military institution and its values and traditions are venerable. However, the hypermasculine culture and heretofore exclusionary policies underlie harassment and assault (Bagilhole, 2014: Dunivan, 1994; Sorcher, 2013). Senior leaders are key to changing the sexist tone and eliminating military sexual aggression (DoD, 2015; Tepe, Yarnell, Nindl, van Arsdale, & Deuster, 2016).

Sex-based discrimination and hostility are not unique to the military. "When women enter occupations that were previously seen as the preserve of men, they encounter hostility, both overt and covert opposition, and resistance to their success" (Bagilhole, 2014, p. 403). Sexual harassment and assault are more prevalent when the sex ratio is unequal and there are large power differentials (Bagilhole, 2014; Burke, 2014). Male-dominated organizational culture and leadership are inextricably linked to the prevalence of sexual aggression within an organization (Benschop & Van Den Brink, 2014;

Fielden & Hunt, 2014). Even short of sexual aggression, women are often excluded and marginalized in traditionally male domains. Their leadership is questioned and women who challenge gender stereotypes are seen as odd and are penalized if they excel in masculine domains (Bagilhole, 2014; Burke, 2014). Women have difficulty getting challenging assignments, yet they are likely to get risky assignments in an attempt to set them up for failure (Eagly, Gartzia, & Carli, 2014). As in the military, ill-fitting clothes and safety gear are not uncommon in such settings as construction and firefighting (Burke, 2014). Women experience "boundary heightening," an exaggeration of gender differences between men and token women. Men tend to be threatened by competent women and resent the intrusion of women and the blurred boundaries between masculine and feminine identities (Bagilhole, 2014; Eichler, 2014). The marginalization and devaluation of women takes its toll in terms of decreased job satisfaction, immense psychological distress, and high turnover (Bagilhole, 2014).

THE NEED FOR WOMEN IN THE MILITARY WORKFORCE

"Manning" the US military is no easy task especially at a time when the military continues to be engaged in a long war on terrorism. Despite the numerous benefits and opportunities to be derived from military service, given that military personnel are trained to actively engage in or support a dangerous enterprise and must sacrifice their personal freedom and a stable home life, this is not an overly popular career calling. In fact, approximately 85 percent of the prime recruiting market (eighteen- to twenty-four-year-olds) has a negative propensity toward a military career. In addition to low interest, approximately 58 percent of youth would not meet physical/medical, moral character, or dependent screens (DMR, 2001; DoD, 2015). With recruiting difficulties on the horizon (DoD, 2016), not only must the military actively recruit women but also they must counter the fact that women's propensity to join the military substantially lags their male counterparts. Opening all positions to women, targeting them for recruitment, increasing their representation, and improving career advancement opportunities will strengthen the military (DoD, 2015).

Though combat restrictions have been lifted and three women have completed Ranger training, we must wrestle further with the place of women in the military. To do this requires the transformation of military personnel policy and practice. Through systematic study of job demands (e.g., the relative contributions of cognitive skills, psychomotor skills, self-management skills, and interpersonal skills, as well as physical strength) optimal assessment and team assignments can be achieved. Organizational (and leader) development efforts could work to remove constraints on performance and enhance cohesion, commitment, and effectiveness. USMA and other service academies as well as ROTC are key leader development programs that continue to confront sexist attitudes. Results from USMA's biannual attitude survey of college undergraduates on a variety of social and military issues suggest that existing gender attitudes and social conservativism hinder the full integration of women. Students from military schools, especially the service academies, are less likely than civilian students to approve of women serving in diverse military jobs, especially those involving combat or command positions (Laurence, Milavec, Rohall, Ender, & Matthews, 2016; Matthews, Ender, Laurence, & Rohall, 2009). Intervening early for developing leaders is necessary.

Flexible yet practical personnel policies that deal with institutional and individual exigencies should be devised. Potential solutions to the military—family conflict, such as home basing, active to reserve movement, and sabbaticals, must be devised and can be done without sacrificing breadth or depth of experience (DiSilverio, 2003). To ensure public trust in the US military it must be diverse. And with women accounting for more of the participating public, gender diversity is vital. With the burgeoning international and homeland security needs, the military cannot afford to turn away or waste the talents of any segment of its citizenry—least of all the half of the recruitment pool that are women. Women will make up a larger portion of the available talent in the upcoming decade. It is time to find out why they separate at higher rates and then do something about the phenomenon.

It's time to stop lamenting the fact that the troops are no longer just single men marching off to war and begrudging the social compact and a family friendly climate. Leaders would better promote readiness by attending to human resource issues and thus fostering the volunteer spirit, pride in service, and the perception of military service as a noble profession for men *and* women. All warriors, regardless of gender, must be properly equipped, trained, and prepared for the mission. A zero tolerance for sexual harassment and assault is critical (DoD, 2015). "Changing institutional attitudes is hard. Changing institutional culture is even harder" (DiSilverio, 2003, p. 59).

Women are present and accounted for in the military, but full-integration has not yet been realized. We must strive to fully develop, employ, and deploy our nation's human resources. It is time to move ahead and more fully accept women in service. Military commitments have expanded over the years with fewer people in uniform to fulfill those commitments. Further, recruiting and retention problems make it difficult to fill even the smaller ranks. Certainly, the increased presence of women increases the complexity of personnel management or, at least, alters the organizational environment. There is a need for cultural shift regardless of the number and roles of women in uniform. Such change should not be lamented. The problem is not with women. They are worthy and willing to take up arms and fight for duty, honor, and country. The military should further its progress and accept the challenge of building a band of brothers *and* sisters.

REFERENCES

Abrams, J.R., (2016). Debunking the myth of universal male privilege. *Michigan Journal of Law Reform, 49*(2), 303–334.

Army Research Institute. (1977). *Women content in units force development test (MAXWAC)*. Alexandria, VA: U.S. Army Research Institute for the Behavioral and Social Sciences.

Bagilhole B. (2014). "Challenging gender boundaries: Pressures and constraints on women in non-traditional occupations." In S. Kumra, & R.J. Burke, (Eds.), *The Oxford handbook of gender in organizations* (pp. 393–414). Oxford University Press.

Benschop, Y., & Van Den Brink, M. (2014) Power and resistance in gender equality strategies: Comparing quotas and small wins. In S. Kumra, & R.J. Burke, (Eds.), *The Oxford handbook of gender in organizations* (pp. 333–352). Oxford University Press.

Burke, R.J. (2014). Organizational culture, work investments, and the careers of men: Disadvantages to women? In S. Kumra, & R.J. Burke, (Eds.), *The Oxford handbook of gender in organizations* (pp. 371–392). Oxford University Press.

Campbell, J.P., McCloy, R.A., Oppler, S.H., & Sager, C.E. (1993). "A Theory of Performance." In N. Schmidt & W.C., Borman (Eds.). *Personnel selection in organizations*. San Francisco, Jossey-Bass, pp.35–70.

Cheney, A.M., Reisinger, H.S., Booth, B.M., Mengeling, M.A., Torner, J.C., & Sadler, A.G., (2015). Servicewomen's strategies to staying safe during military service. *Gender Issues, 32*, 1–18. DOI 10.1007/s1247–014–9128–8

Cohn, C. (2000). "How can she claim equal rights when she doesn't have to do as many push-ups as I do?" *Men and Masculinities, 3*(2), 131–151.

Cone, R.W. (2016). Leading gender integration. *Military Medicine, 181*, January Supplement, 4–9.

Congressional Commission on Military Training and Gender-Related Issues. (1999). *Final report: Findings and recommendations* (Volume I). Arlington, VA: Department of Defense.

Dansby, M., Laurence, J.H., & Wetzel, E. (1999). Military Equal Opportunity Climate Survey (MEOCS): Overview of results related to the CMTGRI. In Congressional Commission on Military Training and Gender-Related Issues, *Final report: Research projects, reports, and studies* (Volume IV, pp. 689–723). Arlington, VA: Congressional Commission on Military Training and Gender-Related Issues.

Defense Market Research (DMR) Executive Notes. (2001, February 8) *Changes in the recruit pool.* (www.defensemarketresearch.org/published/notes/execnote. asp?docid=167).

DoD. (1993). *Population Representation in the Military Services, Fiscal Year 1992.* Washington, DC: Office of the Assistant Secretary of Defense (Force Management and Personnel).

Department of Defense [DoD]. (2015). *Defense Advisory Committee on Women in the Services: 2015 Report.* Alexandria, VA: Defense Advisory Committee on Women in the Services. http://dacowits.defense.gov/Portals/48/Documents/Reports/2015/Annual%20Report/2015%20DACOWITS%20Annual%20Report_Final.pdf

DoD. (2016). *Population Representation in the Military Services: Fiscal Year 2014 Summary Report.* Washington, DC: Office of the Under Secretary of Defense, Personnel and Readiness. Published in 2016. Accessed May 18, 2016. http://www.cna.org/research/pop-rep

Dichter, M.E., & True, G. (2015). "This Is the Story of Why My Military Career Ended Before It Should Have": Premature Separation From Military Service Among U.S. Women Veterans. *Affilia,* 30(2), 187–199. Published online before print October 15, 2014, doi:10.1177/0886109914555219

DiSilverio, L.A.H. (2003, August). *Winning the retention wars: The Air Force, women officers, and the need for transformation.*(Fairchild Paper). Maxwell AFB, AL: Air University Press.

Dunivin, K.O. (1994). Military culture: Change and continuity. *Armed Forces & Society,* 20(4), 531–547. DOI: 10.1177/0095327X9402000403

Eagly, A.H., Gartzia, L., & Carli, L.L. (2014). Female advantage: Revisited. In S. Kumra, & R.J. Burke, (Eds.), *The Oxford handbook of gender in organizations* (pp. 153–174). Oxford University Press.

Eden, J. (2015). Women in combat: The question of standards. *Military Review,* March-April, 39–47.

Eichler, M. (2014). Militarized masculinities in international relations. *Brown Journal of World Affairs, XXI*(I), 81–93.

Eitelberg, M.J. (1988, April). *Manpower for military occupations.* Washington, DC: Office of the Assistant Secretary of Defense (Force Management and Personnel).

Ender, Morten G., David E. Rohall, and Michael D. Matthews. (2014). *The Millennial Generation and National Defense: Attitudes of Future Military and Civilian Leaders.* Basingstoke and NY: Palgrave Pivot.

Fielden, S.L., & Hunt, C. (2014). Sexual harassment in the workplace. In S. Kumra, & R.J. Burke, (Eds.), *The Oxford handbook of gender in organizations* (pp. 353–370). Oxford University Press.

Friedl, K.E. (2016). Biases of the incumbents: What if we were integrating men into a women's Army? *Military Review,* March-April, 69–75.

French, D. (2015, October 5). Social justice at war: Ignoring differences between the sexes will cost lives. *National Review,* 25–26.

Harrell, M.C., Beckett, M.K., Chien, C.S., & Sollinger, J.M. (2002). *The status of gender integration in the military: Analysis of selected occupations.* Santa Monica, CA: RAND.

Harrell, M.C., & Miller, L.L. (1997). *New opportunities for military women: Effects upon readiness, cohesion, and morale.* Santa Monica , CA: RAND.

Hosek, S.D., Tiemeyer, P., Kilburn, R., Strong, D.A., Ducksworth, S., & Ray, R. (2001). *Minority and gender differences in officer career progression.* Santa Monica, CA: RAND.

Kamarck, K.N. (2015, December 3). *Women in combat: Issues for Congress* (R42075). Washington, DC: congressional Research Service.

Katt, M. (2014). Blurred lines: Cultural Support Teams in Afghanistan. *Joint Forces Quarterly, 75*(4), 106–113.

Laurence, J.H., & Estrada, A.X. (2003, September). *Content analysis of DACOWITS site visit reports.* Washington, DC: Defense Department Advisory Committee on Women in the Services.

Laurence, J.H., Milavec, B.L., Rohall, D.E., Ender, M.G., & Matthews, M.D., (2016). Predictors of Support for Women in Military Roles: Military Status, Gender, and Political Ideology. *Military Psychology, 28*(6), 488–497.

Laurence, J.H., Wright, M., Keys, C. S. & Giambo, P. A. (1999, July). "Focus group research." In *Final Report-Volume IV: Research Projects, Reports, and Studies.* Arlington, VA: Congressional Commission on Military Training and Gender-Related Issues.

Matthews, M.D., Ender, M.G., Laurence, J.H., & Rohall, D.E. (2009). Role of group affiliation and sex on attitudes toward women in the military. *Military Psychology, 21*(2), 241–251.

Miller, L.L. (1997). Not just weapons of the weak: Gender harassment as a form of protest for Army men. *Social Psychology Quarterly, 60*(1), 32–51.

Miner-Rubino, K., Settles, I. H., & Stewart, A. J. (2009), More than numbers: Individual and contextual factors in how gender diversity affects women's well-being. *Psychology of Women Quarterly, 33*, 463–474). doi: 10.1111/j.1471–6402.2009.01524.x

Mottern, J., Foster, D., Brady, E., & Marshall-Mies, J. (1997). *The 1995 gender integration basic combat training study* (Study Report 97–01). Alexandria, VA: U.S. Army Research Institute for the Behavioral and Social Sciences.

National Center for Veterans Analysis and Statistics. (2011, November). *America's Women Veterans: Military Service History and VA Benefit Utilization Statistics.* National Center for Veterans Analysis and Statistics, Department of Veterans Affairs, Washington, DC. http://www.va.gov/vetdata/docs/SpecialReports/Final_Womens_Report_3_2_12_v_7.pdf

Nicolas, A. (2015). What the Female Engagement Team experience can teach us about the future of women in combat. *Military Review*, March-April, 56–61.

Rice, C.E. (2015). Women in the infantry: Understanding Issues of physical strength, economics, and small-unit cohesion. *Military Review*, March-April, 48–55.

Salhani, J. (2015, August 20). The military's outdated gender standards are finally breaking down. *Think Progress.* http://thinkprogress.org/world/2015/08/20/3693191/women-are-finally-breaking-through-the militarys-outdated-gender-standards/ Accessed April 7, 2016.

Segal, D.R. (1989). *Recruiting for Uncle Sam: Citizenship and military manpower policy.* University Press of Kansas.

Segal, M.W., Lane, M.D., & Fisher, A.G. (2015). Conceptual model of military career and family life course events, intersections, and effects on well-being. *Military Behavioral Health*, 1–5.

Segal, M.W., Smith, D.G., Segal, D.R., & Canuso, A.A. (2016). The role of leadership and peer behaviors in the performance and well-being of women in combat: Historical perspectives, unit integration, and family issues. *Military Medicine, 181,* January Supplement, 28–39.

Smith, C. P., & Freyd J.J. (2014). Institutional betrayal. *American Psychologist, 69*(6), 575–587. Doi.org/10.1037/a0037564

Sorcher, S. (2013, September 9). How the military's 'bro' culture turns women into targets. *The Atlantic.* http://theatlantic.tumblr.com/tagged/Bro-Culture

Tan, M. (2015, October 16). 3rd woman, and 1st female Reservist, dons Ranger tab. *Army Times.* https://www.armytimes.com/story/ . . . woman . . . 1st . . . ranger . . . /74070360/

Tepe, V., Yarnell, A., Nindl, B.C., van Arsdale, S., & Deuster, P.A. (2016). Women in combat: Summary of findings and a way ahead. *Military Medicine, 181,* January Supplement, 109–118.

Chapter 7

Lesbian and Gay Service Members and Their Families

David G. Smith and Karin De Angelis

In 2011, the repeal of the 1993 policy on homosexuality in the military referred to as "Don't Ask, Don't Tell, Don't Pursue" and later shortened to "Don't Ask, Don't Tell," became the first of many significant changes to Department of Defense (DoD) policy and federal laws related to gays and lesbians serving in the US armed services. In the five-year period after 2011, lesbian, gay, and bisexual (LGB) military personnel were allowed to serve openly, receive the same federal benefits as their heterosexual peers, and legally marry as a same-sex couple in every state and be recognized as such. Military installations now observe PRIDE month and equal opportunity offices are allowed to handle complaints of discrimination due to sexual orientation. Recently, President Obama nominated and Congress approved the appointment of the Honorable Eric Fanning, an openly gay man, as the Secretary of the Army. These have been important and meaningful changes impacting quality of life for LGB service members today, but the path to recognition, equality, and opportunity was not without challenges and barriers.

Integration and inclusion of minority groups in our military has historically been limited through the concept of professional closure (Segal & Kestnbaum, 2002). The military has generally attempted to reproduce itself demographically as heterosexual, white, and male while also preventing equality of opportunity and service for other minority groups. While professional closure functioned well under conscription and periods where demand for manpower was low, the military has relaxed exclusionary policies during periods of high personnel needs, such as wartime. This pattern of recruitment and accession holds true for race/ethnicity, gender, and sexuality. Arguments to support exclusion of minority groups have consistently focused on unit readiness, effectiveness, and cohesion. Broader issues related to recruiting and retention also are highlighted as challenges during the current all-volunteer force.

These concerns were widely held and perpetuated across the military and society with little evidence to support their validity.

LGB service members have a long history of honorably serving in our nation's military to include every war in the past two centuries. In this chapter, we trace the historical events and policies leading up to current policy. We also highlight policy areas to address for full integration of LGB service members, especially with regard to their families. Arguments for exclusion and inclusion will be reviewed to provide a foundation for understanding how prejudice and discrimination may continue to exist in today's military. More importantly, we examine the quality of service of LGB military personnel, current challenges, concerns and outcomes. Finally, we examine LGB same-sex families' experiences and how they may differ from their heterosexual peers.[1]

Throughout this chapter, we use the terms sex, gender, and sexual orientation/sexuality as distinctly different concepts. We commonly understand sex as being biologically determined through chromosomal makeup and genitalia for males and females (Fausto-Sterling, 2012). In the social sciences, gender is considered a socially constructed identity of described and prescribed cultural characteristics that people use to identify as feminine or masculine. People's sexuality/sexual orientation refers to who they are attracted to sexually. These are basic definitions designed to help the reader understand the meanings and subtleties of how these terms may be employed throughout the chapter.

HISTORY OF LGB MILITARY PERSONNEL

The laws regarding LGB individuals and military service have fluctuated over time largely in response to broader social forces (Shilts, 1994). Historians point to the existence of same-sex behaviors among military service members during the country's independence through its expansionist history (Katz, 1992). Most notably, Baron Friedrich von Steuben, a Prussian military member and known gay man, worked with General George Washington to train troops in Valley Forge in 1778. He also wrote the Army's first drill instruction manual. Commodore Stephen Decatur, a naval hero of the War of 1812, also was gay, although he was married to a woman (Shilts, 1993).

During the time of von Steuben and Decatur's service, there was not the abundance of laws, oversight, and punitive actions that emerged during the early- to mid-20th century on homosexuality. During World War I, the military did not concern itself with sexual orientation. It was commander-driven how troops who identified as homosexual were to be integrated into their units, which led to variability in treatment, and oftentimes, an overlooking of homosexual behavior. Following World War I, the first governing regulations concerning homosexual conduct emerged under the Articles of War of 1916, which limited the use of sodomy charges to assault cases that involved the act, or the intent to commit (Katz, 1992). Clinical psychologists and psychiatrists viewed homosexuality as an illness during this time so efforts were made to identify and treat homosexuals. Those whose behavior did not change with treatment were removed for being psychologically unfit for duty. Oversight and regulations focused on homosexual behaviors, rather than identity and orientation; thus, service members who identified as being gay were allowed to serve (Herek, 1996).

As documented by historian Allan Bérubé (1990), LGB individuals served in World War II, at least initially, under these lax prohibitions; however, there were limitations on their service. Commanders placed LGB individuals, whether self-identified or perceived, into jobs viewed as not requiring masculine characteristics and deliberately removed them from the combat arms. During this time, the medical and psychological communities continued to view homosexuality as an illness that required treatment. Following World War II, changes within the Uniform Code of Military Justice led to a ban of sodomy among all service members, regardless of the sex of the partner (Lever & Kanouse, 1994).

It was not until the mid-1970s when the institutional perspective on LGB individuals moved beyond commander discretion and the treatment and separation model. Under President Jimmy Carter, the DoD issued a new policy that explicitly stated that "homosexuality is incompatible with military service" and called for the mandatory separation of all homosexuals (General Accounting Office, 1992, p. 2). It was perceived that LGB individuals threatened good order and discipline, violated privacy norms, and soiled public respect for the military (National Defense Research Institute, 1993). This change in policy reflected society's renewed focus on homosexuality as a depraved behavior and that the best way to stop it was via punitive measures. This shift was further supported by the American Psychiatric Association's (APA) classification of homosexuality as sexual deviance in the first iteration, published in 1952, of the Diagnostic and Statistical Manual of Mental Disorders (DSM), and reaffirmed in the publication of the second iteration of the DSM in 1968. Due to research, professional deliberation, and political protest, the APA's Board of Trustees voted to remove homosexuality from DSM-II and to replace it with the diagnosis of "sexual orientation disturbance" for individuals who experienced distress in connection to their sexuality. This classification was further refined to "ego-dystonic homosexuality," or a sexual orientation, that is, at odds with one's self-image in DSM-III before it was removed completely in 1973 (Spitzer, 1981).

The DoD's new directive prevented homosexuals from enlisting or serving in the armed forces. Those in violation of this directive faced administrative discharge, or if in violation of the Uniform Code of Military Justice, of court-martial with the possibility of a dishonorable or bad conduct discharge. Thus, post-World War II and at a time when the military was transitioning to an all-volunteer force, homosexuals observed a closing of the institution and were banned from military service because of institutional concerns and irrespective of individual behavior. The investigative organizations of each service branch (e.g., Naval Criminal Investigative Service) aggressively pursued individuals considered to be in breach of this policy (Burrelli & Feder, 2009; Shilts, 1994).

This policy of mandated separation of homosexuals, regardless of conduct or self-identification, did not change until President Clinton directed the 1993 implementation of the "Don't Ask, Don't Tell, Don't Pursue" policy, which military sociologist Charles Moskos helped author. LGB individuals were allowed to serve in the military; thus, orientation alone was not a bar to service. Admission of homosexual orientation or homosexual conduct, however, led to a mandated investigation, and if proven, resulted in discharge. By making sexual orientation a private matter, this policy prevented the "witch hunt" investigations of the past and furthered the idea that homosexual orientation alone should not prevent enlistment or continued service. This policy was vastly critiqued because it assumed that the conduct of LGB individuals—regardless of the actual behavior itself—had a negative effect on the military's ability to fulfill its mission. The policy also required LGB individuals to purposefully mask their sexual orientation, even if it required deceit, to stay in compliance (Benecke, Corbett, & Osburn, 1999). However, proponents of the policy argued that it granted LGB individuals the right of military service by preventing investigations based on hearsay. They also argued that it protected the rights of service members uncomfortable with serving alongside LGB individuals. The Palm Center estimates that approximately 11,000 service members were discharged under Don't Ask, Don't Tell and that rates of discharge increased each year through 2005 when manpower needs were strained under the demands of Operations Enduring and Iraqi Freedom (Bonilla, 2006). This included the discharge of at least fifty-eight Arabic linguists at a time when the military was experiencing grave difficulty in finding qualified service members to fulfill these critical roles (see Benjamin, 2007 for a first person account serving as a gay linguist; also see Palm Center, 2007 for detailed reporting on this issue).

Calls to repeal Don't Ask, Don't Tell continued through the next decade, but were not seriously heeded until President Obama announced in 2010 that he would work with Congress and the DoD to repeal the policy. At that time, the Pentagon began to loosen enforcement guidelines; it also published a scientifically sound study arguing that the repeal of Don't Ask, Don't Tell would have minimal to no impact on military effectiveness (DoD, 2010). Citing this research as justification, as well as broader appeals to the human rights and dignity of LGB service members, a Democratic-led House and Senate voted to repeal Don't Ask, Don't Tell in December 22, 2010. President Obama signed the repeal into law a week later, but gave the Joint Chiefs of Staff time to prepare all service members for the policy change. The repeal officially went into effect on September 20, 2011.

Although the repeal of Don't Ask, Don't Tell allowed LGB service members to serve openly without fear of investigation or discharge, they still experienced inequities in accessing benefits available to heterosexual service members and their families due to the Federal government's Defense of Marriage Act. Withheld benefits included health care, housing, and next of kin casualty notification. The Supreme Court ruled a critical provision in the Act unconstitutional in 2013 in *United States v. Windsor*, allowing the families of LGB service members access to federal benefits. Further changes happened in 2015 when the Supreme Court ruled in *Obergefell v. Hodges* that same-sex marriage would be legal in all states. Current policy now allows for the open service of LGB service members, and if legally married, provides equal benefits to their spouses and children (Wright, 2013).

CURRENT COMPOSITION OF THE FORCES

A primary obstacle to completing research on LGB service members and their families is the absence of accurate demographic data. Until the repeal of Don't Ask, Don't Tell, it was very dangerous—and ethically questionable—for researchers to ask about sexual orientation and sexual behaviors because admittance to homosexuality was grounds for dismissal. As a way of protecting their partners, spouses of LGB personnel had to remain uncounted as well. Under Don't Ask, Don't Tell, demographer Gary Gates (2010) of UCLA's Williams Institute estimated that 2.2 percent of military personnel, or 71,000 individuals, were lesbian, gay, or bisexual with a higher percentage serving in the reserve forces (3.4 percent) than active duty (0.9 percent). Although women were only 14 percent of active duty personnel during this time, Gates (2010) also estimated that lesbian and bisexual women accounted for 43 percent of the military LGB population. These estimates suggest that the proportion of LGB service members, at only 0.6 percent for active duty men and 2.9 percent of active duty women, was lower than their percentage in the general population, which was 3.3 percent for men and 5.2 percent for women.

Since the repeal of Don't Ask, Don't Tell, many of the formal, legal, and ethical barriers to collecting demographic data on LGB personnel have been removed. However, in recognition of the private nature of sexuality, the DoD does not track the sexual orientation or behaviors of its personnel, nor does it track whether LGB personnel are married and/or have children. Official counts on the number of LGB personnel as well as their race, ethnicity, gender, marital status, and branch of service are not known. Gates (2010) estimates that the repeal of Don't Ask, Don't Tell could have attracted approximately 36,000 LGB personnel to the military, but there are no data to confirm or dispute this estimate. The DoD currently estimates that there are 18,000 LGB couples in the military, but does not know how many are married or will seek to marry with the Supreme Court rulings in *United States v. Windsor* and *Obergefell v. Hodges* (Maze, 2013). Of these couples, an estimated 37 percent of active duty LGB and 20 percent of LGB guard and reserve personnel report living in a home with children (Oswald & Sternberg, 2014). This current stance on not tracking the sex of married couples or the sexual orientation of individual service members potentially can be defended as ensuring privacy. However, it makes it difficult to assess the unique stressors of LGB service members and their families and certainly prevents the distribution of "LGB-affirming resources" (Oswald & Sternberg, 2014, p. 133).

IMPACTS OF THE END OF DADT

Prior to the 2011 policy changes, opponents of open service and full integration of LGB service members framed their opposition in two ways: the individual competencies of LGB individuals as deficient and, after that argument faded, focusing on the perceived negative consequences LGB service members would have on their units.

Individual Deficiencies

Initially, opponents of full inclusion claimed that LGB service members were physically weak and morally compromised; their sexuality, it was argued, made them incompetent and a security risk (Sarbin, 1996). Both in the past and today, gay men are associated with feminine traits, such as physical weakness, that are not valued within the combat-driven armed forces. Additionally, scientific opinions, such as past characterizations in the Diagnostic and Statistical Manual of Mental Disorders, linked homosexual orientation and behaviors to psychological and social illness and emphasized the need for rehabilitation and military separation. In addition to past mental characterizations, gay men also had to negotiate the stereotypically associated behavior of sexual deviance and promiscuity (Burrelli, 1994). Although gay men contend with the perception of lacking masculinity, and by extension the aggressiveness necessary for military effectiveness, they also experience the characterization of being sexual deviants that undermine privacy and subvert the heteronormative, masculine behaviors of the military. Lesbians, in contrast, are stereotypically portrayed as too masculine and, therefore, as threats to the hegemonic masculinity of the military. From an attraction perspective, arguments have been made that both gays and lesbians were drawn to military service to overcome their attraction to same-sex people (i.e., "make a man out of them") in the case of men, and to seek out other women like themselves for lesbians (Bérubé, 1990; Campbell, 2013). These arguments fell out of favor in the early 1990s when performance reviews demonstrated that LGB service members, in the aggregate, performed at the comparably same level as their colleagues (Bérubé, 1990).

Social and Task Cohesion

Once individual performance concerns were addressed, the dominant argument for excluding LGB personnel focused on their potentially negative impact on the social cohesion, and as a consequence, the overall effectiveness of military units. There was concern that gay men and women disrupted the social norms and rituals found in single-sex military units critical for group solidarity (MacCoun, 1996). Survey research in the early 1990s showed that service members, and especially young, male enlistees, were markedly against the open service of LGB personnel, which they viewed as disruptive and a threat to privacy (Segal, Gade, & Johnson, 1994). In 2010, the DoD noted a marked shift in these attitudes as a majority of service members and their spouses reported that the open service of LGB personnel would have little to no impact on cohesion.

There is modest evidence that highly cohesive groups are more effective in task accomplishment than less cohesive groups. At its basic level, cohesion traditionally is defined as a type of social glue that keeps individuals tied to the group; it is conceptualized mainly in terms of peer relationships. Methodological and theoretical advances have led to increased specification of different types of cohesion, with the greatest difference existing between "social cohesion" and "task cohesion." Social cohesion describes positive interpersonal attractions where individuals develop group friendships. This affective bonding extends beyond formal military duties to informal interactions; the individuals, in short, are friends and like to spend time together. Socially cohesive groups tend to be socially homogeneous as well. In contrast, task cohesion is the shared dedication to a goal and the ability of the group to come together for its completion. Rather than relying on social homogeneity, task cohesion relies on group recognition that each individual brings a different, yet valued, skill set. The focus on social cohesion not only overstates the importance of homogeneity and affective bonding but also overlooks the importance of task cohesion, and the role of each individual member in completing the group's goals. With the integration of gay men and lesbians (as well as other minority groups), the military has had to rely more on task cohesion than on social cohesion; a decrease in military effectiveness as was feared with this change has not been noted (Segal & Bourg, 2002).

Reasons for including gay men and lesbians in the military focus more on individual rights and responsibilities. The military often is viewed as a desired employer, particularly because it offers "pull factors" such as standardized pay, equal entry at the bottom ranks, and a willingness to train unskilled personnel. Additionally, in the citizen-soldier tradition of the United States, military participation is viewed as a civic duty, like voting, that implies shared responsibilities in exchange for equal citizenship. As a result, LGB individuals have sought to join the military as a way to benefit from its economic stability as well as to demonstrate their willingness to serve as equal citizens. At the organizational level, allowing gay men and women to serve openly moves the policies of the US military to be more in line with twenty-five other countries[2] that already allow open service. Since many military missions now involve international coalitions—the International Security Assistance Force in Afghanistan has involved most of these twenty-five countries—our service members already were serving alongside openly gay men and lesbians from allied countries. Of note, military personnel are routinely deployed and stationed outside the United States in countries that do not allow for openly gay military service (e.g., Afghanistan, Iraq, Japan, Malaysia, South Korea, Singapore, Thailand) (Palm Center, 2009).

Military Readiness

Opponents of the repeal of Don't Ask, Don't Tell and allowing homosexual service members to serve openly predicted that repeal would lead to a decline in military readiness and effectively render the military incapable of performing its mission. Of note, military personnel serve alongside LGB civilian federal workers and contractors. Their arguments were based on the belief that heterosexuals would not fight alongside openly gay service members resulting in reduced unit cohesion, lower recruitment and retention, and increased assaults and harassment. These attitudes were believed to be popular within the civilian population and more strongly held within the military. In 2009, 1,063 military general and flag officers signed a statement of support for maintaining Don't Ask, Don't Tell:

> Our past experience as military leaders leads us to be greatly concerned about the impact of repeal [of the law] on morale, discipline, unit cohesion, and overall military readiness. We believe that imposing this burden on our men and women

in uniform would undermine recruiting and retention, impact leadership at all levels, have adverse effects on the willingness of parents who lend their sons and daughters to military service, and eventually break the All-Volunteer Force.

While these senior military officers were convinced of the deleterious effects of repealing Don't Ask, Don't Tell, post-repeal research data provide evidence portraying a different reality.

Findings from research conducted a year after the repeal of Don't Ask, Don't Tell show that there was no evidence of any impact to military readiness, recruiting, retention, unit cohesion, assaults, or harassment (Belkin et al., 2012). Not only did military readiness remain unchanged from pre-repeal levels but also recruiting remained steady as the nation entered the eleventh consecutive year of combat operations. Predictions of mass departures of heterosexual service members unwilling to serve with openly gay and lesbian peers proved to be unfounded. Overall force morale did not change, although morale improved for some people and declined for others resulting in no net change (Belkin et al., 2012). Surveys of service members' spouses provided similar results with a majority of spouses reporting that their service members' units did not experience a decrease in unit cohesion or readiness, and that service members experienced no decrease in their intention to reenlist, ability to perform their job, or attend unit functions (Greentree et al., 2013). Interestingly, research showed subjective improvements in military units with increased openness and honesty in how service members viewed the quality of their service (Belkin et al., 2012). Leaders reported that they were also better able to resolve issues related to harassment and bias after the repeal of Don't Ask, Don't Tell. Overall, quality of service for both LGB and heterosexual service members improved through a more positive command climate and ability to serve with dignity, respect and honor as is customary in the military profession.

POST-DADT ISSUES

Policy Considerations

The evidence indicates that the repeal of Don't Ask, Don't Tell was effectively implemented across the military and produced positive results at the unit and individual levels. However, the unintended consequences of the repeal left LGB service members and their families to contend with federal and state laws governing marriage and family benefits that conflicted with military policy. In 2011, state laws governed the ability to marry and recognize same-sex marriages, which was not legal in many states. Additionally,

federal benefits were not available to LGB service members and their spouses
in same-sex marriages based on the 1996 Defense of Marriage Act (DOMA).
These benefits included: DoD-dependent identification cards, TRICARE
health care, basic allowance for housing, government family housing, Com-
missary and Exchange access, family separation allowance, Service Members
Group Life Insurance beneficiaries, Death Gratuity, Survivor Benefit Plan
beneficiaries, Thrift Savings Plan beneficiaries, Wounded Warrior designated
caregiver, casualty notification, eligibility to receive effects of deceased service member, flag presentation at funeral, hospital visitation rights, and joint
duty assignments for dual military couples.

The repeal of DOMA occurred on June 26, 2013 in the US Supreme Court
case *United States v. Windsor* that ruled the restriction to marriage as being
heterosexual was unconstitutional (Smith, 2014). The repeal of DOMA pre-
cipitated military policy change extending all military benefits and entitle-
ments to same-sex couples married prior to June 26, 2013 with an effective
date of June 26, 2013. It was another two years before the Supreme Court
ruled in *Obergefell v. Hodges* on June 26, 2015 that same-sex couples had
the same fundamental right to marry under the Fourteenth Amendment of
the Constitution (Perry, 2015). While the repeal of DOMA allowed for equal
military benefits, this ruling was pivotal for same-sex military couples residing in states without nondiscrimination laws. These states are now required to
recognize same-sex marriages and protect these families from discrimination
related to employment, housing, and other community services.

Legal barriers and challenges for LGB military service members and their
families in the United States have largely been resolved, but tours of duty
outside the United States in countries that do not recognize same-sex families are still problematic. Service members are required to have command
sponsorship of family members for them to accompany the service member to overseas duty stations. Command sponsorship regulations in foreign
countries are based on the negotiated Status of Forces Agreement (SOFA)
between the United States and the foreign country. SOFAs provide dependent
family members with exceptions to passport and visa requirements as well as
access to the military installation. LGB service members are not allowed to
have their same-sex spouses accompany them to duty stations in countries
that do not recognize same-sex marriage. The State Department negotiates
SOFAs and continues to progress in reducing the number of countries with
US military installations that do not allow same-sex couples. Germany, Italy,
and South Korea were the most recent SOFA additions to allow same-sex
military families. There are currently seventeen countries pending approval
and thirty-four denying access.

Although laws and policy have changed to rectify the pre-Don't Ask, Don't
Tell repeal environment, there are indications that the effects of bias and

prejudice may continue for LGB service members and their families. Because the military does not track or ask service members or their dependents to identify their sexual orientation, it is difficult to study and conduct research related to these effects. However, after sexual orientation was included as a category for equal opportunity issues related to harassment and discrimination in June 2015, there may be future opportunities to measure the extent that these behaviors are being reported. Mental health care providers should be observing more stress-related symptoms in this stigmatized group. As with research in the civilian community, early military research finds that LGB service members are uncomfortable disclosing their sexual orientation to medical healthcare providers which may reduce care and readiness. Distrust still persists between LGB military families and military health care providers despite the repeal of policies such as Don't Ask, Don't Tell and DOMA (Goldbach & Castro, 2016). Institutional, social and cultural change may require a longer track record of equality, dignity, and respect before trust improves.

Sexual Stigma

Attitudes toward homosexuality and gay parenthood have become increasingly more positive and accepting in the United States as evidenced in national surveys and studies showing same-sex couples seeking parenthood are experiencing less conflict, barriers, and stigma (Goldberg & Garcia, 2015; Taylor, 2013). Despite these positive attitudinal trends, sexual stigma is still evident and foundational to any investigation of the experiences and outcomes of same-sex families. Sexual stigma refers to the negative perceptions or lower status of anyone who embodies or associates with nonheterosexual relationships, behavior, identities, or groups (Herek, Gillis, & Cogan, 2015). Sexual stigma that is culturally embedded in social institutions including the military through a prevailing heterosexual ideology coupled with negative affect toward homosexuality is referred to as heterosexism (Herek et al., 2015). Lesbians and gay men in a heterosexist environment such as the military may experience diminished influence, power, personal control, and access to resources than their heterosexual peers (Herek, 2009). In terms of how sexual stigma affects same-sex military families, the Minority Stress Model "posits that minority group members are at risk for some kinds of psychological problems because they face unique, chronic stressors as a result of their disadvantaged status in society" (Herek & Garnets, 2007, pp. 259–260). These minority stressors have been associated with three fundamental types of stigma: enacted stigma (behaviors directed at homosexuals), felt stigma (belief that they will be treated unfairly), and internalized stigma (accepting the stigma as legitimate) (Herek, 2009; Meyer, 2003).

Although these stigmas are directly associated with gay men and lesbians, these stigmas can also apply to military family members, friends, and allies by association (Herek, 2009).

While there is no post-Don't Ask, Don't Tell evidence of minority stressors for military personnel, their partners, or children, prior surveys provide evidence that LGB service members did experience harassment, discrimination, or assault based on perceived sexual orientation. It is more than likely that while the policy regarding sexuality has changed and improved the military work environment for LGB service members, there are still people who harbor heterosexist attitudes and prejudices. Beyond minority stressors, the military profession has other stressors that could have unique effects on LGB service members and their families. Inherent to military service are demands placed on service members and their families for frequent job relocations and separations for deployment and training. These demands in particular create challenges related to disclosure and social support as LGB families must choose each time they relocate whether and to whom they feel comfortable disclosing their sexual identity. Reestablishing support networks at each new duty station can be challenging since these are not explicit and public forms of support provided by the military. Separations for children and partners may also prove to be arduous depending on identity concealment, support available, perceived heterosexist environment, and relationship quality. Stigma as it relates to the interaction of the military professional context and LGB families has not been studied and may provide meaningful insight to military family policy makers.

These forms of stigma often act as mediators and moderators and may produce several types of positive- and negative-coping mechanisms to cope with these stigmatized outcomes. As sources of chronic stress, stigma in heterosexist environments and the associated outcomes may be perceived as presenting barriers and challenges to military family formation, which include stereotypes, social norms, laws/policies, social support, disclosure, and family structure.

Despite the changing public attitudes and acceptance of lesbians and gays in society, stereotypes still exist and present challenges in the military. The enduring and prevalent stereotype that gay men are prone to molest children is often invoked in antigay discourse and policies related to family formation. This felt stigma may be used to preclude gay men from adoption or other childcare-related activities especially in the hypermasculine military context (Herek, 2009).

In addition to stereotypes, social norms may represent barriers to parenthood for lesbians and gay men. Societal norms stigmatize family formation outside heterosexual marriage (D'Emilio, 2002). Enacted stigma in the form of legal barriers, social pressure, and restrictions toward parenthood and adoption are often encountered by lesbians and gay men despite recent changes to law and policy in many states (Patterson, 2009). Attitudes and practices such as overlooking, denying, or being disrespectful by attorneys, adoption agencies or reproductive health care providers are perceived as barriers to parenthood and remind these aspiring parents of their stigmatized sexual identity.

Laws and policies related to parenthood in the military are only one contributing factor of perceived social support. Other important forms of social support include the workplace, family, friends, school, and community/neighborhood. Working and living in an environment where gay men and lesbians feel their families are accepted and welcomed often results in more positive individual and family outcomes. Little is known about how military leaders' attitudes and values affect the command climate and organizational culture for LGB families' quality of service.

Closely linked to a supportive social environment is whether and when lesbians and gay parents disclose their sexual identity. The "coming out" process is complex and involves all family members in deciding when, where, and who to come out to. This information management is crucial to maintaining personal and psychological safety. The military context of moving every two to three years adds another level of complexity in changing support networks and potential allies. For parents this also means being able to communicate what to say and not to say to their children. The sequence of disclosure and parenthood may also be influential as there is evidence that gay men as parents who have children after they have disclosed their sexual identity have more positive outcomes than those who have children before disclosure (Tornello & Patterson, 2015). These fathers were also more likely to perceive their identity was accepted if they were in a relationship and therefore provided social support as a parent.

Same-sex family research provides evidence of the mediating and moderating relationships of the chronic stressors of stigma and the resulting stigmatized outcomes. For gay men and lesbians with higher internalized stigma, studies find that lower perceived social support is related outcomes such as increased psychopathology (anxiety, depression), alcohol and substance abuse, suicide attempts, and decreased well-being, self-esteem, and relationship quality (Goldberg & Smith, 2011; Lick, Tornello, Riskind, Schmidt, & Patterson, 2012; van Dam, 2004; Weber, 2008). Perceived social support in the military may be challenging for those LGB families most in need. Disclosure is generally related to better outcomes, but may also lead lesbians and gay men and their children to fear losses of relationships and jobs, hostile reactions (e.g., personal violence, bullying, teasing, harassment), reprisals and social sanctions, and not seek help or resources (van Dam, 2004; Lindsay et al., 2006). On a positive note, military units may provide a safer environment in terms of fewer incidents related to hostility, harassment, and violence with a focus on discipline and respect for others.

To ameliorate the stigmatized outcomes, gay men and lesbian parents may use a variety of coping mechanisms as strategies. Again, disclosure or maintaining a level of secrecy about sexual identity and family structure may be an option in some cases depending on the perceived community support, military support, and state laws. For parents who choose to disclose, teaching their children how to talk about their family structure is important. Developing diverse and dense support networks of family, friends, neighbors, allies, and other gay and lesbian parents provides the social support these families need (Moore & Stambolis-Ruhstorfer, 2013). Children may employ coping mechanisms that may include challenging or confronting heterosexism, secrecy, finding support groups, educating others, and helping reshape school curricula (Lindsay et al., 2006).

LEADERSHIP IMPLICATIONS

Inclusion and recognition of LGB service members and their families in today's all-volunteer force has largely demonstrated that sexual orientation is not relevant to the mission of the military. While mission success continues to be the overarching goal, it is crucial for military leaders to understand how social trends interact with their sphere of influence including command climate and organizational culture. Ultimately, LGB service members' quality of service will be influenced by their social interactions and perceptions of the workplace environment. Developing and maintaining LGB service member commitment and retention are areas of focus that military leaders should consider in how they create an inclusive workplace and team that values diversity.

The military as a "greedy institution" in that it is demanding in terms of loyalty and personal resources, maintains normative constraints that dictate proper behavioral norms for service members in a heteronormative, masculine environment (Segal, 1986). The conservative gender role beliefs that these norms are based on present leadership challenges even in a modern military with more progressive social attitudes. Formal military policy that essentially assumes a neutral stance toward sexual orientation hinders leaders' ability to engage LGB service members' needs to ensure high levels of readiness and performance. LGB service members' trust in valuable resources such as chaplains, medical and health care providers is a particularly important leadership challenge. As a stigmatized group, they often feel marginalized and restricted in their full expression of social citizenship, humanity, and personhood. Being more susceptible to bias and prejudice, mental health care providers would expect to observe more stress-related symptoms. Stigma directly contributes to increased risk for substance abuse, anxiety, and depressive illness (Weber, 2008). While there is a unique need within this population, early research shows that LGB service members are not comfortable disclosing their sexual orientation to medical health care providers that may lead to inadequate care. One study found LGB service members to be only 70 percent comfortable with disclosure even though it could not be used against them. Only 56.7 percent felt that the military cared for health and well-being (Biddix, Fogel, & Black, 2013). There is a documented culture of mistrust in need of reparation.

Building on these trends, and because both research and experience demonstrate a connection between family satisfaction and service member commitment and retention, support mechanisms in place for military families employ a combination of formal and informal programs. Formal programs include family readiness and child development centers located at each military installation. These centers are open to all military personnel and their families regardless of family structure. Informal programs include social networks like spouses' clubs that typically develop in connection to a military unit. Military leaders often rely on these groups to disseminate information connected to family support. Although these support mechanisms are open to all family types, we do not know if LGB service members feel welcomed and use these resources for support. For example, the informal spouse networks are considered to be numerically dominated by wives.

Military leaders should be cognizant of the importance of informal support networks and affinity groups to LGB families. Maintaining access to these support networks can be uniquely influenced by military policies related to mobility and Permanent Change of Station (PCS) moves, deployments, and living environments (both at home and deployed). Because many of these support networks and affinity groups are informal, they are not typically visible to those who do not belong. PCS moves and deployments may act as barriers to access these important resources for LGB families without necessarily "outing" themselves to leaders in the chain of command.

Finally, family formation for LGB couples relies on adoption and alternative medical technologies. These options are often lengthy and expensive processes that may be negatively affected by PCS moves and deployments. While the military is rapidly advancing in social and health care policies to include many alternative medical technologies and adoption leave, not all expenses are covered yet and time away from work can be difficult based on training and operational deployment schedules. Again the military's policy of sexual orientation neutrality is a leadership challenge given the need for LGB-affirming resources. Despite changes to law and policy, the lingering and silencing effects of Don't Ask, Don't Tell may render these service members and their families invisible. However, the military provides basic human rights and protection from discrimination and harassment that is socially progressive and an exemplar for other civilian institutions to follow suit.

NOTES

1. Although LGB and transgender individuals often are grouped together, their acceptance and integration in the US military are different, especially in legal terms. This entry deals with LGB personnel only.

2. Australia, Austria, Belgium, Canada, Czech Republic, Denmark, Estonia, Finland, France, Germany, Ireland, Israel, Italy, Luxembourg, the Netherlands, New Zealand, Norway, Slovenia, South Africa, Spain, Sweden, Switzerland, the United Kingdom, and Uruguay, as of 2009. Retrieved from: http://archive.palmcenter.org/files/active/0/CountriesWithoutBan.pdf.

REFERENCES

Belkin, A., Ender, M., Frank, N., Furia, S., Lucas, G. R., Packard Jr, & Segal, D. R., (2012). *One year out: An assessment of Don't Ask, Don't Tell repeal's impact on military readiness*. University of California, Los Angeles, Palm Center.

Benecke, M.M., Corbett, K.M., & Osburn, C.D. (1999). In M.F. Katzenstein & J. Reppy (Eds.), *Beyond zero tolerance* (pp. 213–224), Lanham, MD: Rowman & Littlefield Publishers.

Benjamin, S. (2007, June 8). Don't ask, don't translate. *The New York Times*. Retrieved from http://www.nytimes.com/2007/06/08/opinion/08benjamin.html?_r=1.

Bérubé, A. (1990). *Coming out under fire*. Chapel Hill, NC: University of North Carolina Press.

Biddix, J. M., Fogel, C. I., & Perry Black, B. (2013). Comfort levels of active duty gay/bisexual male service members in the military healthcare system. *Military Medicine, 178*(12), 1335–1340.

Bonilla, D. (2002). *Facts and figures on the "Don't Ask, Don't Tell" Statute*. Palm Center. Retrieved from http://www.palmcenter.org/press/dadt/in_print/facts_and_figures_on_the_dont_ask_dont_tell_statute.

Burrelli, D. F., & Feder, J. (2009). *Homosexuals and the U.S. military: Current issues* (RL30113). Washington, DC: Congressional Research Service.

Burrelli, D. F. (1994). An overview of the debate on homosexuals in the U.S. military. In W.J. Scott & S.C. Stanley (Eds.). *Gays and lesbians in the military: Issues, concerns, and contrasts* (pp.17–32). New York: Aldine de Gruyter Press.

Campbell, D. A. (2013). Women's lives in wartime: The American Civil War and World War II. In J. M. Wilmoth & A. S. London (Eds.). *Life course perspectives on military service* (pp. 48–67). New York: Routledge.

Department of Defense [DoD]. (2010). *Report of the comprehensive review of the issues associated with a repeal of "don't ask, don't tell."* Washington, D.C.

D'Emilio, J. (2002). *The world turned: Essays on gay history, politics, and culture.* Duke University Press.

Fausto-Sterling, A. (2012). *Sex/gender: Biology in a social world.* London: Routledge.

Gates, G.J. (2010). *Lesbian, gay, and bisexual men and women in the U.S. military: Updated estimates.* The Williams Institute at the UCLA School of Law.

General Accounting Office. (1992). *Defense force management: DOD's policy on homosexuality.* Washington, DC: Author. (Document GAO/NSIAD-92–98).

Goldbach, J.T. & Castro, C. A. (2016). Lesbian, Gay, Bisexual, and Transgender (LGBT) Service Members: Life after Don't Ask, Don't Tell. *Current psychiatry reports, 18*(6), 1–7.

Goldberg, A. E., & Garcia, R. (2015). Predictors of relationship dissolution in lesbian, gay, and heterosexual adoptive parents. *Journal of Family Psychology, 29*(3), 394–404.

Goldberg, A.E. & Smith, J. Z. (2011). Stigma, social context, and mental health: Lesbian and gay couples across the transition to adoptive parenthood. *Journal of Counseling Psychology, 58*(1), 139–150.

Greentree V. W, Bradbard, D., Dagher, L., Lee, K., Levingston, K., LoRe, C. E., . . . & Resnick, S. (2013). Military Family Lifestyle Survey. Retrieved from http://mldc.whs.mil/public/docs/report/pr/BSF_2013-Military-Families-Lifestyle-Survey-Comprehensive-Report.pdf.

Herek, G. M., & Garnets, L. D. (2007). Sexual orientation and mental health. *Annual Review of Clinical Psychology,* 3, 353–375.

Herek, G. M., Gillis, J. R., & Cogan, J. C. (2015). Internalized stigma among sexual minority adults: Insights from a social psychological perspective. *Stigma and Health,* Vol 1(S), 18–34.

Herek, G. (1996). Social science, sexual orientation, and military personnel policy. In G. Herek, J.Jobe, & R. Carney (Eds.), *Out in Force: Sexual Orientation and the Military* (pp. 3–14). Chicago: University of Chicago Press.

Herek, G. M. (2009). Sexual stigma and sexual prejudice in the United States: A conceptual framework. In J. Bailey & D. Hope (Eds.), *Contemporary perspectives on lesbian, gay, and bisexual identities* (pp. 65–111). Springer.

Katz, J.N. (1992). *Gay American history: Lesbians and gay men in the U.S.A.* New York: Meridian.

Lever, J. & Kanouse, D. (1994). Sexual orientation and proscribed sexual behaviors. In G. Herek, J.Jobe, & R. Carney (Eds.), *Out in Force: Sexual Orientation and the Military* (pp. 15–38). Chicago: University of Chicago Press.

Lick, D. J., Tornello, S. L., Riskind, R. G., Schmidt, K. M., & Patterson, C. J. (2012). Social climate for sexual minorities predicts well-being among heterosexual off-spring of lesbian and gay parents. *Sexuality Research and Social Policy, 9*(2), 99–112.

Lindsay, J., Perlesz, A., Brown, R., McNair, R., De Vaus, D., & Pitts, M. (2006). Stigma or respect: Lesbian-parented families negotiating school settings. *Sociology, 40*(6), 1059–1077.

MacCoun, R.J.. (1996). Social science, sexual orientation, and military personnel policy. In G. Herek, J. Jobe, & R. Carney (Eds.), *Out in force: Sexual orientation and the military* (pp. 157–176). Chicago: University of Chicago Press.

Maze, Rick. (2013, June 28). Same-sex marriage: 18 questions answered. *Air Force Times.*

Meyer, I. H. (2003). Prejudice, social stress, and mental health in lesbian, gay, and bisexual populations: Conceptual issues and research evidence. *Psychological Bulletin, 129*(5), 674–697.

Moore, M. R., & Stambolis-Ruhstorfer, M. (2013). LGBT sexuality and families at the start of the twenty-first century. *Annual Review of Sociology*, 39, 491–507.

National Defense Research Institute. (1993). *Sexual orientation and U.S. military personnel policy: Options and assessment.* Santa Monica, CA: RAND.

Oswald, R.F., & Sternberg, M.M. (2014). Lesbian, gay, and bisexual military families: Visible but legally marginalized. In S. MacDermid Wadsworth & D.S. Riggs (Eds.) *Military deployment and its consequences for families (pp. 133–147).* New York: Springer.

Palm Center (2007). Military fires three more gay Arabic linguists as shortfall continues. Retrieved from http://archive.palmcenter.org/press/dadt/releases/military_fires_three_more_gay_arabic_linguists_as_shortfall_continues.

Palm Center (2009). *Countries that allow military service by openly gay people.* Palmcenter.org. Retrieved from http://archive.palmcenter.org/files/active/0/CountriesWithoutBan.pdf.

Patterson, C. J. (2009). Children of lesbian and gay parents: Psychology, law, and policy. *American Psychologist, 64*(8), 727–736.

Perry, R. M. (2015). *Obergefell v. Hodges: Same-sex marriage legalized.* Congressional Research Service Report, R44143.

Taylor, P. (2013). *A survey of LGBT Americans: attitudes, experiences and values in changing times.* Pew Research Center: Washington, DC. Retrieved from http://www.pewsocialtrends.org/files/2013/06/SDT_LGBT-Americans_06–2013.pdf.

Sarbin, T.R. (1996). Social science, sexual orientation, and military personnel policy. In G. Herek, J. Jobe, & R. Carney (Eds.), *Out in force: Sexual orientation and the military* (pp. 177–196). Chicago: University of Chicago Press.

Segal, M.W. (1986). The military and the family as greedy institutions. *Armed Forces & Society, 13*(1), 9–38.

Segal, D.R., Gade, P. A., & Johnson, E. M. (1994). An overview of the debate on homosexuals in the U.S. military. In W.J. Scott & S.C. Stanley (Eds.). *Gays and lesbians in the military: Issues, concerns, and contrasts* (pp.33–52). New York: Aldine de Gruyter Press.

Segal, D.R., & Kestnbaum, M. (2002). Professional closure in the military labor market: A critique of pure cohesion. In L.Matthews (Ed.) *The future of the Army profession.* (pp. 441–458). Boston: McGraw-Hill.

Segal, M. W., & Bourg, C. (2002). Professional leadership and diversity in the Army. In D. M. Snider, G.L.Watkins, & L.J. Matthews (Eds.), *The Future of the Army Profession* (pp. 505–520). New York: McGraw Hill.

Shilts, R. (1994). *Conduct unbecoming.* New York: Ballantine Books.

Smith, A. M. (2014). Same-sex marriage: A legal background after United States v. Windsor. *Current Politics and Economics of the United States, Canada and Mexico, 16*(1), 1–8.

Spitzer, R. L. (1981). The diagnostic status of homosexuality in DSM-III: A reformulation of the issues. *American Journal of Psychiatry, 138*(2): 210–215.

Tornello, S. L., & Patterson, C. J. (2015). Timing of parenthood and experiences of gay fathers: A life course perspective. *Journal of LGBT Family Studies, 11*(1), 35–56.

U.S. Department of Defense, Support to the DoD comprehensive review working group analyzing the impact of repealing 'Don't Ask, Don't Tell,' *Volume 1: Findings From the Surveys.* Pentagon, Washington, DC, November 2010.

van Dam, M. A. A. (2004). Mothers in two types of lesbian families: Stigma experiences, supports, and burdens. *Journal of Family Nursing, 10*(4), 450–484.

Weber, G. N. (2008). Using to numb the pain: Substance use and abuse among lesbian, gay, and bisexual individuals. *Journal of Mental Health Counseling, 30*(1), 31–48.

Wright, J. L. (2013). *Further guidance on extending benefits to same-sex spouses of military members* [Memorandum]. Washington, D.C.: Office of the Undersecretary of Defense. Retrieved from https://www.army.mil/e2/c/downloads/321863.pdf.

Chapter 8

The Integration of Trans People into the Military

Judith E. Rosenstein

On June 30, 2016, US Secretary of Defense, Ash Carter announced that transgender military service members may now serve openly (Department of Defense, 2016b). The United States joins at least 18 other countries in allowing transgender service members to serve their country (Elders, Brown, Coleman, Kolditz, & Steinman, 2015).

This policy shift directly impacts the estimated up to 15,500 trans people on active duty or in the Guards or Reserves, not to mention transgender family members (Gates & Herman, 2014). While the exact number of transgender people in the United States is unknown, estimates consistently put the number as less than one percent, with one report offering the estimate of up to 1.4 million transgender people in the United States (Flores, Herman, Gates, & Brown, 2016, Schaefer et al., 2016). With trans people becoming more comfortable revealing their gender identity, the chance that each of us will know someone who is transgender increases. They may be in our units (if you are a service member), they may be friends or family, or they may be family members of people we know.

The aim of this chapter is to provide background on what it means to be transgender; review concerns that have been raised regarding allowing open transgender people to serve in the military, along with relevant research; and offer suggestions for how commanders can best serve their transgender service members or transgender family members. This chapter will cover definitions, discuss various cultural ideas about transgender people, touch on the history of trans people in the United States both broadly and in the military, provide an overview of the process many transgender people go through to transition from one gender to another, and offer some suggestions for creating an inclusive work space. While some policies will be discussed, that is not the focus of the chapter, nor have they been fully articulated.

WHAT DOES "TRANS" MEAN?

The terminology related to sex, gender, and sexuality is varied and can be confusing. In this section I will define some of the basic terms.

Sex, "biological sex," "sex at birth," "assigned sex," or "assigned gender" is the sex someone is born with. It is biological, largely determined by chromosomes (e.g., XX, XY) and hormones, and is primarily reflected in genitalia. While we tend to consider sex to be binary (i.e., male, female), there are people who are born intersex.[1] Intersex people are "born with a reproductive or sexual anatomy that doesn't seem to fit the typical definitions of female or male" (Intersex Society of North America, n.d.-b). There are a variety of forms of intersexuality, but some include people with chromosomal combinations other than XX and XY (e.g., X0, XXY), people with XX or XY chromosomes whose body does not process hormones correctly (e.g., androgen insensitivity disorder, congenital adrenal hyperplasia), and people who have ambiguous genitalia (e.g., a very large clitoris, a very small penis, etc.). Sometimes intersexuality is apparent at birth, sometimes it becomes noticeable later in life (e.g., puberty), and sometimes people never know (Intersex Society of North America, n.d.-a).

Gender, in contrast, is cultural or social; it is what it means to be a man or a woman (or whatever categories are relevant) in a given society. While in the United States there are two widely recognized genders, referred to as the gender binary, that we generally expect to correlate with a person's assigned sex at birth (i.e., men are masculine and women are feminine), there is significant global variation. This is easy enough to see, for example, when looking at standard "normal," expected behavior for men in the US versus men in the Middle East. Moreover, many societies have a third or even fourth gender, as will be discussed later.

How we identify, the label we give ourselves, is our gender identity. While most people are born with congruence between their biological sex and gender identity (called cisgender or cissexual), such that people assigned male at birth identify as men, and people assigned female at birth identify as women, there are some people for whom these labels do not fit. These people may identify as agender, genderfluid, genderqueer, transsexual, transgender, or something else. People who are agender do not identify as having a gender, people who are genderfluid have a gender identify that varies by time and/or place, while people who are genderqueer do not identify with conventional definitions of gender. What genderqueer means can vary by person, so some people who identify as genderqueer may identify as neither man nor woman or a combination of the two, while others may identify as genderless (i.e., agender) or genderfluid. Transsexuals are people who feel that their physical body does not match their gender identity (i.e., they are in the wrong body), consequently many want to live as the gender with which they identify; they want to transition (Brown & Rounsley, 1996). While some trans people undergo surgery, many more take hormones, and some rely strictly on clothes and make-up. As far as terminology, trans men are people assigned female at birth and identify as men (sometimes referred to as FTM, female-to-male), while trans women are people assigned male at birth and identify as women (sometimes referred to as MTF, male-to-female). "Trans" refers to people being transgender or transsexual, and "man"/"woman" refers to the gender with which they identify.

Transgender, or trans, is an umbrella term that includes the "full range of individuals who have a conflict with or question about their gender" (Brown & Rounsley, 1996, p. 18). At its broadest, the spectrum includes people who are questioning; those who cross-dress[2] (regardless of their own identification); people who do not identify with the gender they were assigned at birth, but still live as their assigned gender; all the way to people who completely transition (Brown & Rounsley, 1996; Stryker, 2008). At this point, it does not appear that the military is considering the full transgender spectrum, but instead focusing on transsexuals.

The final component is sexuality. Sexuality is about sexual desire (attraction), sexual behavior, and/or sexual identity. Some categories with which people identify include gay, lesbian, bisexual, heterosexual, pansexual (attraction not based on potential partner's sex or gender), and asexual (not interested in sex at all or not sexually attracted to other people). Sexuality is distinct and independent from both biological sex and gender (Stryker, 2008). For instance, just like cis people, trans people may be attracted to and/or have sex with men, women, men and women, or trans people (Stryker, 2008).

BACKGROUND AND HISTORY

Transgender in a Global Context

The idea that some people want to live in ways inconsistent with societal dictates for their sex assigned at birth is not new. For instance, in places with strict rules about gendered behavior, living as a man sometimes meant greater freedom for women, regardless of whether they actually identified as a man (Feinberg, 1996; Stryker, 2008). Even in places like 17th-19th century Europe where there were often harsh penalties for "cross dressing" (with the exception of socially sanctioned situations like festivals) there were people for whom it was a way of life (Feinberg, 1996). In some societies, women could become men to meet their family's need for a male figure, regardless of the individual's identity (e.g., the sworn virgins of the Balkans, woman/woman marriage among the Nandi [Nanda, 2000; Oboler, 1980]). Other societies have acknowledged that not everyone's identity matches the body in which they are born. In some of these societies, people assigned male at birth can become women and vice versa; while other societies have a third, or even fourth, gender category (e.g., hijras in India, katheoys in Thailand, māhū in Tahiti and Hawaii, fa'afafine in Samoa, nádleeh among the Navajo, alyha and hwame among the Mohave, hetaneman among the Cheyenne) (Nanda, 2000).

Transgender People in the United States

Within the United States, gender is largely viewed as binary. There are men and there are women. In the United States, there is evidence of people cross-dressing dating back to at least the Revolutionary War (Leonard, 1999). However, according to Stryker (2008), the 1850s were the first time policies were enacted to bar people from wearing clothes of the other sex. While variants of the term "transgender" started appearing in the late 1960s, it began to be more widely used in the early 1990s (Stryker, 2008). Transgender people have been gaining attention in the United States, most notably through Barbara Walters' interviews with transgender children, television shows such as *Orange is the New Black*, and celebrities like Laverne Cox and Caitlyn Jenner.

Laws and legislation regarding trans people vary dramatically across the country. So-called "bathroom bills," such as the one passed in North Carolina in February 2016 (commonly referred to as HB2), and laws allowing the denial of services for LGBT people based on religious grounds (e.g., Mississippi House Bill 1523, which was blocked by a federal judge on June 30, 2016 [Domonoske, 2016]) have been gaining in popularity. The frequent lack of legal protection for trans people is clear in that as of July 2016, only 20 states and the District of Columbia had laws prohibiting employment and housing discrimination based on gender identity, and 19 states and the District of Columbia had laws banning discrimination in public accommodations. Three states had laws prohibiting nondiscrimination laws or their enforcement (Movement Advancement Project, 2016). At the national level, the federal government considers gender identity protected against discrimination under Title VII of the Civil Rights Act of 1964, Title IX the Education Acts Amendment of 1972, and the Violence Against Women Reauthorization Act of 2013, according to a letter and subsequent lawsuit filed by the Justice Department against North Carolina's HB2 (Gupta, May 4, 2016).

Transitioning—What's Involved

Being transgender is not easy. Many trans people struggle with questions about their identity: Who am I? What am I? Why am I different? Then there are questions about who to tell and what to tell them: How will people react? What will loved ones say? These are legitimate concerns, as many trans people experience rejection and disownment from loved ones (Grant et al., 2011). Trans youth are especially vulnerable, and many end up on the street, homeless, after facing rejection from their families (Durso & Gates, 2012). The frequent questions, fear, shame, isolation, and self-hate that many trans people experience all contribute to explaining why about 41 percent of trans adults attempt suicide, in sharp contrast to less than 4 percent of the general population (Grant et al., 2011; Substance Abuse and Mental Health Services Administration, 2015).

When people identify as transgender they face a range of choices with how to proceed. While some people choose to do nothing, many others begin transitioning by dressing and presenting themselves as their identified gender, even if only on weekends (for many people this stage occurs before they come out to others). If they decide to start hormone replacement therapy (HRT), preferably under the care of a trained medical professional, their bodies will begin changing: breast growth, change in fat deposits (e.g., hips), facial and body hair growth, voice change, muscle development, etc. A small portion of people also elect surgical procedures (Grant et al., 2011). These are classified colloquially as "top" and "bottom" surgeries. Top surgeries, which can include facial procedures (e.g., shaving brow ridges, sharpening cheek bones), shaving the Adam's apple, and breast reduction or augmentation, are more common than bottom surgeries (e.g., genital removal and reconstruction).

Besides the not insignificant physical, emotional, and financial costs of medically transitioning, many trans people want to pass as their identified gender. If they want to pass, many trans people have to learn how to dress, how to walk, how to talk, how to apply make-up, and generally how to behave so that no one questions who they are. While not everyone wants to or even can pass, the consequences of not passing are potentially severe, as trans people are at significant risk of being targets of violence (Grant et al., 2011; Stotzer, 2009).

TRANSGENDER PEOPLE IN THE MILITARY

The United States

The US military's approach to gender identity differed from its approach to sexuality. Don't Ask, Don't Tell (DADT, 10 USC. § 654 [2010]) was specific to sexuality, so its repeal had no impact on transgender service members. Gender identity, in contrast to sexuality, has been encapsulated under

DoDI 6130.03 which provides medical accession standards (Department of Defense, 2010, incorporating change, September 12, 2011). According to DoDI 6130.03, "transsexualism" and "transvestism" ("psychosexual conditions") (Enclosure 4 29r) and "change of sex" (a "major abnormalit[y] or defect of the genitalia") (Enclosure 4 14f and 15r) prohibited accession, and were grounds for dismissal, involuntary separation, and denial of reenlistment/continuation (Department of Defense, 2016d).[3] (For more information see Elders & Steinman, 2014.) The idea that being transgender was a "psychosexual condition" stems, at least in part, from the American Psychiatric Association's former classification of gender dysphoria (GD) and gender nonconformity as mental illness in its *Diagnostic and Statistical Manual of Mental Disorders* (DSM-IV). However, in 2013 the DSM-5 was released and the classifications of gender dysphoria and gender non-conformity were changed so that they are no longer considered mental illnesses (Elders & Steinman, 2014), and will not in and of themselves be grounds for denying accession, involuntary separation, or denial of reenlistment/continuation. According to a memo released by the Secretary of Defense, DoDI 6130.03 will be updated no later than July 1, 2017 to reflect the revised policy (Department of Defense, 2016b).

The DoD instruction 1300.28 outlines the new policy regarding transgender service members (Department of Defense, 2016a). Effective immediately, people will no longer be discharged, involuntarily separated, or denied reenlistment for being transgender (Department of Defense, 2016b). As of September 30, 2016 service members for whom transitioning is medically necessary (determined by a military medical provider) are allowed to transition and upon transitioning will be subject to the standards of their preferred gender (e.g., uniform and grooming, PRT, etc.) (Department of Defense, 2016a, 2016c, 2016d). The *Transgender service in the US military: An implementation handbook* (Department of Defense, 2016c) provides guidance to transitioning service members and commanders on the transition process and requirements and respective roles and responsibilities. As previously mentioned DoDI 6130.03 (medical accession standards) will be updated no later than July 1, 2017 (Department of Defense, 2016b).

Within the US Armed Forces, there is evidence that gender non-conformists have served since the Revolutionary War. The majority appear to be women who served as men. Whether these people would identify as transgender as we now understand it, is unclear. Since women could not serve in the military, some clearly cross-dressed to appear as men and later resumed life as women again after leaving the military. While others lived out the remainder of their lives as men, and might today define themselves as transgender (Leonard, 1999). More recently, there are numerous examples of trans people who served in the military and transitioned after leaving, with some attempting, usually unsuccessfully, to reenlist post transition (Whittle, 2007).

One interesting case involved Sister Mary Elizabeth who served in the US Navy and Navy Reserve for 17 years as a man. She transitioned following her discharge in the early 1970s, reenlisted with the Army Reserve openly identifying herself as a transgender woman, and was later discharged based on medical fitness standards (see Whittle, 2007).

In May 2015, MAJ Jamie Lee Henry became the first known active duty military service member to be granted a name and gender change within the US military (Geidner, 2015). Since then, some openly transgender service members have received support from their commands, while others have faced discharge, and yet others are in limbo ("Let transgender troops serve openly [Editorial]," 2015). For those on hormones, this limbo can mean having the physical characteristics of the gender with which they identify (e.g., facial hair, breasts, etc.), but having to adhere to the uniform and grooming standards of their sex at birth (Eilperin, 2015).

Recent estimates from RAND suggest that there up to 10,790 people on active duty or in the selected reserves, with the number possibly much lower (Schaefer et al., 2016).[4] According to data from the National Transgender Discrimination Survey, transgender individuals are twice as likely to serve in the US military than cisgender individuals (Grant et al., 2011). Although trans people were not previously allowed to serve openly, 35 percent of trans veterans who tried were able to update their discharge papers (DD Form 215[5]) to reflect their change in gender. An even smaller number were recently able to change their DD 214 to reflect their correct name and gender (Grant et al., 2011; LGBT Bar, 2015). This appears likely to change immediately with the new policy (Department of Defense, 2016d).

There is limited research on the experiences of transgender people in the US Armed Forces. In a small study of transgender personnel, participants indicated a range of experiences including both supportive and unsupportive leadership and colleagues, challenges navigating the military's gendered regulations (e.g., uniform and grooming standards, pronoun and titles, etc.), and the need to make extra effort to prove oneself professionally (Parco, Levy, & Spears, 2014).

In a separate paper, Parco and colleagues present a case study of a transgender woman, a "former [US] military officer in an active-duty military context" (2016, p. 5). As a civilian federal employee, the study subject was allowed to transition and be openly transgender in a military environment. While not all coworkers were equally comfortable with her transition, the workplace remained professional, and the woman described the "experience as 'very positive'" (p. 8). The authors attribute this success to leaders guided by policy, who lead by example (p. 10).

Strong leadership is also likely to be essential in broader military contexts. In a survey comparing attitudes of military academy cadets to civilian students and ROTC cadets, Ender, Rohall, and Matthews (2016) found that while the majority of all students believed there would be no impact on their job if they had transgender colleagues, the future military officers were more supportive of a military ban on trans people than civilian students.

Militaries around the Globe

According to Elders and her colleagues (Elders et al., 2015), there are at least 18 countries that allow transgender people to serve openly in the military: Australia, Austria, Belgium, Bolivia, Canada, Czech Republic, Denmark, Estonia, Finland, France, Germany, Israel, Netherlands, New Zealand, Norway, Spain, Sweden, and United Kingdom, (n. 1 p. 212). While there is variation in how these countries approach transgender military service, along with cultural differences, there is much we can learn from them. (See Yerke & Mitchell, 2013 for an overview of different military models.)

CONCERNS OVER TRANS PEOPLE IN MILITARY SERVICE

Many concerns have been presented about allowing transgender people to serve in the US armed forces. In this section I will review some of those concerns and briefly discuss relevant evidence and research. Much of the evidence draws on the experiences of other militaries which do allow transgender people to serve.

Unit Cohesion and Effectiveness

As with other forms of integration, a commonly expressed concern about allowing transgender people to serve openly is unit cohesion and effectiveness. Following an analysis of the Canadian Forces, Okros and Scott (2015) report that "all available evidence suggests that Canada's decision to allow transgender individuals to serve openly did not compromise operational effectiveness" (pp. 252–3). While the report by Okros and Scott is one of the only documentation on the impact of open transgender military service, Ross (2014) notes that "of the countries that allow transgender service members, none have reversed that decision" (p. 207). Moreover, in a study examining the impact of LGBT military members' sexual orientation concealment and disclosure, Moradi (2009) determined that disclosure of sexual orientation was associated with perceptions of higher social and task cohesion, and concealment with perceptions of lower social and task cohesion.

Within US operations, transgender civilian contractors have deployed and been embedded with US troops in a variety of conflict zones (Fulton, Robinson, & Tannehill, 2015). More importantly, some deployed transgender service members have been out to their units with no identified adverse impact on unit performance (Dawson, 2015).

Medical Concerns

Issues related to medical care are a common concern raised when discussing allowing transgender people to serve in the military. These issues can be broken down into three categories: mental health of trans service members, implementation and impact of administering hormone replacement therapy, and implementation and impact of surgical procedures. (See Elders et al., 2015 and Elders & Steinman, 2014 for a more complete discussion.)

While mental health is a significant concern for all military service members, many trans people suffer from significant distress (e.g., depression, suicidal ideation, etc.) due to the incongruence of their identity and assigned sex. However, evidence indicates that addressing the incongruence can significantly alleviate the dysphoria (Coleman et al., 2012; Parco et al., 2014). For many people, transitioning through the use of hormones and/or surgery can address mental health concerns.

Another concern is the implementation and impact of hormone replacement therapy on a service member's ability to perform their job. First, it is worth noting that many cisgender service members take hormones for a variety of medical conditions and they are not barred from service (Elders & Steinman, 2014). Moreover, cross-sex hormone therapy has a low risk of complications (Elders et al., 2015). As with any medication regime, there can be a period of adjustment, but once that has been achieved, hormone therapy is likely to have little impact on service members' ability to deploy (Elders & Steinman, 2014).

Surgical gender reassignment procedures are similar to other surgical procedures in that they require a recovery period and personnel would not be deployable during this time (Elders et al., 2015). In the long run, barring any complications, service members should be able to return to full duty status. Based on experiences of other militaries, transgender service members are likely to not be deployable for medical reasons for less than six months (Fulton et al., 2015).

According to new guidance, service members are to receive "all medically necessary care related to their gender transition," with specifics to follow (Department of Defense, 2016d, p. 1). There is as of yet, no information on what will be available to family members; however, transition related medical care will likely be covered, as to do otherwise may be in violation of the Affordable Care Act (Belkin, personal communication).

As for accessions, starting in July 2017, people with gender dysphoria will be allowed to access if medical providers determine they are clinically stable

for 18 months. For those people who have begun or completed transitioning, they will be allowed to access if they have completed medical treatment
(including surgery if applicable) and/or received hormones and been stable
for 18 months (Department of Defense, 2016a).

Barracks, Berthing, and Bathrooms

Some of the most common questions people ask when discussing trans people
serving openly in the military are "Where will they sleep?" and "Which bathroom will they use?" Within the civilian sector, bathroom usage has received
more attention than housing. Supporters of allowing trans people to use the
bathroom of their choice contend that it is about equal protection (i.e., nondiscrimination) (Steinmetz, 2016). Opposition appears to be largely centered
around fear of predators in women's restrooms, privacy concerns, and belief
in the immutability of sex/gender (e.g., FoxNews.com, 2016; Sprigg, 2010).
Contrary to safety concerns, there is little evidence that cisgender people are
at particular risk when transgender people use the same bathroom. In fact,
the reverse is true—transgender people are more likely to be at risk in public
restrooms than cisgender people (Herman, 2013).

Lodging has been discussed less than bathrooms. In an examination of
transgender student experiences on college campuses, Seelman (2014)
reports that a high number of students were "not allowed to access gender-
appropriate housing . . . and/or appropriate bathrooms and other facilities" (p.
198); moreover, being denied access to bathrooms and lodging was associated with a greater likelihood of attempted suicide (Seelman, 2016). Fears
expressed about lodging are the same as those about bathrooms. Evidence
from transgender-inclusive homeless shelters indicates that there is no difference in the types of assaults committed by trans and cisgender women and
no evidence of cisgender men wearing women's clothing to gain admittance
to women's housing (Mottet & Ohle, 2006).

According to DoDI 1300.28, when people have completed their transition
(defined as when they change their gender marker in DEERS and are "recognized in the preferred gender") they "will use those berthing, bathroom,
and shower facilities associated with the preferred gender" (Department of
Defense, 2016a, p. 7). This is consistent with policies of other militaries
(Palm Center, 2013). Commanders are offered the additional guidance that
they are to "employ reasonable accommodations . . . to respect the privacy
interests of Service members" (Department of Defense, 2016c, p. 29).

Physical Fitness

Another concern about full inclusion of trans people into the military involves
physical fitness standards and whether trans people should be required to

meet the standards for their sex at birth or their identified gender. While gender neutral standards should not be an issue, standards that differ by gender might raise a question of fairness. Transgender US service members "will be responsible for meeting all applicable military standards in the preferred gender" once they have completed their transition, as described above (Department of Defense, 2016a, p. 7). Similarly, Australia, Canada, and the UK all require trans people who have been on HRT to meet the standards of their identified gender (Palm Center, 2013), which is consistent with NCAA and International Olympic Committee policies for transgender athletes (International Olympic Committee, 2015; NCAA, 2011). This makes sense, because hormones modify a person's physiology (including increasing or decreasing muscle mass) initial competitive advantages associated with being born male are significantly reduced or eliminated and the converse for females (Gooren & Bunck, 2004).

CREATING AN INCLUSIVE WORK SPACE

The new policy makes it clear that transgender service members are now welcome to serve openly in the military (Department of Defense, 2016a). However, all of the specifics of this integration have not yet been articulated. While forthcoming instruction will certainly be developed, we can also look to other sectors for direction, such as guidelines for civilian federal employees and materials produced for the Australian Defense Force (ADF, Australian Air Force, 2013; Australian Department of Defence, 2011; Office of Personnel Management, 2011). The remainder of this chapter will examine those best practices that have not already been addressed, offer insight into additional issues that may arise for transgender service members, and suggest ways that military leaders can best serve trans service members and trans family members.

Leadership

In many ways, recommendations for leader behavior when there is a trans person in the unit are no different than for any other form of diversity. Two essential recommendations for leaders identified by Parco et al. (2016), which are echoed in the ADF materials, are "collaborating with the transgender member as soon as it becomes known that he or she desires to transition" and "[modeling] behavioral expectations without fanfare" (p. 10). Additional leadership challenges include ensuring confidentiality and privacy, as well as minimizing and addressing gossip and rumors (Office of Personnel Management, 2011).

Communication in all directions is important. Not only do the leader and the person transitioning need to be conversing, but the leader also needs to be open to communication and questions from others in the unit. It is appropriate and desirable to ask a trans person what name and pronouns they want. Once it is known that a person in the unit is transgender, at least initially, there are likely to be questions. It may prove useful to have open dialogue about what this means and what will happen. However, communication with the unit needs to be managed so as to ensure the person's privacy and squash gossip and rumors.

Language

Language can prove particularly challenging as it is so entrenched. At the same time, appropriate language shows respect, while intentional misuse can not only be hurtful, but may constitute harassment.

The best practice is to use the name, title, and pronouns with which the person identifies (Office of Personnel Management, 2011; Parco et al., 2016). This may be most challenging when the person identifies with pronouns inconsistent with traditional grammar (e.g., "it," "they," and "them") or not commonly used (e.g., "xe," "sie," "hir"). It may take some time to become accustomed to using new pronouns, names, etc., especially if the person was known prior to their transition. That is understandable. However, the *intentional* misuse of names and pronouns is highly disrespectful and often painful to an individual and may "be construed as sexual harassment" (Palm Center, 2013, p. 6; see also Office of Personnel Management, 2011).

It is also worth keeping in mind that "trans" and "transgender" are adjectives rather than nouns (GLAAD, n.d.; Palm Center, 2013). It is both grammatically incorrect and inappropriate to refer to "transgenders" or someone as "transgendered" (GLAAD, n.d.). Instead, we should refer to "transgender people," "transgender men," "trans men," "transgender women," or "trans women," etc.

Finally, as always, be alert for derogatory terms and language. Problematic terms and terminology largely unique to transgender people include, but are not limited to: "tranny," "she-male," "it," "he/she," "shim," "deceptive," "fooling," "pretending," "posing," "trap," "masquerading," and "chicks with dicks" (GLAAD, n.d.; Mottet & Ohle, 2006).

Situational Awareness

Outside of the relatively controlled military environment, there may be challenges that trans service members and civilians may face. If, as a leader, one is aware of these situational problems it may be possible to mitigate or address them with minimal negative impact.

The level of protection afforded transgender people varies dramatically by country and region. As previously mentioned, the majority of US states do not offer protection from discrimination for people who are transgender. Moreover, less than half of the states with hate crime laws include protection for trans people (Movement Advancement Project, 2016). A number of states have explicit policies that penalize or even criminalize trans people living and acting in accordance with their affirmed gender (e.g., North Carolina). Regardless of formal policies, trans people report high levels of discrimination and harassment (Grant et al., 2011). Around the world, nations offer different levels of protection for trans people. The State Department recommends reviewing country information before travel (e.g., US Department of State)

Within the US many trans people have had negative experiences with staff at airports, including harassment and discrimination (Grant et al., 2011). Besides the resulting stress of such experiences, they can also delay travel and cause travelers to miss their flights (Queally, 2015).

Negative experiences with medical care are common for trans people. In the National Transgender Discrimination Survey, 19 percent of respondents were refused medical care, 28 percent were harassed in "medical settings," and 50 percent had to educate their "medical providers about transgender care" (Grant et al., 2011, p. 72). One egregious case garnered national attention. In 1995 Tyra Hunter, a 24 year old trans woman, was in a car accident in Washington D.C. Upon discovering that she had male genitalia emergency medical staff made derogatory remarks and were reported to have withdrawn care. Hunter later died at a local hospital and courts ruled that her death was due to mistreatment by emergency medical workers and malpractice at the hospital (Bowles, 1995; GLAA, 2000). While trans military members and their families often receive routine medical care through the military, where they will hopefully not receive negative treatment, emergency medical care is a concern.

For children who identify as trans or are otherwise gender non-conforming, schools can be a particularly challenging experience. Grant and colleagues concluded that "harassment and discrimination against transgender and gender non-conforming students is severe and pervasive in [grades K-12]" (Grant et al., 2011, p. 46). Of those surveyed, three quarters of students experienced harassment or bullying by other students, more than a third were assaulted by other students, and almost a third experienced harassment by teachers (Grant et al., 2011). Negative treatment continues into higher education (Grant et al., 2011).

RECOMMENDATIONS FOR LEADERS AND TRANS SERVICE MEMBERS

Recommendations for interacting with trans people are fairly straightforward and fundamentally similar to general recommendations for good leader behavior. Beyond those discussed below, the *Transgender service in the US military: An implementation handbook* (Department of Defense, 2016c) offers additional tips from allied foreign military services.

It is important to be respectful and humble. While this may seem obvious, in the context of trans people, this specifically means using the name and pronouns with which a person identifies. It is okay to make mistakes—but afterwards, acknowledge, apologize, and correct.

Ask questions. Many questions are acceptable and appropriate. What pronouns do you use? What do you need from me? What can I do to support you personally and professionally? How can I help you best integrate into the unit? How do we help you perform at your best? Is there anything I need to know? What concerns do you have? Note, that it is generally inappropriate to ask about a person's body (e.g., what "parts" they have). Similarly, encourage conversation and dialogue as appropriate and necessary, with the individual and the unit. This may involve seeking and providing education.

Pay attention to language, so as to avoid outing someone and to be alert for rumors and gossip. If rumors or gossip do occur, then they need to be addressed. This is no different than other topics/issues. Depending on the situation, conversation and/or further education might be warranted.

Be aware of situations or environments that may pose particular challenges for trans service members or their families, such as location, travel, medical care, etc. As previously discussed, there are many situations that may prove challenging for trans people that are not challenging for cisgender people.

The *Transgender service in the US military: An implementation handbook* (Department of Defense, 2016c) also offers guidance for transitioning service members about the process of transitioning while in-service and suggestions with interactions with superiors and peers. These recommendations include "being open and honest with leadership" (p. 20) and communication with colleagues, including some considerations about disclosing one's gender identity. Transitioning service members are also advised to find a mentor for the transition process. This mentor can then offer guidance and support on transition related issues/decisions, including considering the impact a transition will have on one's career and assignments. Additional tips from allied foreign military services include "honesty," "being professional," "empowering those around you," "being confident," "trust," and "planning" (Department of Defense, 2016c, pp. 22–23).

NOTES

1. Estimates of the number of people who are intersex vary, with one estimate going as high as 2 percent of live births (Blackless et al., 2000).
2. Cross-dressing is the process of wearing clothes of another gender.

3. Many people who are intersex are also disqualified due to "hermaphroditism" and "pseudohermaphroditism" (Enclosure 4 14f and 15r). The new policy does not appear to change accession standards for people who are intersex.

4. These estimates are lower than those reported by Gates and Herman (2014), who estimated 15,500 trans people on active duty or in the Guards or Reserves, and more than 134,000 transgender veterans and retired service members.

5. DD Form 215 is used to correct or update DD Form 214, through an addendum, although it does not impact the original DD 214 (http://www.dd214.com/dd214_dd_form_215).

REFERENCES

10 U.S. Code, § 654 (2010).

Australian Air Force. (2013). *Air Force diversity handbook: Transitioning gender in Air Force.* Air Force Workforce Diversity, April.

Australian Department of Defence. (2011). *Understanding transitioning gender in the workplace.*

Blackless, M., Charuvastra, A., Derryck, A., Fausto-Sterling, A., Lauzanne, K., & Lee, E. (2000). How sexually dimorphic are we? Review and synthesis. *American Journal of Human Biology, 12*(2), 151–166.

Bowles, S. (1995, December 10). A death robbed of dignity mobilizes community. *The Washington Post.* Retrieved July 7, 2016 from https://www.washington-post.com/archive/local/1995/12/10/a-death-robbed-of-dignity-mobilizes-a-community/2ca40566–9d67–47a2–80f2-e5756b2753a6/

Brown, M. L., & Rounsley, C. A. (1996). *True selves: Understanding transsexualism . . . : For family, friends, coworkers, and helping professionals.* San Francisco, CA: Jossey-Bass Inc Pub.

Coleman, E., Bockting, W., Botzer, M., Cohen-Kettenis, P., DeCuypere, G., Feldman, J., . . . Meyer, W. J. (2012). Standards of care for the health of transsexual, transgender, and gender-nonconforming people, version 7. *International Journal of Transgenderism, 13*(4), 165–232. doi:10.1080/15532739.2011.700873

Dawson, F. (Director). (2015). Transgender, at war and in love. F. Dawson, G. Silverman, & J. Coughlin (Producer): New York Times. Retrieved July 11, 2016, http://www.transmilitary.org/watch/

Department of Defense. (2010, incorporating change, September 12, 2011). *Medical standards for appointment, enlistment, or induction in the military services (DoD Instruction 6130.03).* Washington, D.C.: Author. Retrieved July 8, 2016 from http://www.dtic.mil/whs/directives/corres/pdf/613003p.pdf

Department of Defense. (2016a). *In-service transition for transgender service members (DoD Instruction 1300.28).* Washington, D.C.: Author. Retrieved July 8, 2016 from http://www.defense.gov/Portals/1/features/2016/0616_policy/DoD-Instruction-1300.28.pdf

Department of Defense. (2016b). Secretary of Defense Ash Carter announces policy for transgender service members [Press release]. Retrieved July 1, 2016 from http://www.defense.gov/News/News-Releases/News-Release-View/

Article/821675/secretary-of-defense-ash-carter-announces-policy-for-transgender-service-members

Department of Defense. (2016c). *Transgender service in the U.S. military: An implementation handbook*. Author. from http://www.defense.gov/News/Special-Reports/0616_transgender-policy

Department of Defense. (2016d). Transgender service member policy implementation fact sheet. Retrieved July 1, 2016 from http://www.defense.gov/Portals/1/features/2016/0616_policy/Transgender-Implementation-Fact-Sheet.pdf

Domonoske, C. (2016). Judge blocks Mississippi law protecting religious objections to gay marriage. Retrieved July 1, 2016 from http://www.npr.org/sections/thetwo-way/2016/07/01/484291451/judge-blocks-mississippi-law-protecting-religious-objections-to-gay-marriage

Durso, L. E., & Gates, G. J. (2012). *Serving our youth: Findings from a national survey of services providers working with lesbian, gay, bisexual and transgender youth who are homeless or at risk of becoming homeless*. Los Angeles: The Williams Institute with True Colors Fund and The Palette Fund.

Eilperin, J. (2015). Transgender in the military: A Pentagon in transition weighs its policy. *The Washington Post*. Retrieved May 10, 2016 from https://www.washingtonpost.com/politics/transgender-in-the-military-a-pentagon-in-transition-weighs-its-policy/2015/04/09/ee0ca39e-cf0d-11e4–8c54-ffb5ba6f2f69_story.html

Elders, J., Brown, G. R., Coleman, E., Kolditz, T. A., & Steinman, A. M. (2015). Medical aspects of transgender military service. *Armed Forces & Society, 41*(2), 199–220. doi:10.1177/0095327X14545625

Elders, J., & Steinman, A. M. (2014). *Report of the transgender military service commission*. Palm Center.

Ender, M. G., Rohall, D. E., & Matthews, M. D. (2016). Research note: Cadet and civilian undergraduate attitudes toward transgender people. *Armed Forces & Society*, 427–435. doi:10.1177/0095327X15575278

Feinberg, L. (1996). *Transgender warriors: Making history from Joan of Arc to RuPaul*. Boston: Beacon Press.

Flores, A. R., Herman, J. L., Gates, G. J., & Brown, T. N. T. (2016). *How many adults identify as transgender in the United States*. Los Angeles, CA: The Williams Institute. Retrieved July 12, 2016 from http://williamsinstitute.law.ucla.edu/research/how-many-adults-identify-as-transgender-in-the-united-states/

FoxNews.com. (2016). North Carolina Gov. McCrory responds to "bathroom bill" backlash. Retrieved June 17, 2016 from http://www.foxnews.com/politics/2016/04/29/north-carolina-gov-mccrory-responds-to-bathroom-bill-backlash.html

Fulton, B. S., Robinson, A. D., & Tannehill, B. (2015). Transgender military service: Frequently asked questions. Retrieved June 28, 2016 from http://www.spartapride.org/learn_more

Gates, G. J., & Herman, J. L. (2014). *Transgender in the military service in the United States*. The Williams Institute. Retrieved May 10, 2016 from http://williamsinstitute.law.ucla.edu/research/military-related/us-transgender-military-service/

Geidner, C. (2015, June 8). The first out transgender active duty U.S. army officer: "My story is not unique". *BuzzFeed*. Retrieved September 16, 2015 from https://

www.buzzfeed.com/chrisgeidner/the-first-out-transgender-active-duty-us-army-officer-my-sto?utm_term=.tx5abq95#.lx6qebRd

GLAA. (2000). District settles Hunter lawsuit for $1.75 million [Press release]. Retrieved July 7, 2016 from http://www.glaa.org/archive/2000/tyrasettlement0810.shtml

GLAAD. (n.d.). GLAAD media reference guide—transgender issues. Retrieved June 29, 2016 from http://www.glaad.org/reference/transgender

Gooren, L. J. G., & Bunck, M. C. M. (2004). Transsexuals and competitive sports. *European Journal of Endocrinology, 151*(4), 425–429.

Grant, J. M., Mottet, L., Tanis, J. E., Harrison, J., Herman, J., & Keisling, M. (2011). *Injustice at every turn: A report of the national transgender discrimination survey.* Washington, D.C.: National Center for Transgender Equality and National Gay and Lesbian Task Force.

Gupta, V. (May 4, 2016). *Letter to Governor Pat McCrory.* Washington, D.C. Retrieved May 11, 2016 from https://www.documentcloud.org/documents/2823498-Doj-Letter-Nc.html

Herman, J. L. (2013). Gendered restrooms and minority stress: The public regulation of gender and its impact on transgender people's lives. *Journal of Public Management & Social Policy, 19*(1), 65–80.

International Olympic Committee. (2015). *IOC consensus meeting on sex reassignment and hyperandrogenism.* Lausanne, Switzerland. Retrieved June 28, 2016

Intersex Society of North America. (n.d.-a). Retrieved May 9, 2016 from http://www.isna.org/

Intersex Society of North America. (n.d.-b). What is intersex? Retrieved May 9, 2016 from http://www.isna.org/faq/what_is_intersex

Leonard, E. D. (1999). *All the daring of the soldier: Women of the Civil War armies* (Vol. 1). New York: W.W. Norton & Co.

Let transgender troops serve openly [Editorial]. (2015, June 4). *New York Times.* Retrieved May 10, 2016 from http://www.nytimes.com/2015/06/04/opinion/let-transgender-troops-serve-openly.html

LGBT Bar. (2015). LGBT Bar announces legal victory for transgender veterans [Press release]. Retrieved June 16, 2016 from http://us1.campaign-archive2.com/?u=0d4bedbf3d0ee0b80639584c0&id=9ea4556598

Moradi, B. (2009). Sexual orientation disclosure, concealment, harassment, and military cohesion: Perceptions of LGBT military veterans. *Military Psychology, 21*(4), 513–533. doi:10.1080/08995600903206453

Mottet, L., & Ohle, J. (2006). Transitioning our shelters: Making homeless shelters safe for transgender people. *Journal of Poverty, 10*(2), 77–101. doi:10.1300/J134v10n02_05

Movement Advancement Project. (2016). Equality maps: Non-discrimination laws. Retrieved July 11, 2016 from http://www.lgbtmap.org/equality-maps/non_discrimination_laws

Nanda, S. (2000). *Gender diversity: Crosscultural variations.* Long Grove, IL: Waveland Press.

NCAA. (2011). *NCAA inclusion of transgender student-athletes* Retrieved June 28, 2016 from http://www.ncaapublications.com/p-4335-ncaa-inclusion-of-transgender-student-athletes.aspx

Oboler, R. S. (1980). Is the female husband a man? Woman/woman marriage among the Nandi of Kenya. *Ethnology, 19*(1), 69–88.

Office of Personnel Management. (2011). *Guidance regarding the employment of transgender individuals in the federal workplace.* Retrieved June 20, 2016 from https://www.opm.gov/policy-data-oversight/diversity-and-inclusion/reference-materials/gender-identity-guidance/

Okros, A., & Scott, D. (2015). Gender identity in the Canadian Forces: A review of possible impacts on operational effectiveness. *Armed Forces & Society, 41*(2), 243–256. doi:10.1177/0095327X14535371

Palm Center. (2013). *Overview of regulations for transgender military personnel from the UK, Canada, and Australia.* San Francisco, CA.

Parco, J. E., Levy, D. A., & Spears, S. R. (2014). Transgender military personnel in the post-DADT repeal era: A phenomenological study. *Armed Forces & Society,* 221–242. doi:10.1177/0095327X14530112

Parco, J. E., Levy, D. A., & Spears, S. R. (2016). Beyond DADT repeal: Transgender evolution within the US military. *International Journal of Transgenderism, 17*(1), 4–13. doi:10.1080/15532739.2015.1095669

Queally, J. (2015, September 22). Transgender woman says TSA detained, humiliated her over body "anomaly". *Los Angeles Times.* Retrieved June 29, 2016 from http://www.latimes.com/nation/nationnow/la-na-nn-tsa-transgender-20150921-story.html

Ross, A. (2014). The invisible army: Why the military needs to rescind its ban on transgender service members. *Southern California Interdisciplinary Law Journal, 23,* 185–215.

Schaefer, A. G., Iyengar, R., Kadiyala, S., Engel, C. C., Kavanagh, J., Williams, K. M., & Kress, A. M. (2016). *Assessing the Implications of Allowing Transgender Personnel to Serve Openly.* Santa Monica, CA: Rand Corporation.

Seelman, K. L. (2014). Transgender individuals' access to college housing and bathrooms: Findings from the National Transgender Discrimination Survey. *Journal of Gay & Lesbian Social Services, 26*(2), 186–206.

Seelman, K. L. (2016). Transgender adults' access to college bathrooms and housing and the relationship to suicidality. *Journal of Homosexuality,* 1–22. doi:10.1080/00918369.2016.1157998

Sprigg, P. (2010). "Gender identity" protections ("bathroom bills"). Retrieved June 17, 2016 from http://www.frc.org/onepagers/gender-identity-protections-bathroom-bills

Steinmetz, K. (2016, May 2). Why LGBT advocates say bathrom "predators" argument is a red herring. *Time.* Retrieved June 17, 2016 http://time.com/4314896/transgender-bathroom-bill-male-predators-argument/

Stotzer, R. L. (2009). Violence against transgender people: A review of United States data. *Aggression and Violent Behavior, 14*(3), 170–179. doi:10.1016/j.avb.2009.01.006

Stryker, S. (2008). *Transgender history.* Berkeley, CA: Seal Press.

Substance Abuse and Mental Health Services Administration. (2015). *Results from the 2013 national survey on drug use and health: Mental health findings.* (NSDUH

Series H-49, HHS Publication No. (SMA) 14–4887). Rockville, MD: Substance Abuse and Mental Health Services Administration.

U.S. Department of State. LGBTI travel information. Retrieved July 7, 2016 from https://travel.state.gov/content/passports/en/go/lgbt.html

Whittle, S. (2007). Military service. In J. Barrett (Ed.), *Transsexual and other disorders of gender identity: A practical guide to management* (pp. 269–276). New York: Radcliffe Publishing.

Yerke, A. F., & Mitchell, V. (2013). Transgender people in the military: Don't ask? Don't tell? Don't enlist! *Journal of Homosexuality, 60*(2–3), 436–457. doi:10.1080 /00918369.2013.744933

Additional Resources

Department of Defense. (2016). *Transgender service in the U.S. military: An implementation handbook*. Author. Available at http://www.defense.gov/News/ Special-Reports/0616_transgender-policy.

Department of Defense Instruction 1300.28. *In-service transition for transgender service members*. http://www.defense.gov/Portals/1/features/2016/0616_policy/ DoD-Instruction-1300.28.pdf.

Intersex Society of North America (http://www.isna.org/). An organization advocating for intersex people.

SPART*A (http://www.spartapride.org/, https://www.facebook.com/SPARTA-ArmedForces). An organization for LGBT military service members, veterans, families, and allies.

Transgender American Veterans Association (TAVA) (http://transveteran.org/). An organization focused on transgender veterans.

Chapter 9

Religious Diversity in the US Armed Forces

Michelle Sandhoff

Military service and religion have a long history together. Considering medieval combat through World War I, Keegan (1976) argued that religious ritual has historically been common in the preparation for battle. Watson (2006) described the religious practices of British and German troops in World War I, and in their study of American soldiers in World War II, Stouffer et al. (1949) identified prayer as a common strategy for coping with combat.

In the United States, religion has always been a part of the military. Within weeks of the establishment of what would become the US Army in 1775, a chaplain corps was established (Murray, 2009). The roles of military chaplains have shifted over the years; in some eras chaplains were charged with motivating troops in combat, in others with addressing social problems like racism or public health concerns such as substance abuse. Chaplains have also been seen as important for improving the quality of life for service members (Loveland, 2004). Although the specific roles of chaplains have shifted, religion has long been seen as a way to enhance the power of the US military; serving as what Waggoner (2014) refers to as "a multiplier of military force" (p. 702).

The importance of religious diversity to the US military can be understood in two ways: as necessary for social legitimacy and as a practical tool for achieving the mission. The military is a representative of the nation and its values. Religious freedom is a defining concept for the United States, and as such, the military must be seen to embody this ideal in order to continue to be accepted as legitimate. Greenslit (2006) commented on this, "If a widespread perception emerges, both among the American public and the international community, that religious freedom is lacking in our military, then America's moral standing among the community of nations is diminished" (p. 2). Within this context, the military has intensely grappled with questions of what religious freedom means for those in the service.

The second broad reason why religious diversity plays an important role in the US military relates to practicalities such as recruitment and retention. Huerta and Webb (2001) characterized religious accommodations in the military as a way to boost morale among recruits. Similarly Hansen (2012) argued that religious accommodation is important because it enables the service of minorities and also demonstrates the acceptance and inclusion of a diverse American population. Recent conflicts have also made it increasingly clear that religious diversity has benefits for achieving the military mission. Carlson (2008) argued that "getting religion" is essential to military success in contemporary conflicts:

> If one lesson of Vietnam was that winning hearts and minds was essential to victory in counterinsurgency warfare, then the emerging corollary from the Iraq War and other struggles in the global war against terror may be that getting religion is central to winning those hearts and minds (p. 87).

Although religion has a long history in the US military, it has also at times been contested. The most famous example was in the 1980s when two Harvard law students brought a case against the Department of Defense (DoD) arguing that the use of federal money to maintain the military chaplaincy was a violation of the Establishment Clause of the Constitution. In the resultant case *Katcoff v. Marsh* (1985), the US Court of Appeals for the Second Circuit ruled that the existence of the chaplaincy does not violate the Establishment Clause and deferred to the legislative branch, which has consistently affirmed the existence of the military chaplaincy by providing funding. During the case, the Army argued that the military chaplaincy protected first amendment rights of service members to free exercise of religion (Hansen, 2012).

RELIGIOUS DIVERSITY IN THE US MILITARY

The military reflects the religious diversity found throughout the United States. Table 9.1 presents data on the religious diversity of the active duty force and of the general US population. The religious composition of the armed forces is similar to the population as a whole. The majority of both service members and Americans generally identify as Christian, rates of unbelief and no religious preference are similar across the populations,

Table 9.1   Religious Diversity

	Active-duty force (Jan 2015)	US population (2014)
Christian (total)*	70.9%	70.6%
Catholic	19.6%	20.8%
Protestant	23.5%	46.5%
No denominational preference	26.5%	N/A
Latter Day Saints (LDS)	1.3%	1.6%
Atheist/agnostic/no religious preference	22.0%	22.8%
Judaism	0.4%	1.9%
Islam	0.3%	0.9%
Buddhism, Hinduism, and other religions**	0.6%	1.7%
Other faiths	N/A	1.5%
Unclassified/unknown	5.8%	0.6%

*In the Pew data, total Christian population includes measures for Orthodox Christians (0.5%), Jehovah's Witnesses (0.8%) and other Christians (0.4%), which are not included here.
**Kamarck uses the category "Buddhism, Hinduism, and other eastern religions" while Pew reports separate data for Buddhist (0.7%), Hindu (0.7%), other world religions (0.3%), and includes an additional category "other faiths" (1.5%) that includes Unitarians, New Age religions, Native American religions, and others.
Sources: For active duty forces: Kamarck, K. N. (2015). Diversity, inclusion, and equal opportunity in the armed services: Background issues for Congress. Congressional Research Service 7–5700. Retrieved from: https://www.fas.org/sgp/crs/natsec/R44321.pdf; For US Population: Pew Research Center. (2015). America's changing religious landscape. Retrieved from http://www.pewforum.org/2015/05/12/americas-changing-religious-landscape/.

while minority religious traditions such as Judaism, Islam, Buddhism, and Hinduism are slightly underrepresented in the military.

Military Chaplaincy

To become a military chaplain, an individual must meet military requirements of education, age, and fitness and be endorsed by a recognized civilian faith group (Hansen, 2012). The endorsement requirement in particular can pose a barrier for minority religious groups that do not have the formal hierarchical structure of many Christian denominations. For example, aspiring chaplains who are Buddhist, Hindu, Muslim, and Pagan may have few or no recognized endorsing agencies.

Today, chaplains overrepresent evangelical Protestant faith groups (Townsend, 2011). This mismatch reflects shifts in the civilian world. There has been declining interest in religious service, including military chaplaincy, among Catholic and mainline Protestant groups; additionally some Protestant groups have experienced reduced interest in military chaplaincy due to ideological opposition to the current conflicts. While Catholics and mainline

Protestants have struggled to provide chaplains to the military, evangelical groups have not. Ideological differences in worldview, growth in evangelical communities generally, combined with encouragement for evangelicals to see the military as a mission field has led to an abundance of evangelical chaplains in the military.

Despite these challenges, the military chaplaincy has seen dramatic increases in diversity recently. As Hansen (2012) reported, 175 different religious groups had chaplains by 2009. Buddhist, Hindu, and Muslim chaplains were commissioned in the 1990s and 2000s. Other groups such as Wiccans and Humanists have submitted candidates, but as of the time of writing have not successfully had a chaplain commissioned.

There are far fewer chaplains than service members, and, especially for smaller religious faiths, chaplains are spread thin. For regular worship and community-building, lay leaders play and important role. These volunteer service members are not members of the clergy but are approved by the military and/or their religious groups to provide some religious services. Service members may also be directed to the civilian community for their religious needs where feasible.

Religious Accommodation

Freedom of religious practice and encouragement of worship are traditions in the US military. Hansen (2012) explained:

> While military personnel surrender some of their basic rights when they enlist, such as the right to trial by jury, the right to free exercise of religion is not one they have to give up. Allowing military personnel to worship as they please, or almost as they please, while in uniform is considered helpful for recruitment and retention, as well as for morale (p. 37).

The needs of the military have been legally established to have greater authority than the individual right to religious freedom. The Supreme Court has ruled that although military service members retain their first amendment rights, they can be limited for military necessity, "the Court is not saying what military necessity is and under what conditions military commanders can evoke military necessity to limit the free exercise or religion. Currently, the interpretation and decision is determined by the commander" (Huerta & Webb, 2001, p. 86). DoD issued a directive on religious accommodation (1300.17) in 1988; a modified version of the instruction remains in effect. The policy allows accommodation that does not interfere with military necessity: "Requests for religious accommodation [. . .] will be approved when accommodation would not adversely affect mission accomplishment, including military readiness, unit cohesion, good order, discipline, health and safety, or any other military requirement" (Department of Defense, 2014, p. 4e).

THE CHALLENGES OF RELIGIOUS DIVERSITY

In the following section I provide an overview to some common religious accommodation issues. This section is designed as an overview and is not a comprehensive consideration of all religious accommodation issues that may be encountered. It is important to keep in mind that religions are internally diverse; not everyone who identifies with a specific religion will have the same needs. The issue of internal diversity has been addressed by the Supreme Court with regard to religious accommodation in the military, "practices based on religious conviction, even if not universally followed, are protected by the free exercise clause" (*Goldman v. Secretary of Defense,* 1984, para. 8). This means that it is individual conviction that matters, not the majority opinion within the religious community.

As I examine the following religious accommodation issues, several themes will be become apparent. In debating diverse religious accommodations, concerns about cohesion, morale, and safety repeatedly arise as individuals and the courts try to determine the balance between free exercise of religion and good order and discipline in the military setting.

Uniformity and Religious Expression

Uniformity is an important characteristic of the military. This is also an area where religious diversity is likely to be visible as many religious traditions require or encourage appearance or apparel that is not a part of the US military uniform. An area where religious accommodation has been an issue is grooming standards, specifically military requirements that males maintain short hair and be clean shaven. Growing a beard is common religious practice among Jews, Muslims, and Sikhs. Additionally, Sikh men wear their hair long and tied in a turban. Religious meanings of these practices vary. Jews often grow beards based on religious laws that prohibit using a razor to shave the face and as a marker of Jewish identity. Muslim men often grow a beard as a *sunnah* practice, meaning it is a way to emulate the Prophet Muhammad. Sikhs are enjoined to wear their hair unshorn, a practice referred to as *kes,* as a way of respecting God's creation.

Until 1974, Jewish and Sikh service members were allowed to wear beards for religious reasons. However, in the 1980s, stricter appearance standards ended this practice. Those service members already serving were allowed to retain their beards, but all new recruits had to seek individual exceptions. These were generally denied. The first person to be granted an exception was Major Kamaljeet Singh Kalsi who, in 2009, was allowed to wear a beard and turban. It took Kalsi two years to be granted the special exception by the Army (Dao, 2013). Kalsi expressed his frustration with the difficulty of getting the accommodation, "asking a person to choose between religion and country, that's not who we are as a nation. We're better than that. We can be Sikhs and soldiers at the same time" (Dao, 2013). Following Kalsi, a handful of others have been granted the same accommodation. Those granted the accommodation have generally had particular leverage as experts in needed fields such as medicine or language (Dao, 2013).

The military rationale for denying accommodation for beards focuses on the potential detrimental effects of nonuniformity on morale and cohesion as well as safety concerns, particularly concerns that beards would prevent a gas mask from functioning properly and that a helmet would not fit over a turban (Dao, 2013). The recent acceptance of accommodations for beards and turbans raises questions about the validity of the concerns used to deny these accommodations for so long. In 2015, a US district court judge rejected the safety justification noting that thousands of service members are allowed to grow beards due to medical conditions (Philipps, 2015). Additionally, the British, Canadian, and Indian militaries all permit Sikhs to wear long hair, turbans, and beards and they have not found issues with safety or morale (Dao, 2013).

A common example of religious apparel is headwear. Examples of religious headwear include the Jewish *yarmulke* or *kippa*, the skullcap called a *kufi* or *taqiyah* worn by some Muslim men, the Sikh turban, *hijab* worn by some Muslim women, and *tichel* worn by some Jewish women. The religious reasons for wearing these vary, but often relate to ideas of modesty and acknowledgement of an omnipresent God.

A pivotal legal case was fought over accommodations for wearing a yarmulke in the 1980s. Simcha Goldman began his military career as a chaplain in the Navy in 1970 and in 1977 joined the Air Force as a psychologist. An Orthodox Jew, Goldman wore a yarmulke while in uniform. While the yarmulke was not an issue for many years, in 1981 the installation commander prohibited Goldman from wearing his yarmulke. Goldman refused to remove it and was threatened with court-martial. Goldman filed suit arguing that his first amendment rights were violated by this order. The subsequent legal case traveled through the US District Court for the District of Columbia, The US Court of Appeals for the District of Columbia Circuit, and finally to the Supreme Court. The Air Force provided several arguments in defense of the prohibition, including that allowing Goldman to wear a yarmulke would "crush the spirit of uniformity, which in turn will weaken the will and fighting ability of the Air Force" (affidavit submitted by Major General Emanuel as cited in Levine, 2010, p. 214). They also raised safety concerns, specifically that unauthorized headgear "might fly into a jet engine and cause it to malfunction and explode" (testimony by General Usher as cited in Levine, 2010, p. 215). In 1986, the Supreme Court ruled 5–4 in favor of the Air Force explicitly deferring to the military's "professional judgment" that strict uniformity of dress was a military necessary (*Goldman v. Secretary of Defense*, 1984).

This ruling against religious accommodation in uniform was quickly challenged by Congress. The 1985 Defense Authorization Bill included the requirement that the Secretary of Defense form a study group "to examine ways to minimize the potential conflict between the interests of members of the Armed Forces in abiding by their religious tenets and the military interest in maintaining discipline" (Sullivan, 1988, p. 137). The study group raised concerns about group cohesion and safety, issues that continue to define discussions of religious accommodation in the military. After failed attempts to legislate a requirement for accommodation of religious apparel in 1986 and 1987, the 1988 Defense Authorization Bill included a religious apparel accommodation provision that granted service members the right to wear "neat and conservative" religious apparel while in uniform, while giving the service secretaries discretion in determining specific apparel that would be allowed or disallowed (Sullivan, 1988). In 2014, this policy was revised in a way that has made it easier for service members to receive permission for accommodations in grooming standards and for religious apparel (Defense, 2014). For example, the current policy allows Sikh men to wear a smaller turban, which can fit under their helmets when in ACUs, and while in garrison a black turban in place of a beret (Kappler, 2010).

Women who want to cover their head have routinely been denied this accommodation until recently. As with other religious headgear, justifications for this prohibition included morale, cohesion, and safety. For example, in 1996, a spokesperson for a base where two service members were denied permission to wear hijab explained the denial as a concern about dehydration and safety around equipment where the scarf could be caught (Jowers, 1996). As with the Sikh turban, the armed forces and police forces of other nations have demonstrated that there are practical ways to accommodate head covering. Police in Australia, Britain, Canada, Norway, and Sweden are allowed to wear hijab (Meehan, 2009). American service women in Afghanistan and Iraq are also permitted to wear a headscarf while in uniform, a policy that has been defended by the DoD as something that can help these women achieve their mission (Shaughnessy, 2011). The 2014 updates to military religious accommodation policy allow requests to wear hijab in uniform to be made and they will be evaluated on a case-by-case basis (Somers, 2014).

Some religions encourage members to wear specific undergarments (e.g., *kachera* worn by some Sikhs or the Latter Day Saints [LDS] *Temple Garments*). These items will generally fit under the military uniform and so seem to raise few issues. The LDS Church even produces special Temple Garments for military members that are designed to meet military requirements (Church of Jesus Christ of Latter-Day Saints, n.d.).

Religious requirements of dress can also include nonclothing items. For example, Sikh men are expected to carry a ceremonial dagger (*kirpan*) and to wear a steel bracelet (*karha*). I have found no information about how these religious requirements are treated in the military.

Dietary restrictions are another common area where religious accommodation issues are relevant. Some dietary restrictions take the form of rules about what can be eaten, such as requirements that food be halal, kosher, or vegetarian. Another form of dietary restriction is fasting, which is practiced in many different ways.

Everyday dietary restrictions are varied. Some religious groups encourage vegetarianism, others encourage practitioners to follow strict ritual guidelines such as kosher (*kashrut*). A common challenge for service members is avoiding meat and particularly pork. Pork is a common ingredient in military meals, and pork grease may be used to flavor side dishes; shared serving utensils are also common. Some groups expect members to abstain only from particular substances (e.g., alcohol or caffeine). Some of these may seem very unusual for those outside the faith, for example, LDS are encouraged to avoid "hot drinks."[1]

A service member unable to eat the food regularly served at the installation may be able to get "com rats," extra cash allowing them to buy their own food. However, com rats are not feasible while the service member is in the field or at sea. Kosher, halal, and vegetarian MREs (meals ready to eat) are available if a request is made. It is the chaplain's responsibility to make sure the unit deploys with appropriate MREs (Hansen, 2012).

Religious fasting takes a myriad of forms. For some religious groups, fasting refers to abstaining from particular ingredients, most commonly meat. For example, during Lent, Catholics abstain from meat on Fridays. Some Buddhists also abstain from meat at set times in the lunar calendar.

Fasting can also take the form of limiting intake of food. For example, LDS are encouraged to fast one Sunday per month by abstaining from food and drink for two consecutive meals (Church of Jesus Christ of Latter Day Saints, 2011). In Catholicism, Ash Wednesday and Good Friday are fast days during which worshippers eat one full, but meatless, meal as well as smaller meals or snacks that combined are less than a full meal (US Conference of Catholic Bishops, n.d.). Some Buddhists also practice a similar form of fasting by eating only one meal (generally consumed before noon). Protestant traditions of fasting tend to be less formalized and are largely defined by the individual.

Judaism and Islam practice highly ritualized and strict fasting. The holiest day of the year in Jewish tradition is Yom Kippur (Day of Atonement), which occurs in autumn. This day is marked with a twenty-four-hour fast in which worshippers abstain from all food and drink. The fast also includes limitations about what clothing can be worn (e.g., wearing leather shoes is prohibited) (Urkin & Naimer, 2015). In Islam, the month of Ramadan is marked by abstaining from all food and drink from dawn until sunset. This usually lasts for twenty-eight to thirty days. Because the Islamic calendar is lunar, Ramadan does not occur at the same time every year.

The possibility of accommodation and the form it takes varies depending on the type of fast. In previous work on Muslims in the military, I found two basic approaches: service members who accommodated their religious practice to their military duties, for example, fasting only on days they had lighter duties, and those who accommodated their military duties to their religious practice, for example, by seeking formal accommodation to complete the fast (Sandhoff, 2013). For those whose duties permit it, a possible accommodation is rescheduling physical training (PT) to a time when the individual can consume water. For example, one of the Muslim service members in my study was allowed to complete her PT at the gym after the fast ended for the day, but was still required to attend early morning PT where she passed out water and recorded run times. This allowed her to practice her religion while not excluding her from the group (Sandhoff, 2013).

In general the use of controlled substances by service members is prohibited, even as part of their religious practice. The one exception to this is the ritual use of peyote by members of the Native American Church. In 1997 peyote use was approved for service members who are enrolled tribal members and members of a Native American Church. Peyote use must occur off-base and must be stopped at least twenty-four hours before returning to duty (Brooke, 1997).

Worship and Ritual

Different faith groups have very different forms of worship. In this section, I outline some common ritual practices with a focus on what tools, space, and accommodations might be necessary.

Christian rituals are likely the most familiar in the US setting, but it is important to recognize the diversity within these traditions. In an attempt to address this diversity, the military often divides Christianity (and Christian chaplains) into three groups: Catholics, liturgical Protestants (abbreviated as LitProts), and nonliturgical protestants (NonLitProts). Hansen (2012) described the differences:

> LitProts tend to come from denominations where the clergy wear vestments, whose worship follows a set order, and where worship is typically solemn and peaceful. They include Episcopalians, most Lutherans, and many Methodists. [. . .] NonLitProts are more likely to preach in a business suit than robes and to conduct spontaneous worship services that are enthusiastic, even boisterous. They include the Assemblies of God and most Baptists (p. 171).

These different groups (and the different denominations within them) will have specific needs in terms of space and ritual items for their religious practice.

Communion (also called the Eucharist by Catholics, Anglicans, Lutherans, Orthodox, and Presbyterians) is a common Christian ceremony in which the Last Supper is commemorated through ritualized eating and drinking. The form of this ritual and the elements required vary across denominations. For example, Catholic use a wheat-based wafer referred to as the "host" and sacramental wine, Baptists tend to use bread and grape juice, while LDS use bread and water. The frequency of the ritual also varies; Catholics may partake in communion up to twice a day. Many denominations offer communion at least once a week; Baptists and Lutherans often observe the ritual once of month while Jehovah's Witnesses practice it only once per year. There is also variation in whether communion is "open" (meaning it is available to all Christians) or limited to members of the specific group.

Baptism is another common Christian ritual practice with variation across denominations. Some denominations practice infant baptism and others eschew the practice and only baptize those who are old enough to profess their faith (the lower limit varies, e.g., LDS set the minimum age at eight while some Baptist groups recommend waiting until the child is at least a teenager). The distinction between denominations that practice infant baptism and those that reject it is a meaningful one within the military where Christian chaplains are often divided into "baby-baptizers" a common name for Catholic and liturgical Protestant chaplains and "nonbaby-baptizers." Hansen (2012) jokingly commented on the predilection for acronyms in the military, "I consider it a near miracle that no one has reduced this to NonBabBap" (p. 171). The method of baptism also varies, the most common methods are sprinkling or pouring water on the head or full immersion. These differences may matter if the military chapel contains only a baptismal font, which is not designed for full immersion. This is interpreted by some as a bias toward Catholic and mainline Protestant practices (Hansen, 2012).

Jewish men are encouraged to pray three times a day: morning, afternoon, and nightfall. These prayers are highly ritualized. Men are expected to cover their head with a yarmulke or hat. Depending on the denomination and on which prayer is being offered, a prayer shawl (*tallit*) and *tefillin*, a set of black leather boxes that are tied to the forehead and arm, may be used. Jews generally read prayers from a prayer book, called a *siddur*. It is considered best to pray communally (*minyan*), which requires at least ten adults, something that may be difficult to arrange regularly in the military where Jews are a small minority. Women's ritual practice will vary depending on their denomination. Some interpret women's religious obligations to be the same as men, while others argue that women should observe distinct rituals.

Jews are enjoined to observe a weekly Sabbath, or day of rest. Sabbath (*Shabbat*) begins at nightfall on Friday and ends at nightfall on Saturday. Jews observe the Sabbath in a variety of ways, but common practices involve lighting of candles and recitation of prayers, partaking in a special meal, and avoiding labor during the twenty-four-hour period.

Muslims are enjoined to pray at fixed times of the day. To do this they require only access to water for ablutions (*wudu*), and a clean place to pray. It is common to use a prayer rug for this purpose. It is time rather than space that may need accommodation for Muslims in the military. Although the prayers themselves are quick (around five minutes) the timing may be difficult. The first prayer is before dawn, the second around noon, then the late afternoon, sundown, and about ninety minutes after sundown. In addition to daily prayers, Muslim men are expected to attend communal prayers on Friday. This is referred to as *jummah*. A possible accommodation is allowing Muslim service members to work on a Sunday rather than Friday or to grant the service member a break around midday. Jummah is not a whole-day requirement, but rather a midday sermon and prayer service that typically lasts an hour.

Buddhists are likely to engage in solitary practice, both as an aspect of the religion and as a practical issue given the small number of Buddhists in the military. These practices emphasize meditation and mindful contemplation of Buddhist teachings. Buddhist meditation can take many forms, the external requirements are quite similar although the internal experience varies. The meditator needs a location that is quiet (but not necessarily silent) where they will be undisturbed. The meditator may use cushions, pillows, bolsters or a chair to achieve a suitable posture. Where there is a community, communal services are often held weekly and include practices such as recitation, chanting, singing, religious education, and meditation. There is one dedicated Buddhist chapel in the US military, a 300-square-foot chapel specially constructed at the US Air Force Academy (Brady, 2009).

Hindu worship centers on a shrine. Most Hindu households have their own shrine, which vary in size and content. The primary form of Hindu worship is *puja* (adoration). Puja utilizes symbols for divinity, often an image or statue. Divine energy is ritually summoned to this object, which then becomes the focus of ritual adoration. Household puja is generally performed at least once a day. During the household puja it is common to wash and beautify any statues, and provide offerings of flowers, fruits, food, and incense. More elaborate and longer puja rituals are performed at temples where a priest conducts the puja and worshippers observe and then receive some of the food and water, which has been blessed by the deity (Smithsonian Institution, 1997).

Contemporary Paganism is extremely diverse; rituals vary depending on the specific faith tradition (often referred to as a "path"). Pagans may practice alone or with a group (sometimes called a *coven*). Pagan rituals often take place outdoors. Many Pagans use ceremonial tools in their worship. The most common are a disc or dish engraved with magickal[2] symbols, most commonly the five-pointed star called a pentacle, a chalice, and an athame (a ceremonial dagger). Barner (2008) warns that when stationed overseas, local laws may prohibit Pagan soldiers from bringing their religious objects. She recommends that when deploying, practitioners should assume they will have no ritual tools, or plan to make new tools from materials available. She gave an example of this:

> I've been told of one particularly effective ritual held in Baghdad, where the pentacle was drawn in the dust of the ground, the athame was one participant's utility knife, the wand was a piece of wooden debris, and the chalice was a CamelBak of water passed amongst the participants (p. 166).

Pagans may face challenges in finding space to worship on base. Hansen (2012) found that many chaplains did not allow Pagan groups to use the chapel. Pagans also face particular challenges in maintaining a community; study groups and covens can quickly dissipate as members are deployed or change duty station (Barner, 2008; Hansen, 2012).

Holidays and Celebrations

Holidays may also shape religious accommodation. Federal holidays reflect the Christian majority culture of the United States, for example, by recognizing Christmas as a legal holiday as well as through the structure of the Monday through Friday workweek with Sundays off. Recognizing the ways in which Christianity is assumed is important for being prepared to effectively include those of different faith backgrounds. Familiarity with the major holidays of diverse faiths is necessary for making sure ritual needs are met. If holidays will occur during a deployment, chaplains can prepare by stocking any necessary ritual elements ahead of time (Hansen, 2012).

One should also be aware of reinforcing Christian norms under the guise of neutrality. For example, it is common in the military and civilian society to host "holiday" parties in December. One of the Muslims interviewed by Sandhoff (2013) explained:

> Everybody tries to be politically correct now, it's no longer a Christmas party, it's a holiday party, but every holiday party has a Santa Claus and a [Christmas] tree. And I'm like really, a holiday party? [. . .] I was like, whose holiday is it? Whose holiday is in December? It's a Christmas party, we get it (p. 107).

There is not necessarily a problem with hosting a holiday party, and some non-Christians may enjoy attending these festivities. However, it should not be assumed that by removing the word "Christmas" the celebration is religiously neutral. More importantly, those of higher rank should be cautious about making these celebrations seem mandatory. Although some non-Christians[3] are happy to participate in these festivities, others will feel uncomfortable or even offended if they are required to attend.

Many faith traditions have predictable religious calendars for those who know to ask about them. For example, the Jewish calendar has aligned lunar and solar calendars so that holidays occur in the same season each year, though the exact date in the Gregorian calendar varies (Urkin & Naimer, 2015). Buddhism and Hinduism also tend to use a "lunisolar" calendar that aligns with the seasons of the Gregorian calendar. On the other hand, the Islamic calendar is solely lunar, meaning that annual holidays move relative to the Gregorian calendar.

The Pagan religious calendar is aligned with the seasons of the year, with the spring and autumn equinoxes and the summer and winter solstices typically celebrated as great festivals. These dates are fixed in the Gregorian calendar, which makes these holidays predictable (Barner, 2008).

End of Life, Funerary, and Burial Practices

End-of-life issues and funeral arrangements often bring discussions of religion to the forefront. Religion may influence the decisions patients make about end-of-life care, for example, decisions about the aggressiveness of care and the use of life support (Sharp, Carr, & Macdonald, 2012; Shinall & Guillamondegui, 2015). Religious beliefs may also influence organ donation and other decisions family members must make. DoD provides a casualty officer to help bereaved families; however, this person is likely to be unfamiliar with the beliefs and practices of minority faiths.

There are differences in beliefs and customs around death, how the body is handled, and funeral customs. Beliefs about the nature of the universe and the afterlife may shape end-of-life experiences, and are important to respect both for the dying and for surviving family and friends. The Abrahamaic faiths Judaism, Christianity, and Islam view the universe as linear in nature. Humans are born, live, die, and then enter the afterlife through various means. Faiths like Buddhism and Hinduism conceptualize the universe in a nonlinear fashion.

In Christianity there is general agreement about the existence of an afterlife, though the details of how this afterlife is reached vary. A fundamental disagreement between denominations is whether salvation is by "works" or "grace." As the majority religion in the United States, familiarity with some of these different views is generally high, and it is relatively easy to locate a chaplain or other religious leader who can provide specific guidance. Ritual practices surrounding death also vary. Catholics may practice "Last Rites," a set of sacraments including anointing, confession, and communion (this final administration of the Eucharist is referred to as *Viaticum*). Protestant practices at the time of death vary. It is common to have a religious leader present for at least some time during the end of life and for various prayers to be offered.

Funerary practices also vary. Burial and cremation are both generally accepted. The official Catholic rituals involve several separate funeral practices: the vigil service (also called the wake), the Funeral Mass, and the Rite of Committal. Traditionally, during the Funeral Mass the body or remains should be present and there is no eulogy (Bahr, 2015). Variation in Protestant practices include the expected mood of the funeral (grief, celebration of life, etc.), whether the remains are present, and whether there is a formal ceremony.

In Judaism, the emphasis is on the current life rather than the next, and religious law is followed as a way to improve life on earth, not as a way to achieve a better afterlife. Some Jews believe in an afterlife characterized by peace and tranquility in which one may reunite with God and departed loved one. Other Jews believe that there is no afterlife (Ponn, 1991).

In Jewish custom, a dying person should be constantly attended and never alone, and their comfort should be paramount. After death, the eyes and mouth should be closed, preferably by the son or closest relative, and the body is placed in a ritual position. These ritualistic practices are not important to all Jews, but the emphasis on care and constant attention that they demonstrate is generally valued. According to Jewish law, the body is to be buried, cremation is not generally accepted. Burial should occur as quickly as possible, although delays are allowed when the family must travel or when there are other logistical hurdles. The corpse is ritually cleansed (*tahara*), then dressed in a plain white shroud and buried in a plain wooden coffin. It is not customary to view the body. Flowers and music are generally limited. Funerals cannot occur during the Sabbath. The service is designed to evoke grief and sadness, and it is customary for mourners to express grief. The bereaved are expected to observe a formalized mourning period of three to seven days (referred to as "sitting shiva"); during this time the needs of the bereaved are attended to by friends and family (Ponn, 1991).

In the Islamic worldview good and bad deeds done during earthly life determine the fate in the afterlife, though entrance into heaven is understood to be through God's mercy. In Islamic tradition, heaven (*jannah*) is described as a garden and is conceptualized as a place of peace, pleasure, and fulfillment.

It is common for a dying person to be read to from the Qur'an. Some Muslims may give the dying person drops of water or honey as a way of fending off temptation from the devil (Idleman Smith, 1991). After death, the eyes and mouth are closed and, as in Jewish tradition, the body is placed in a ritual position. The body is ritually washed (*ghusl*); if possible relatives of the same gender as the deceased should be involved in this process. The body is then wrapped in a white shroud and placed in a simple wooden coffin (no coffin is preferred if it is allowed by local law). Serving as a pallbearer is considered a sign of piety, and multiple relatives and friends may wish to help in this process. Burial is the norm, and cremation is not generally practiced. Burial should occur within twenty-four hours if possible. The body is buried with the face in the direction of Mecca. Many Muslims believe that the body can still experience pain and so treatment of the corpse is careful. Expectations around mourning vary. Some believe that dramatic expressions of grief are forbidden in Islam; however, some Islamic cultures have highly ritualized mourning practices that include weeping and wailing (Idleman Smith, 1991).

Buddhist theology conceptualizes the universe in cyclical fashion, a beginning-less process of birth, death, and rebirth; it is only by achieving enlightenment (*bodhi*) that this cycle will end. At the time of death, consciousness gathers in the heart and then leaves the physical body. During this time, the dying person is expected to have eight visions, which correspond with consciousness leaving specific parts of the body. Discipline developed in life through meditation may allow the person to have some control over this process, perhaps even allowing them control over their next rebirth (Klein, 1991).

Family and friends are advised to say their farewells to the dying person, preferably without any displays of strong emotions, as they do not want the dying person to feel regret or longing, which could lead to an unfortunate rebirth. In Buddhism, the state of mind of the dying person is an important determinant of their rebirth. A religious teacher may read or recite to the dying person to remind them to remain calm and aware of approaching death. Prayers, mantra recitation, and incense may also be used at the end of life to calm the mind of the dying person. In Buddhism, there is no belief in a bodily resurrection, and the physical corpse is not considered to have special meaning. Cremation is common. Cremation or burial may be preceded by a wake, which may involve rituals such as chanting; alternatively, a memorial service may be held after cremation or burial. After death of the body, the consciousness remains in a state between death and rebirth for up to forty-nine days. Prayers are offered during this time to remind the deceased that they are in this intermediate state and to facilitate a fortunate rebirth (Klein, 1991).

Similarly, Hinduism conceptualizes existence as a cyclical process of birth, death, and rebirth. Hopkins (1992) explained, "Progress toward salvation is not, for most Hindus, a matter of a single lifetime, but a long-term process involving repeated rebirths until one reaches the necessary level of development" (p. 145). Liberation (*moksha*) from this cycle can be achieved by spiritual practice. Hindus tend to distinguish "good" deaths from "bad" deaths, and see this as being significant for the fate of the soul. A good death is one that occurs at the proper time and place. A sudden or traumatic death is often seen as a bad death; additionally the presence of feces, vomit, or urine at death is often seen as a sign of a bad death. To avoid this, some terminally ill patients will fast at the end of life (Firth, 2005).

Hymns or mantras may be sung or chanted to encourage the dying person to focus on God. If possible, the dying person should be laid on the ground with the head north. Due to the symbolic importance of the river Ganges, the Ganges water kept especially for this purpose may be offered to the dying person, and placed on the lips after death. Traditionally, the body is ritually washed (*abhisegam*), preferably by family members, placed in a ritual position, and shrouded in either white or red (depending on gender and marital status). It is common to hold a brief viewing of the body, which is followed by cremation. This should occur as soon as possible, customarily by the next dusk or dawn. After death the soul travels through a series of hells (and perhaps heavens) where it expiates its sins. Important rituals are required for surviving relatives in the days following death, culminating in a ritual on the twelfth day after death where the deceased relative is transformed into an ancestor (Firth, 2005).

Pagan beliefs about the nature of the universe and death are diverse. Some may identify with a linear conceptualization where life is followed by an afterlife; others subscribe to a cyclical conceptualization of life, death, and rebirth. As such, the rituals at end of life vary. It is demonstrably possible to combine pagan rituals with military rituals. Sgt. Patrick Stewart, a Wiccan member of the Nevada National Guard, was killed in Afghanistan in 2005. Stewart's widow, Roberta was supported by the Christian chaplain who served Stewart's unit and by Nevada's congressional delegation as she fought for the Wiccan pentacle to be recognized by the Department of Veterans Affairs (VA). Although it took several years to get the symbol recognized, Roberta was able to integrate Wiccan and military elements in the funeral. In Barner (2008), Roberta Stewart described the funeral:

> Patrick's funeral was military with full honors and I incorporated our Wiccan faith; a circle was cast and wrapped with red, white, and blue ribbon with one entry. The entry was lined with Indian rocks that Patrick had collected, and after they brought his casket in the circle the Honor Guard closed the circle with those rocks. It was the most beautiful ceremony. We had our spiritual advisor and friend along with other friends and the military speak. My local military and the state of Nevada truly honored our faith in all aspects of Patrick's death. They truly honored Patrick completely (Barner, 2008, p. 256).

For veterans buried in the cemeteries maintained by the VA, a government-approved religious symbol may be used to mark their grave (or used on other official memorials). The VA currently recognizes sixty-one "emblems of belief" that may be placed on the government-issued headstone of a veteran (National Cemetery Administration, 2015). In the past few years, the number of available emblems has dramatically increased. A decade ago, only thirty-eight symbols were recognized. In 2007, a group of Wiccan families took the VA to court over delays in approving a Wiccan symbol. The VA settled and approved the symbol and also streamlined the process of having new symbols approved (Banerjee, 2007). In addition to a variety of crosses, the Star of David, and an Islamic crescent, veterans and their families may now also select a Wiccan pentacle, a hammer of Thor, or an image of a dancing sandhill crane, a symbol added in 2013 as a personal representation of the relationship of an Oregon couple who hope others will also find meaning in the image (Francis, 2013).

CONCLUSION

Religious diversity is an important, if often overlooked, aspect of diversity in the US military. The freedom of religious practice is recognized as important for recruitment and retention and also as a form of social legitimacy. As a symbol of the American way of life at home and abroad, the military has a unique duty to uphold the values and ideals of the nation. In recent years, the importance of religious diversity and the associated necessity of accommodation have gained increased attention. As I have outlined here, the increased recognition of this diversity can be seen in changed policies that now make it easier for service members to request accommodations in grooming and uniform standards, increased inclusion of minority chaplains, and increased diversity in religious symbols used in military cemeteries.

By addressing the history of religious diversity in the US Armed Forces and by briefly introducing what some of that diversity of faith looks like in a practical way, I hope that this chapter will serve as a starting point for questions and discussions. Just as there are many differences between faith traditions, there are also many commonalities. By embracing these shared experiences while respecting the differences, the unique strengths of the American ideal of freedom of religion can be honored in the military.

NOTES

1. "Hot drinks" have been formally codified as tea and coffee; however, some interpret this to include all forms of coffee and tea regardless of caffeine content, others interpret it as a ban on caffeine which has led to a spirited ongoing debate about

whether caffeinated soda is permitted (Church of Jesus Christ of Latter Day Saints, 2002).

2. The spelling "magick" is used by many Pagans to distinguish their ritual practices from stage magic.

3. These comments primarily pertain to non-Christians; however some Christian groups do not celebrate Christmas, most notably Jehovah's Witnesses, as well as some Baptist and Pentecostal groups and Churches of Christ. Orthodox Christian churches celebrate Christmas using a different calendar, meaning it often occurs one to two weeks after December 25.

REFERENCES

Bahr, K. (2015). Good mourning. *U.S. Catholic, 80*(11), 12–17.

Banerjee, N. (2007, April 24). Use of Wiccan symbol on veterans' headstones is approved. *The New York Times*. Retrieved from http://www.nytimes. com/2007/04/24/washington/24wiccan.html?_r=1&

Barner, S. E. (2008). Faith and magick in the armed forces: A handbook for Pagans in the military. Woodbury, MN: Llewellyn Publications.

Brady, J. (2009, October 13). Military Buddhist chapel represents tolerance. *Morning Edition* Retrieved from http://www.npr.org/templates/story/story. php?storyId=113501618

Brooke, J. (1997, May 7). Military ends conflict of career and religion. *The New York Times*. Retrieved from http://www.nytimes.com/1997/05/07/us/military-ends-conflict-of-career-and-religion.html

Carlson, J. D. (2008). Winning souls and minds: The military's religion problem and the Global War on Terror. *Journal of Military Ethics, 7*(2), 85–101.

Church of Jesus Christ of Latter-Day Saints. (n.d.). Resources for Military Members. Retrieved from https://www.lds.org/callings/military-relations/resources-military-leaders

Church of Jesus Christ of Latter Day Saints. (2002). *Doctrine and Covenants Student Manual*. Retrieved from https://www.lds.org/manual/doctrine-and-covenants-student-manual/section-81–89/section-89-the-word-of-wisdom

Church of Jesus Christ of Latter Day Saints. (2011). *Gospel Principles*. Salt Lake City, UT: Intellectual Reserve, Inc. Retrieved from https://www.lds.org/manual/gospel-principles/chapter-25-fasting

Dao, J. (2013, July 9). Fitting faith into the army; Dress code is keeping Sikhs who want to enlist out of the U.S. military. *International Herald Tribune*.

Department of Defense. (2014). *Accommodation of religious practices within the military services*. (Number 1300.17). Retrieved from http://www.dtic.mil/whs/directives/corres/pdf/130017p.pdf

Firth, S. (2005). End-of-life: A Hindu view. *Lancet, 366*(9486), 682–686.

Francis, M. (2013, July 1). Coming to VA cemetery headstones: The sandhill crane. *The Oregonian*. Retrieved from http://www.oregonlive.com/pacific-northwest-news/index.ssf/2013/07/coming_to_va_cemetery_headston.html

Goldman v. Secretary of Defense. (Supreme Court 1984). Retrieved from http://openjurist.org/734/f2d/1531/goldman-v-secretary-of-defense

Greenslit, L. P. (2006). *Religion and the military: A growing ethical dilemma.* USAWC Strategy Research Project. Retrieved from http://handle.dtic.mil/100.2/ADA448671

Hansen, K. (2012). *Military chaplains and religious diversity.* London: Palgrave Macmillan.

Hopkins, T. (1992). Hindu views of death and afterlife. In H. Obayashi (Ed.), *Death and afterlife: Perspectives of world religions* (pp. 143–155). Santa Barbara, CA: Praeger.

Huerta, C. C. & Webb, S. C. (2001). Religious accommodation in the military. In Dansby, M. R., Stewart, J. B., and Webb, S. C. (Eds.), *Managing diversity in the military* (pp. 77–96). New Brunswick, NJ: Transaction Publishers.

Idleman Smith, J. (1991). Islam. In C. Johnson & M. McGee (Eds.), *How different religions view death and afterlife* (pp. 185–204). Philadelphia, PA: The Charles Press.

Jowers, K. (1996, November 11). Army rules Muslim soldier can't wear religious scarf. *Navy Times.*

Kappler, S. (2010, November 10). Keeping faith: Sikh solider graduates basic training. *Army.mil* Retrieved from http://www.army.mil/article/47924/keeping-faith-sikh-soldier-graduates-basic-training

Kamarck, K. N. (2015, December 23). Diversity, inclusion, and equal opportunity in the armed services: Background issues for Congress. *Congressional Research Service* 7–5700. Retrieved from https://www.fas.org/sgp/crs/natsec/R44321.pdf

Katcoff v. Marsh (United States Court of Appeals, Second Circuit 1985). Retrieved from http://openjurist.org/755/f2d/223/katcoff-v-o-marsh

Keegan, J. (1976). *The Face of Battle.* New York: Penguin Books.

Klein, A. (1991). Buddhism. In C. Johnson & M. McGee (Eds.), *How different religions view death and afterlife* (pp. 85–108). Philadelphia, PA: The Charles Press.

Levine, S. J. (2010). Untold stories of Goldman v. Weinberger: Religious freedom confronts military uniformity. *Air Force Law Review, 66*(1), 205–224.

Loveland, A. C. (2004). From morale builders to moral advocates: U.S. Army chaplains in the second half of the twentieth century. In D. L. Bergen (Ed.), *The sword of the lord: Military chaplains from the first to the twenty-first century* (pp. 233–250). Notre Dame, IN: University of Notre Dame Press.

Meehan, M. (2009, January 8). Maha's uniform. *Star News.* Retrieved from http://www.starnewsgroup.com.au/story/68688

Murray, R. (2009, July 9). Army chaplains corps: Serving 'God and country' for 234 years with 25,000 chaplains. *Army.mil.* Retrieved from http://www.army.mil/article/24086/army-chaplains-corps-serving-god-and-country-for-234-years-with-25000-chaplains/

National Cemetery Administration. (2015). Available emblems of belief for placement on government headstones and markers. Retrieved from http://www.cem.va.gov/cem/docs/emblems.pdf

Pew Research Center. (2015). America's changing religious landscape. Retrieved from http://www.pewforum.org/2015/05/12/americas-changing-religious-landscape/

Philipps, D. (2015, December 13). Sikh solider allowed to keep beard in rare Army exception. *New York Times*. Retrieved from http://www.nytimes.com/2015/12/14/us/sikh-soldier-allowed-to-keep-beard-in-rare-army-exception.html

Ponn, A. (1991). Judaism. In C. Johnson & M. McGee (Eds.), *How different religions view death and afterlife* (pp. 205–227). Philadelphia, PA: The Charles Press.

Sandhoff, M. L. (2013). Service, sacrifice, and citizenship: The experiences of Muslims serving in the U.S. military. (Unpublished doctoral dissertation). University of Maryland, College Park, MD.

Sharp, S., Carr, D., & Macdonald, C. (2012). Religion and end-of-life treatment preferences: Assessing the effects of religious denomination and beliefs. *Social Forces, 91*(1), 275–298.

Shaughnessy, L. (2011, April 4). Headscarves for female soldiers in Afghanistan defended. *CNN*. Retrieved from http://religion.blogs.cnn.com/2011/04/04/headscarves-for-female-soldiers-in-afghanistan-defended/

Shinall Jr., M. & Guillamondegui, O. (2015). Effect of religion on end-of-life care among trauma patients. *Journal of Religion and Health, 54*(3), 977–983.

Smithsonian Institution. (1997). Puja: Expressions of Hindu devotion. *Guide for educators*. Retrieved from https://www.asia.si.edu/pujaonline/puja/start.htm

Somers, M. (2014, January 23). Obama's Pentagon relaxes dress code to allow turbans, scarves. *Washington Times*. Retrieved from http://www.washingtontimes.com/news/2014/jan/23/pentagon-relaxes-dress-code-allow-turbans-scarves

Stouffer, S. A., Lumsdaine, A. A., Lumsdaine, M. H., Williams Jr., R. M. W., Smith, M. B., Janis, I. L., Star, S. A. Cottrell Jr., L. S. (1949). Combat motivations among ground troops. In *The American soldier: Combat and its aftermath* (pp. 105–191). Princeton, NJ: Princeton University Press.

Sullivan, D. H. (1988). The congressional response to *Goldman v. Weinberger*. *Military Law Review 121,* 125–152.

Townsend, T. (2011, January 9). Military chaplains are faith mismatch for personnel they serve. *St. Louis Post-Dispatch*. Retrieved from http://www.stltoday.com/lifestyles/faith-and-values/military-chaplains-are-faith-mismatch-for-personnel-they-serve/article_19c66ee6–82b8–59f7-b3d5-fd3cc05bc538.html

United States Conference of Catholic Bishops. (n.d.). Questions and answers about Lent and Lenten practices. Retrieved from http://www.usccb.org/prayer-and-worship/liturgical-year/lent/questions-and-answers-about-lent

Urkin, J. & Naimer, S. (2015). Jewish holidays and their associated medical risks. *Journal of Community Health, 40*(1), 82–87.

Waggoner, E. (2014). Takin religion seriously in the U.S. Military: The chaplaincy as a national strategic asset. *Journal of the American Academy of Religion 82*(3), 702–735.

Watson, A. (2006). Self-deception and survival: Mental coping strategies on the Western Front, 1914–18. *Journal of Contemporary History 41*(2), 247–268.

Part III

INTERSECTIONS: LINKING STATUSES

Chapter 10

The Intersections of Race, Class, Gender, and Sexuality in the Military

David E. Rohall, Morten G. Ender and
Michael D. Matthews

Never has there been a dull moment to study diversity and inclusion in the US military. The early 21st century is no exception. The outgoing US Secretary of Defense Ash Carter formally announced the opening of all positions in the military including combat and special operations forces to women (Brook & Michaels, 2015). The three Army women successfully completing Ranger School might serve as a cultural change marker (Tan, 2015). Further, given the size and scope of US Armed Forces around the world, the change may have global implications. Other Western all-volunteer military services allow women to serve in most, if not all, positions but few will likely engage as many women or have as active a military presence around the world as the US forces. What happens in the US military has monolithic implications for both other military forces but the civilian world as well because US forces are scrutinized both by policy makers domestically and globally.

Concomitantly, similar changes have occurred in the US military over the last several years. President Barack Obama announced an end to the *Don't Ask, Don't Tell* policy in 2011 allowing gay, lesbian, and bisexual service members to serve openly in the military and to receive spousal benefits for the first time. While the military has been out front (i.e., race/ethnicity) and lagged far back (i.e., sex, gender, and sexual orientation) on diversity issues, it broke through on formal inclusion once those barred became fully recognized. That is, the military formally changed its policies and, remarkably fast, created diversity initiatives, diversity and inclusion training and education, equal employment opportunity, and equal opportunity programs that the civilian sector might aspire to.

The third major transition (pun intended) area for military personnel relates to transgender/gender nonconforming service members. As Judith Rosenstein

191

points out in Chapter 8 of this book, the Secretary of Defense announced that transgender military service members may now serve openly as of June 30, 2016 with accessions expected to begin in the summer of 2017 (Department of Defense, 2016). The United States joins at least eighteen other countries in allowing transgender service members to serve their country (Elders, Brown, Coleman, Kolditz, & Steinman, 2015). This number is important because there are 193 members in the UN, moving the United States among the top twenty nations with regard to transgender integration in the military.

Yet, it is noteworthy to highlight that traditionally disenfranchised groups, such as people of color and women, have had long civilian social movements and served in segregated military units as they marched toward full inclusion. In contrast, GLB service members have had a relatively short historical civil rights movement and they have always served in traditional military units albeit more or less clandestinely. Seemingly similar to their GLB peers, transgender service members are relatively unable to hide their gender nonconformity. Transgender service inclusion in the military moved far faster than GLB integration. For example, DADT remained in place seventeen years, giving a generation of military people ample time to adjust to the possibility of full inclusion. The transgender civil rights movement is short and fast, providing transgender service members with less of a time cushion. This may explain why cisgender (i.e., people whose gender corresponds to their sex) service members are somewhat apprehensive about their comfort levels serving alongside transgender service members (Ender, Ryan, Atkins, Spell, & Nuszkowski, 2017). Other groups remain on the horizon who will seek full American citizenship status through military service including people with physical anomalies, the aged, undocumented immigrants, and perhaps even foreign nationals. Their level of acceptance and integration should be examined accounting for the length and impact of their social movements and their relative military experiences either openly, segregated, or clandestinely.

Before examining the breadth and depth of diversity and inclusion in the US military put forth in this volume, we should answer the question, why is military diversity so important? First, the US military is one of the largest single employers in both America and the rest of the world. There are just over 3.5 million active and reserve soldiers, sailors, and air men and women including the Coast Guard and Department of Defense civilians and not including contractors.[1] As a result, people take note when the military changes personnel policies. It is a most public, political event, and military leaders recognize that what happens in the military receives significant press, garners vigorous debate, and brings international attention.

Second, the US military has been a model for diversity and inclusion in the workforce going back to the aftermath of World War II and prior to the

Korean War (1948) that ushered in the formal racial desegregation of the armed services. This occurred even before the American educational system (1954) and interracial marriage (1967) but arguably a year after professional baseball formally integrated racially with small numbers of African- and Hispanic-Americans joining the leagues, such as former US Army Lieutenant Jackie Robinson. It was a difficult time for the armed services and it did not go without problems but with time and careful supervision, the armed services has become a model for the rest of the nation and perhaps the world. Charles Moskos aptly noted that the US armed services represent one of the few places where blacks regularly order around whites (Moskos & Butler, 1996). Today, African-Americans in the military are in relative proportion to their civilian numbers. With some underrepresentativeness in the higher-status officer corps, African-American proportions among officers is similar to the proportion of those men who graduate college, a requirement for officer positions. Likewise, their proportions are more or less representative at specific enlisted ranks, sex, and military occupational specialties. Exceptions include lower levels of African-Americans in the combat arms and a higher proportion of African-American women in the senior NCO ranks in combat support and combat service support positions.

The military has also been a stabilizing factor for many minorities in the United States. While African-Americans continue to earn less money and have twice the unemployment rates as Caucasians in the civilian workforce, the military provides equal pay for the same ranks and benefits for all members and their families. Issues of discrimination in the services continue but the military has been a major source of income equality that has led to positive outcomes among African-American military families (Burk & Espinoza, 2012; Teachman & Tedrow, 2008). How each minority group has fared in the military and the lessons learned have application to both the military and the larger society.

Third and perhaps most importantly, if diversity cannot work in the armed services, it may not work anywhere in society. The military is a unique institution in the United States because—despite the rhetoric of democracy and freedom—the military is a very undemocratic institution. Members of the military do not have the same rights and freedoms found in the civilian society. Service members risk punishment if they do not obey all (legal) orders through the Uniformed Code of Military Justice. If a military leader commands soldiers to accept people of different backgrounds, they must accept them or face punishment. While they may not inwardly accept all groups, they cannot show their dislike outwardly. They may be prejudiced but they cannot discriminate. They cannot protest organizational change on the job. The result of this type of organizational structure is that service members must live with the diversity whether they like it or not. If we cannot address

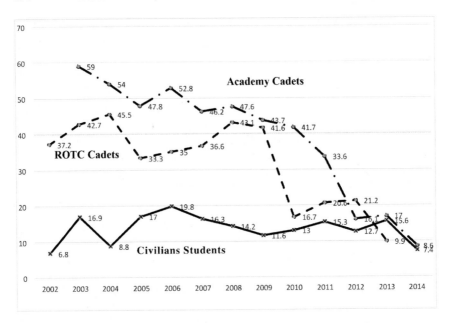

Figure 10.1   Support for Banning Gays from the Military by Military Affiliation, 2002–2014. Adapted from Rohall, D., Ender. M. G., & Matthews, M. D. 2015. From exclusion to inclusion: Changing attitudes toward homosexuals in the military. Paper presented at the 2015 Midwest Sociological Society Meetings, Kansas City, KS March 26–29.

diversity and inclusion in the military organizational structure in which there are high levels of control, it will be even more difficult to get people to accept diversity and inclusion in the civilian world where there is a relative lack of institutional control and sanctions.

Fourth, certainly attitudes toward majority-minority group issues can change. Data from a longitudinal survey of West Point and ROTC cadets shows a marked change in attitudes toward allowing gays to serve in the military (see Figure 10.1). Since 2011, cadets are less likely to support barring gays and lesbians from serving in the military than before that time and they have become increasingly tolerant with time. It is important to note that the majority of civilians in this study never supported barring gays during this time (Rohall, Ender, & Matthews, 2015). These findings suggest that change occurred following the DADT repeal instituted under President Barack Obama in 2011. It appears policy dictates attitudes.

Finally, despite many arguing the military should not be a place for "social experimentation" or "social engineering," the social history since the inception of the nation suggests the opposite. The military represents a natural experiment of sorts. One example of why diversity integration works is the contact hypothesis that states that persistent interaction of people from different, even conflicting backgrounds, can lead to social change and acceptance under some conditions (Allport, 1954). The conditions include (1) a common task (national defense); (2) equity (rank system based on time in grade); (3) supportive supervision (the officer and senior NCO corps); and (4) formal and informal cooperation (working and living together as a team). The US military resonates with elements of the contact hypothesis—more so during a time of war. There is a saying among Marines: "We all bleed green" referring to the fact that black and white Marines share the same combat uniform and need each other to complete their missions. They look different on the outside but they share the same uniform and are the same on the inside. They can only hope that this attitudinal change can occur for all groups who serve in the military and this model has application to civilian contexts as well. And indeed, the move toward diversity and inclusion has shown little to no blowback in terms of backlash or a compromising of military readiness and performance of the mission.

DIMENSIONS OF MILITARY DIVERSITY

Each of the chapters in this book gives us a window into the unique challenges that people from different minority backgrounds face as they embrace the military identity. In the second chapter, JooHee Han starts our journey into military diversity with his chapter on the African-American experience. African-Americans are unique in American history both because they were part of early America and because of their tragic but unique roles as slaves for the mass of America's early history. In some respects, one might argue that African-Americans would want nothing to do with American defense given this history but it is clear that African-Americans have always been part of the military and even dominated it at times in particular ranks and services, at least relative to their size in the civilian population. Changes in African-American civilian status over the last 100 years runs parallel to their changing military status to that of greater participation and inclusion. However, they also moved ahead of their civilian counterparts by ending desegregation before many locations in the United States at the time. We can learn from this experience—that the military can be a leader in diversity or any matter if leaders choose to do so. Yet inclusion—full inclusion—may be another matter. It has historically required time.

Karin De Angelis' work shows the matchless history of Hispanic-American service men and women. She points out that this group has grown in proportion of the military, just like civilian society, but they have dominated the sea services and that female Hispanic accessions have begun to outpace men's accessions. She estimates that there are 35,000 noncitizens in service and that the military serves as a place to socialize such people and, ultimately, obtain citizenship. Another feature that makes the case of Hispanic service members interesting is that this is an ethnic group with many different constituencies. Hispanics from Puerto Rico have different cultural traits than their peers from Mexico and other Latin American countries. Simply separating the group by a common, generic language and massive region will not help to unravel the deep variations housed under the umbrella of Hispanic-American. Indeed, it may be a source of stress as both leaders and comrades use stereotypes from the civilian world in their interactions. Much remains unanswered in the experiences of nuanced groups in the US military including Mexican-Americans, Dominican-Americans, Peruvian-Americans, and Cuban-Americans, among many others.

There are very few scholars of Asian-American soldiers, so Deenesh Sohoni's examination of the topic is both exceptional and insightful. Here we see the legal struggle that Asian-Americans faced as they have tried to enter military service. Similar to Hispanic-Americans, many Asian-American men and women are first-generation Americans and the military serves as a place to both gain and live out their citizenship. Thus, Asian and Hispanic-Americans intersect with regard to their historical role as outsiders who have had to fight for their right to participate in the military. Dr. Sohoni highlights the many court cases utilized to secure these rights as well as the ways that courts interpreted those cases both to withhold and to secure access to the military. On the civilian side, he sites examples such as the Immigration Act of 1917 that put limits on Asian immigration. Other immigrant groups experienced similar exclusions over the years but it is attention-grabbing to see the distinctive ways the laws influenced Asian-American military service participation. Sohoni suggests that Asian-Americans have been "perpetual outsiders" because of their immigrant status and small numbers. For example, they comprised 3.8 percent of the total military force in 2014. While the Congressional Act of July 17, 1862, created military naturalization, he notes that Asian-Americans continued to face barriers to the naturalization process. It appears that people from different races and backgrounds were more or less included in these and other acts, at least as it was interpreted by different courts over the last two centuries. Similar to the generic designation of Hispanic-American, Asian-American requires a dismantling and the exclusive contributions and cultural nuances of varied groups is warranted such as Chinese-Americans, Japanese-Americans, Korean-Americans, Hmong-Americans, and Filipino-Americans among many others.

Issues of race, ethnicity and citizenship are further complicated in the case of Native Americans. Like African-Americans, Native Americans have been associated with both American military and civilian institutions since the inception of the country. Unlike African-Americans who, for the most part, came to America in bondage as slave labor, Native Americans lived on the continent and either served as adversaries to the early colonists or allies against other enemies such as the French or the British. They also participated as members of the US armed services at an early stage. Like many other racial and ethnic groups, Native Americans rarely achieved high status in the military—serving mostly as an outsider status historically—but they did take on inimitable roles from those other groups. Notably, William Meadows presents their unique background both as scouts and, later, as Code Talkers. The stereotype of the Indian scout helped to perpetuate the "Indian Scout Syndrome" whereby Native American soldiers were expected to take on this dangerous position whether they had those specific skills and talents or not. As Code Talkers, individuals from many different tribes helped to maintain secure code transmissions among units as part of staging and implementing attacks against enemies during World War I and World War II. More recently, twenty-three-year-old US Army Specialist Lori Piestewa, a member of the Hopi Nation, became not only the first American woman to die in the War in Iraq in 2003, yet, perhaps somewhat surprisingly, is the first known Native American woman in US history to die in combat while serving on active duty in the US military.

Meadows goes on to address how the warrior ethos or culture that exists in some Native American tribes overlaps with traditional American military culture. In some cases, Native Americans participate, for example, in blessing ceremonies before leaving for service and they may bring special medicine bundles used in combat. Many Native American service members return to their communities with a type of cleansing ceremony as a way to integrate back into civilian life. Like other minorities, Native Americans have experienced any number of prejudices in the services and have turned to legislation to address these problems. The 1924 Indian Citizenship Act gave US citizenship to all Native Americans who served in the military. Similar to other minority groups, military service both exposed Native Americans to other American racial and ethnic groups as well as exposing Caucasians to Native Americans. Similar to Asian-Americans and Hispanic-Americans, there is lacunae of knowledge on the quality and quantity of specific tribe contributions to the US military.

Almost all of the groups reviewed in the first part of the book are clearly minorities with respect to their size and relative status in society. The inclusion of women as minorities may appear odd numerically among civilians because they represent over half of the US population. In the civilian sector, women make less money than men for the same job. Military pay is more equitable; however, overall women have made less because of exclusion from the combat arms, which has pay incentives over combat support and combat service support. Women continue to be minorities in the US military in many respects. They rarely exceed 20 percent of the armed services (16.5 percent of the total force in 2014) and they typically have lower status than male service members since their roles have been limited over the years and they rarely achieve rank levels in the same proportion as men. Janice Laurence's chapter on this topic came along just as women achieved the ability to take combat billets. She points out that job assignments matter to careers in service. Unlike other minorities who, in some cases, were overrepresented in the combat forces and thus casualties, women had to fight for the right to access combat occupations. She points out that these assignments can be very important to obtaining higher level positions over the course of a military career.

David Smith and Karin De Angelis' chapter on gays, lesbians, and bisexuals (GLB) in military service (chapter 7) reminds us that the military is more accepting of minorities when there is greater demand for personnel. Hence, the military is more likely to accept people from diverse backgrounds when there is a greater demand such as a time of war. Under the Obama Administration, the focus seemed to be on task cohesion trumping social cohesion—skills override comradery. Homosexuality has been more or less accepted in the military over time, depending on historical and the context conditions. They suggest that sexuality was less of a formal issue in regulatory history but only emerged in the 20th century, especially after World War II in which the Uniform Code of Military Justice (UCMJ) formally banned sodomy. Deemed an illness or psychological disorder through much of the 20th century—both in the military and in the civilian world—being gay was not necessarily something that warranted a military separation or dismissal. In the mid 1970's the military began more earnestly to separate service members for being gay or lesbian--ironically, this occurred soon after 1973 when the American Psychological Association removed homosexuality as a core sexual disorders from the *Diagnostic and Statistical Manual of Mental Disorders.*

The Don't Ask, Don't Tell (DADT) policy—devised by sociologist Charles Moskos and accepted and implemented by then President Clinton in 1993—promulgated an environment in which gays, lesbians, and bisexuals could serve in the military as long as their sexual orientation status remained hidden. Like gender, the conventional concern among leaders assumed the presence of gays and lesbians could undermine social cohesion in units. Utilizing this logic, diversity of any kind may lead to low cohesion among troops. The authors suggest that one way to deal with diversity in the military is to focus on task cohesion, cohesion that focuses on the success of completing a task rather than emotional cohesion among group members. In this way, the diversity may actually help bring unique skills to resolve problems. Task cohesion would now drive the car and social cohesion simply takes a back seat rather than standing on the curb.

Judith Rosenstein's chapter on transgender military personnel (chapter 8) helps by first differentiating GBL personnel issues from those of "trans" service members. Much like gay and lesbian personnel, transgender tendencies historically fell into a mental health disorders except gender nonconforming came along much later among mental health experts in the 20th and 21st centuries. It was not until 2013 that transgender was removed as a formal pathology from the *Diagnostic and Statistical Manual of Mental Disorders*. As of 2016, military men and women can transition and then become accountable to the standards of their new sex. This fact is interesting in-and-of itself because it suggests that sex/gender differences are still part of the military experience—but remains somewhat elusive. There are no differences, for instance, among men of different races with regard to physical fitness. Gay and lesbian people retain their biological sex thus there are no concerns over gender standards. Now transgender people must identify with one sex or the other—treating gender as a binary rather than along a fluid continuum.

Rosenstein estimates that there are over 10,000 gender nonconforming people in the military today or less than 1 percent of the forces. Despite this small proportion, like women in the military, their numbers are high, given the size of the armed forces—the military could hold the largest concentration of transgender people of any occupation or organization in the United States. Rosenstein suggests that they are more likely to serve than cisgender Americans. If this remains so, then they may share the warrior spirit associated with Native Americans who are also disproportionally overrepresented in the military compared to non-Native Americans. The concerns of transgender personnel are likely to be much different than any other group in part because they change the gender standards of the services but also because there are surgical procedures and medications that they may seek in order to transition their gender identities. We know comparatively little about this group simply because they never received acceptance into the armed forces, did not serve in segregated units prior to inclusion, and likely underwent their major transitioning after they left military service although this is likely to change in the coming years. Some research on transgender veterans has been accumulating over the past ten years and some worthy knowledge is coming from our international, AVF western ally peers (Ender et al., 2017).

The final chapter of this volume deals with religious minorities in the military. There is a natural intersection of religion with race, ethnicity, and gender. People who originate from the continental United States are much more likely to be Christian (and Protestant specifically) than people who originate from the Middle East, which is dominated by Muslims. This simple fact has hefty implications for being a minority in the military because people in the United States are more distant to Muslims and Middle Easterners than other minority groups in the United States today (Parrillo & Donoghue,

2005). Further, at this writing, the United States continues to be at war in Afghanistan—a predominately Muslim country. While not a religious war, the Global War on Terror to some people may feel that way, leading to both internal tensions among Muslims serving in the US military and between people of different religions serving overseas.

As Michelle Sandhoff points out, religious identity is also about organizational structure and religious practices. While other identities may entail certain behaviors, it is clear that religious practices require more attention. She uses the example of the Military Chaplain Corps, which has been part of the armed forces since their inception. Growing religious diversity has caused military leadership to consider adding chaplains to reflect religious variation but the question is how far this organizational requirement should be extended. Should Wiccans and Sadists have chaplains when they represent such a small proportion of service members? A related issue involves tolerance for religious practices. For example, the average workday and military assignments weakly compensate for prayer throughout the day as required by some religious groups. In addition, requirements related to bodily care (e.g., growth of facial hair or fasting) do not fit current military standards and routines. Hence, there are organizational considerations with regard to religious diversity that differ from other forms of diversity.

Different types of diversity overlap in a host of ways. The organizational challenges of religious diversity, for instance, do exist for transgender personnel because changing elements one's sex identity requires a change in organizational standards for those personnel. As the military pays for any psychological and medical requirements associated with sex/gender transitions, it requires that the military consider these issues in its annual budget (Elders et al., 2015). Hence, accommodating diversity is more than simply accepting people with different values, beliefs, needs, and orientations. Diversity must embrace commitments of time, monies, and resources. As a result, military leaders must reflect on and consider the limits of diversity since accepting more diversity may require different utilizations of resources than in the past.

DIVERSITY FOR THE FUTURE

Is there a diversity and inclusion goal for the military? More is not necessarily better. Success in the form of organizational efficiency and completing missions should also be part of the metric; diversity, you can argue, is essential in a global society that is diverse—you need diversity to work with diversity (McDonald & Parks, 2012). We focus on two measures of the future of military diversity regarding inclusiveness. First, there must be consensus as to the limits of diversity, if there is any at all. This point is especially poignant given the current trend toward talent management and task cohesion. At one point, gays and lesbians were restricted from service because of the perception that "deviant" sexual orientations could cause problems with cohesion and morale, ultimately yielding a less productive military force. Clearly, sexual orientation is now a more acceptable form of military diversity (Belkin et al., 2014). What about other groups such as people with disabilities? Arguably, blind or deaf persons could reduce productivity on the battlefield because they are unable to function in the same way as soldiers with full vision or hearing but it is a point of discussion: where do we draw the line? What other roles might he or she perform off the warrior platform? Perhaps people with disabilities can serve in some military capacity without impact on the military's ability to do missions, including any number of support positions. What about undocumented Americans? The elderly? Non-Americans? As we have seen in this book, this process occurred with many other minority groups beginning with the military offering lower status positions before moving toward greater inclusion into evermore positions and ranks. Perhaps this is a changing target as more groups seek acceptance in society. Other groups come along from different sources such as immigration. While African-Americans have been part of the military from the founding of America, the role of Hispanic-Americans has been greatest in the last century with increased migration from Mexico and Central and South America. We are likely to see a growing influence from Hispanic and Asian immigrants in the United States over the next century (Brown, 2015).

Another dimension of military diversity is equality. First, what is the appropriate proportion of people from diverse backgrounds? Should the military organization mirror the US across services, ranks, locales, and military occupational specialties? This is an important question with regard to both pay and status. Unlike the civilian sector, this form of diversity is easier to monitor because of the unique rank structure of the military. The military services divide among the enlisted (lower status) and officer (higher status) ranks, which require a college degree. Is the proportion of diverse populations in the enlisted and officer corps reflective of their numbers in the civilian populations? If not, it is an indicator that something should be done to rectify the situation.

On another level, enlisted and officer ranks are numbered with corresponding names and pay, starting with E-1 (Private making about $18,000 as of 2016) to E-9 (making about $60,000 annually). Similarly, officers range from O-1 (Second Lieutenant, making about $36,000) to O-10 (generals and admirals, making over $100,000). These pay scales can be very complicated because they do not include benefits that could significantly increase income and incomes increase with time in service. That said, it is possible to adjust for all of these variations to ensure that there is an equitable distribution of people from diverse backgrounds at different ranks given time in service and other factors. We know that men outnumber women among higher ranking officers, especially generals and admirals, the highest ranks in the Army and Navy. Like their civilian counterparts, women have historically been underrepresented in these ranks suggesting that there remains a "glass ceiling" for military women—a limit to the highest of rank they can achieve (Ritzer, 2013)—or what Iskra (2008) has referred to as a "brass ceiling" for military women. There are similar disparities for African-Americans (Smith, 2010). Unlike the civilian sector, it is easier to monitor these status differences in the military. In this sense, the military can be a leader by monitoring and rectifying disparities. These numbers are important to ascertaining the relative status of minorities.

Women are underrepresented among CEOs in the civilian world (Warner, 2015)—can the same be said for the equivalent positions in the military? It is as simple as examining the proportion of women in the military to their relative positions in military service ranks. The challenge is to understand the underrepresentativeness and develop strategies to address the problem. The Defense Advisory Committee on Women in the Services (DACOWITS) is an organization that can provide this kind of analysis. Similarly, there are other committees and associations designed to examine minority service member and veteran issues such as the Office of Diversity Management and Equal Opportunity but this group is less visible than DACOWITS (Military Leadership Diversity Commission, 2011). The Defense Equal Opportunity Management Institute can also serve to monitor diversity and inclusion matters across the military services.

Finally, occupational distributions by race and gender, among other characteristics, are important to monitor as well because your occupation has implications for rank later in life. As Janice Laurence points out in her chapter on women in the military, having a combat command is import to achieving higher ranks among officers and simply serving in a combat unit can influence the career achievements for both enlisted men and women and officers. Thus, if a group dominates a noncombat support occupation, it can influence their career outcomes at least as it relates to their rank and pay. Conversely, it is important to remember the history of African-Americans, and more recently, Hispanic-Americans includes over- and underrepresentation among combat casualties and these somewhat flipped in Iraq (Gifford, 2005). In this case, being in combat is a considerable form of discrimination! The lesson here is that diversity is complex and trying to manage diversity and inclusion requires an understanding of how it is manifested in an organization such as the military but also the history of the groups involved in a particular situation. The history of women and African-Americans (and other ethnic minorities) is quite complex as it relates to military service (Burk,

1995). Perhaps a broader question to ask is "Who serves when everyone does not, and more in depth, who is killed and wounded when everyone is not?"

Ultimately, the goal is to help the military achieve its goal of protecting and defending nation while maximizing the potential of people in service. Part of officer training includes the idea that leaders need to take care of the people in their commands. Knowing something about diversity and inclusion should help them manage the unique issues that people face as they carry their civilian traits and characteristics with them. Commanders have always had to deal with unique people who have unique issues in the military organization. In the classic sociological article called, "The Small Warship," George Homans (1946) describes the small ways that officers help their subordinates in establishing a sense of trust among crewmembers and between leaders. In this case, understanding exchanges between technical competence, balance, reciprocity, and communication. Further, knowing the men and women in your command—both individually as well as their social histories—is essential to creating those types of relationships in the modern military. It creates a sense of caring that is reciprocated with trust and fidelity.

We also hope that people with diverse backgrounds can look at the examples of diversity in the military as a microcosm of the larger society. There is a unique history of African-Americans in service, for instance, that both parallels American history but also diverges from it. For instance, the US military has been, and continues to be, a major source of stable employment in the African-American community (Teachman & Tedrow, 2008; Burk & Espinoza, 2012) even though it has an historical reputation for discrimination, like other institutions in American society. The military has also been a place to gain citizenship even in the face of anti-immigrant sentiment among civilians (Burk, 1995). These examples show the unique and formidable context that military leaders can find themselves in, do things differently than the rest of society, and serve as a model for managing diversity and inclusion.

INTERSECTIONS OF MILITARY DIVERSITY

In terms of researching diversity and inclusion in the military, we know comparatively little about the intersections of race, class, gender, and sexuality. This research area may be as simple as examining individuals of mixed race or ethnicity for instance. Other more complex intersections of race and other identities become more complex when we look at issues of race, ethnicity, gender, and sexuality and even religious affiliation. How do enlisted gay men differ from enlisted lesbian women or is being black and transgender different from being white and transgender in the military? What are the experiences of black female, cisgender officers? How do enlisted married gay Asian men fare in the military? What issues might a gay Muslim man have in the military? Different subcultures and issues exist among people from different mixes of status characteristics that have implications for their work lives. All of these issues are pertinent to leaders in the military who need to recognize them to make effective personnel decisions—no different from understanding the role of families on soldiers' morale.

We have reason to believe that the military status intersects with all of these background characteristics. While no study has examined the intersection of being gay in the military relative to being a gay civilian, data on being African-American in the military suggests that the military status does not trump African-American status but it does influence the thoughts and feelings of African-American personnel. As we reviewed in the first chapter, African-Americans affiliated with the military were much more likely to support the wars in Iraq and Afghanistan than their civilian peers—well known for the dissent against these conflicts—but less so than their white peers affiliated with the military (Ender, Rohall, & Matthews, 2015). Why would this be the case? Perhaps blacks who self-select into the services share similar values to their white peers. Alternatively, the military may inculcate the values through training and military culture. It is important to note that African-Americans in this study did not totally agree with whites in the military—they reported less support of the wars compared to whites in the military. It suggests that one identity does not exist at the expense of another one. Rather, the two are "intersectioned." We give the integration of the intersection value more detail below.

The theory of intersectionality provides us a lens from which to assess diversity in the military and view people more holistically rather than unidimensional. Intersectionality refers to the ways in which people take on multiple statuses to make a unique one (Collins, 1990). A working-class black women is not primarily black, working-class, or a women but a combination of all three—a unique position from the other three statuses. Being a female, black sergeant in the Marine Corps is similarly unique to a black, woman manager of a Starbucks. While all Marines may "bleed green," it is important to recognize the unique abilities that people from different groups bring to the military, as well as the institutional barriers that those characteristics harbor may yield in their careers.

Perhaps military leaders can harness the exclusive status of Veteran to create what sociologists call a "master status"—one that overrides other identity statuses in our lives (Strauss, 1996). Following the Marine Corps model, they might emphasize the role of the military as a place for all of its members to call home. Yet, this model will only work if leadership both supports and reflects the diversity that exists within the rank-and-file. Service men and women have to believe that their unique backgrounds are recognized and honored in order to establish and build trust that will ultimately produce the kind of esprit de corps among a highly diverse pool of recruits that is necessary for success in the field. People want to be both different and included—leaders need to understand this seemingly paradoxical notion.

CONCLUSIONS AND RECOMMENDATIONS

Again, it is an exciting time for diversity and inclusion in general—precisely why we deem this book both timely and necessary. The United States is perhaps one of the most diverse countries in the world now. Since the inception of the all-volunteer force in 1973, the US military has depended on diversity to fill its ranks. *Stripes* is a postdraft, early, Hollywood film to address this issue. In the 1981 film, the main character, played by comedian Bill Murray, tries to motivate his fellow soldiers with a speech in which he calls them "mutts" because they are a blend of peoples from around the world. He argues, their diversity makes them strong, providing creative solutions to military problems. While this movie was a comedy, it does provide the sentiment that the military has to manage people from fantastically different walks of life to complete a very important mission: national defense.

While none of us would call soldiers "mutts"—they clearly represent a unique conglomeration of peoples, each with its own irreplaceable history. They bring these atypical gifts to their military service; harnessing this diversity can make the forces even stronger. Conversely, mismanagement of this diversity may lead to low morale and poor performance. We hope that the material in this book will update and highlight the significance of diversity and inclusion that exists in the military and provide assistance to people managing and leading diversity and inclusion in the workplace, whether it be in the military or civilian world.

Increasingly, veteran status is a form of diversity! Not only are veterans a statistical minority with only 13 percent of Americans having any military experience (Newport, 2012), but their historical treatment and acceptance by Americans is mixed at best. World War II veterans received a hero's welcome and treatment, Korean era veterans received little recognition, and Vietnam veterans suffered indignities following their homecomings. Adding other minority statuses to ethnic and other forms of identity makes the study and understanding of these varied lives even more difficult. We do see glimpses of this intersection in this book. Bill Meadows' examination of warrior culture among some Native American tribes shows military status connected to ethnic status. He suggests that there is less of a divide between military and ethnic status among many Native Americans. Perhaps we can adopt this perspective when trying to link other minority statuses to the military with the understanding this may not be possible in some cases. Consider the case of conscientious objectors among religious minorities in the United States such as the Amish (Burk, 1995). They received religious exemption from military service in the past. Yet they too might have a place in military service. For example, at the time of this writing, the 2016 film *Hacksaw Ridge* directed by Mel Gibson tells the story of a medic in World War II, Desmond Morris, a Seventh Day Adventist, who refused to kill anyone yet managed to receive a Medal of Honor for service in a combat unit. This film provides an example of ways in which diversity and inclusion is an asset to the military services—but it requires leadership and management.

The Military Leadership Diversity Council (2011) provides recommendations for the military in the management of diversity for the future. We add inclusion to the mix. Among those recommendations are to:

- Ensure leadership commitment to diversity (and inclusion)
- Increase pools of eligible candidates from diverse backgrounds (and include them)
- Eliminate barriers to advancement
- Institute organizational structures which ensure diversity (and inclusion) goals are being met
- Ensure that leadership structure supports diversity (and inclusion) initiatives

While we support all of these goals, we hope that the work in this book will provide more targeted efforts for the unique groups that exist in service. The barriers to women's progress in the military are different from those of Hispanic men and women and transgender personnel. There is overlap. But we cannot presume that all minorities have the same strengths and weaknesses or we run the risk of creating a bifurcation between majority-minority relations leaving many nuanced issues on the proverbial table. We offer some additional suggestions for military leadership:

- Learn about the unique histories that different minority groups bring to the military
- Address and balance diversity and inclusion
- Treat diversity and inclusion as an asset rather than a liability to overcome
- Encourage other service members to tolerate or even appreciate differences
- Celebrate differences and similarities
- Show everyone the same dignity and respect regardless of their background
- Emphasize the veteran master status that the military experience creates for all of them, regardless of their other statuses

At this moment, the future of diversity in the military appears to be fundamentally positive. The military institution continues to recognize diversity and inclusion in its policies and procedures and there are leaders and organizations within the military trying to ensure that the transition to acceptance is a positive experience for the service men and women in both over- and underrepresented groups while continuing to maintain the military's high standards. We are optimistic that our collective effort here on diversity and inclusion in the US military will contribute to the US Armed Forces being a more proficient, successful, and human-oriented organization.

NOTE

1. Actual numbers are: Department of Defense Active Duty = 1,326,273 (37.3 percent); Coast Guard Active Duty = 39,454 (1.1 percent); Ready Reserve = 1,101,939 (31 percent); Stand-By Reserve = 13,700 (.4 percent); Retired Reserve = 214,784 (6 percent); and Department of Defense Civilians 856,484 (24.1 percent). Source: Department of Defense, 2014).

REFERENCES

Allport, G. W. (1954). *The nature of prejudice.* Cambridge, MA: Perseus Books.

Belkin, Aaron, Morten G. Ender, Nathanial Frank, Stacie Furia, Gary Packard, Tammy Schultz, Steven Samuels, and David Segal (2014). *One Year Out: An Assessment of DADT Repeal's Impact on Military Readiness.* Los Angeles, CA: Palm Center, UCLA (September 20). Reprinted in *The Rise and Fall of DADT Repeal: Evolution of Government Policy Towards Homosexuality in the U.S. Military.* Edited by James E. Parco and David A. Levy (Eds.). Routledge.

Brook, T. V. & Michaels, J. (2015). Military will open all combat jobs to women, Defense secretary announces. *USA Today,* December 3.

Brown, A. (2015). U.S. immigration population projected to rise, even as share falls among Hispanics, Asians. *Pew Research Center.* Retrieved December 16, 2016, from http://www.pewresearch.org/fact-tank/2015/03/09/u-s-immigrant-population-projected-to-rise-even-as-share-falls-among-hispanics-asians/

Burke, J. (1995). "Citizenship status and military service: The quest for inclusion by minorities and conscientious objectors," *Armed Forces & Society,* 21, 4, 503–521

Burk, J. & Espinoza, E. (2012). "Race relations within the US military." *Annual Review of Sociology,* 38: 401–422.

Collins, P.H. (1990). *Black feminist thought: Knowledge, consciousness, and politics of empowerment.* New York: Routledge.

Department of Defense. (2014). *2014 Demographics: Profile of the military community.* Washington, DC: Office of the Deputy Assistant Secretary of Defense (Military Community and Family Policy).

Department of Defense. (2016). Secretary of Defense Ash Carter announces policy for transgender service members [Press release]. Retrieved July 1, 2016 from http://www.defense.gov/News/News-Releases/News-Release-View/Article/821675/secretary-of-defense-ash-carter-announces-policy-for-transgender-service-members

Elders, J., Brown, G. R., Coleman, E., Kolditz, T. A., & Steinman, A. M. (2015). Medical aspects of transgender military service. *Armed Forces & Society, 41*(2), 199–220. doi:10.1177/0095327X14545625

Ender, M. G., Rohall, D. E., & Matthews, M. D. (2015). Intersecting identities: Race, military affiliation, and youth attitudes toward war. *War & Society, 34*(3). Retrieved from http://www.tandfonline.com/doi/full/10.1179/0729247315Z.00000000056

Ender, M. G., Ryan, D. M., Nuszkowski, D. A., Spell, E. S. & Atkins, C. B. 2017. "Dinner and a conversation: Transgender integration at West Point and beyond." *Social Sciences*, 6(1), 27; doi:10.3390/socsci6010027. Available online at: http://www.mdpi.com/journal/socsci/special_issues/focusing_on_the_T_in_LGBT_studies. Gifford, B. (2005). "Combat casualties and race: What can we learn from the 2003–2004 Iraq conflict?" *Armed Forces & Society*, 31, 2, 201–225.

Homans, G.C. (1946). The small warship. *American Sociological Review, 11*, 294–300.

Iskra, D. M. (2008). *Breaking through the brass ceiling: Strategies of success for elite military women.* Germany: VDM Verlag Dr. Müller.

McDonald, D.P. & Parks, K.M. (2012). *Managing diversity in the military: The value of inclusion in a culture of uniformity.* New York, NY: Routledge.

Military Leadership Diversity Commission (2011). *From exclusion to inclusion: Diversity leadership for the 21st century.* Retrieved December 17, 2016, from http://diversity.defense.gov/Portals/51/Documents/Special%20Feature/MLDC_Final_Report.pdf

Moskos, C.C. & Butler, J.S. (1996). *All that we can be: Black leadership and racial integration the Army way.* NY: Basic Books.

Newport, F. (2012). *In U.S., 24% of men, 2% of women are veterans.* Gallup Report. Retrieved December 17, 2016 from http://www.gallup.com/poll/158729/men-women-veterans.aspx

Parillo, V.N. & Donoghue, C. (2005). Updating the Bogardus social distance studies: A New national survey. *The Social Science Journal, 42*, 257–271.

Ritzer, G. (2013). *Introduction to sociology.* Los Angeles and other locations: Sage.

Rohall, D., Ender. M. G., & Matthews, M. D. (2015). *From exclusion to inclusion: Changing attitudes toward homosexuals in the military.* Paper presented at the 2015 Midwest Sociological Society Meetings, Kansas City, KS March 26–29.

Smith III, I. (2010). "Why Black officers still fail," *Parameters*, (Autumn), 1–16.

Strauss, A. (1996). Everett Hughes: Sociology's mission. *Symbolic Interaction, 19*,4, 271–283.

Tan, M. (2015). "3rd women, and 1st female reservist, don's Ranger Tab," *Army Times*, Available online at: https://www.armytimes.com/story/military/careers/army/2015/10/16/3rd-woman-and-1st-female-reservist-dons-ranger-tab/74070360/ (October 16). Retrieved January 1, 2017.

Teachman, J. D., & Tedrow, L. 2008. Divorce, race, and military service: More than equal pay and equal opportunity. *Journal of Marriage and Family*, *70*(4), 1030–1044. Retrieved from http://www.jstor.org/stable/40056316

Warner, J. (2015). *The women's leadership gap: Women's leadership by the numbers*. Center for American Progress. Retrieved December 16, 2016, from https://www.americanprogress.org/issues/women/reports/2015/08/04/118743/the-womens-leadership-gap/

Index

About the Editors

Dr. David Rohall is professor of sociology at Missouri State University and author of over a dozen books and articles related to military service. His most recent book, *The Millennial Generation and National Service: Attitudes of Future Military and Civilian Leaders* (2014) focuses on young persons' attitudes toward the modern military and its missions.

Dr. Morten G. Ender is professor of sociology in the Department of Behavioral Sciences and Leadership at West Point, the United States Military Academy. He teaches qualitative research methods among other courses and co-chairs a new Diversity and Inclusion Studies Minor at West Point. His books include *Military Brats and Other Global Nomads: Growing Up in Organization Families* (2002); *Inequalities: Readings in Diversity and Social Life* with Betsy Lucal (2007); *American Soldiers in Iraq: McSoldiers or Innovative Professionals?* (2009); and with Steve Carlton-Ford *The Routledge Handbook of War and Society: Iraq and Afghanistan* (2010).

Dr. Michael D. Matthews is professor of engineering psychology at the United States Military Academy, USA. He served as president of the American Psychological Association's Division of Military Psychology from 2007–2008 and is a Templeton Foundation Senior Positive Psychology Fellow. In 2014–2015 he served as a fellow with the Army Chief of Staff's Strategic Studies Group. Matthews is the author of several books on military psychology, including *Head Strong: How Psychology is Revolutionizing War* (2014).